MW01252790

Games and Sporting Events in History

Games and Sporting Events in History offers a broad global perspective on sports and games in Europe, North America, Africa and Asia. This anthology covers a diverse set of topics including education, medicine, therapy, body culture, gender, race, cross-cultural flow and political issues, from the late nineteenth century throughout the twentieth century, offering new insights into previously under-researched areas of scholarship relating to physical activity and sport. These essays take a new look at old issues with continued relevance to current works. Some studies explore the use of sports as a political tool in national and inter-national relations; while other investigations cover the sociocultural discourse of the past relative to bodies and physical performances that continue to resonate in modern times.

This book was previously published as a special issue of *The International Journal of the History of Sport*.

Annette R. Hofmann is Professor of Sports Studies at Ludwigsburg University of Education, Germany, president of the International Society for the History of Physical Education and Sport (ISHPES) and Academic Editor, Europe, of *The International Journal of the History of Sport*. She has recently edited *Gertrud: Global Scholar – Global Spirit* (2015) and *License to Jump: A Story of Women's Ski Jumping* (2015).

Gerald Gems is Professor of Health and Physical Education at North Central College in Naperville, USA, and past president of the North American Society for Sport History (NASSH). He is currently vice-president of the International Society for the History of Physical Education and Sport (ISHPES).

Maureen Smith is Professor in the Department of Kinesiology and Health Science at California State University, USA. Smith is an active member in the North American Society for the Sociology of Sport, a past president of the North American Society for Sport History (NASSH) and a vice-president of the International Society for the History of Physical Education and Sport (ISHPES).

Sport in the Global Society: Historical Perspectives

Series Editors: Mark Dyreson and Thierry Terret

Titles in the Series

Sport, War and Society in Australia and New Zealand
Edited by Martin Crotty and Robert Hess

Global Perspectives on Sport and Physical Cultures
Edited by Annette R. Hofmann, Gerald Gems and Maureen Smith

Games and Sporting Events in History
Organisations, Performances and Impact
Edited by Annette R. Hofmann, Gerald Gems and Maureen Smith

Brazilian Sports History
Edited by Maurício Drumond and Victor Andrade de Melo

A Global History of Doping in Sport
Drugs, Policy, and Politics
Edited by John Gleaves and Thomas Hunt

American National Pastimes – A History
Edited by Mark Dyreson and Jaime Schultz

Delivering Olympic and Elite Sport in a Cross Cultural Context
From Beijing to London
Edited by Fan Hong and Lu Zhouxiang

East Asia, Geopolitics and the 2012 London Games
Edited by J. A. Mangan and Marcus Chu

Encoding the Olympics
The Beijing Olympic Games and the Communication Impact Worldwide
Edited by Luo Qing and Giuseppe Richeri

Gymnastics, a Transatlantic Movement
From Europe to America
Edited by Gertrud Pfister

London, Europe and the Olympic Games
Historical Perspectives
Edited by Thierry Terret

'Manufactured' Masculinity
Making Imperial Manliness, Morality and Militarism
J.A. Mangan

Mapping an Empire of American Sport
Expansion, Assimilation, Adaptation
Edited by Mark Dyreson, J.A. Mangan and Roberta J. Park

Militarism, Hunting, Imperialism
'Blooding' The Martial Male
J.A. Mangan and Callum McKenzie

Olympic Aspirations
Realised and Unrealised
Edited by J.A. Mangan and Mark Dyreson

Post-Beijing 2008: Geopolitics, Sport and the Pacific Rim
Edited by J.A. Mangan and Fan Hong

Representing the Nation
Sport and Spectacle in Post-Revolutionary Mexico
Claire and Keith Brewster

Rule Britannia: Nationalism, Identity and the Modern Olympic Games
Matthew Llewellyn

Soft Power Politics – Football and Baseball in the Western Pacific Rim
Edited by Rob Hess, Peter Horton and J. A. Mangan

Sport and Emancipation of European Women
The Struggle for Self-fulfilment
Edited by Gigliola Gori and J. A. Mangan

Sport and Nationalism in Asia
Power, Politics and Identity
Edited by Fan Hong and Lu Zhouxiang

Sport and Revolutionaries
Reclaiming the Historical Role of Sport in Social and Political Activism
Edited by John Nauright and David K. Wiggins

Sport and Urban Space in Europe
Facilities, Industries, Identities
Edited by Thierry Terret and Sandra Heck

Sport, Bodily Culture and Classical Antiquity in Modern Greece
Edited by Eleni Fournaraki and Zinon Papakonstantinou

Sport in the Cultures of the Ancient World
New Perspectives
Edited by Zinon Papakonstantinou

Sport in the Middle East
Edited by Fan Hong

Sport in the Pacific
Colonial and Postcolonial Consequences
Edited by C. Richard King

Sport, Literature, Society
Cultural Historical Studies
Edited by Alexis Tadié, J. A. Mangan and Supriya Chaudhuri

Sport, Militarism and the Great War
Martial Manliness and Armageddon
Edited by Thierry Terret and J. A. Mangan

Sport Past and Present in South Africa
(Trans)forming the Nation
Edited by Scarlet Cornelissen and Albert Grundlingh

The 1984 Los Angeles Olympic Games
Assessing the 30-Year Legacy
Edited by Matthew Llewellyn, John Gleaves and Wayne Wilson

The Asian Games: Modern Metaphor for 'The Middle Kingdom' Reborn
Political Statement, Cultural Assertion, Social Symbol
Edited by J. A. Mangan, Marcus P. Chu and Dong Jinxia

The Balkan Games and Balkan Politics in the Interwar Years 1929–1939
Politicians in Pursuit of Peace
Penelope Kissoudi

The Beijing Olympics: Promoting China
Soft and Hard Power in Global Politics
Edited by Kevin Caffrey

The History of Motor Sport
A Case Study Analysis
Edited by David Hassan

The New Geopolitics of Sport in East Asia
Edited by William Kelly and J.A. Mangan

The Politicisation of Sport in Modern China
Communists and Champions
Fan Hong and Lu Zhouxiang

The Politics of the Male Body in Sport
The Danish Involvement
Hans Bonde

The Rise of Stadiums in the Modern United States
Cathedrals of Sport
Edited by Mark Dyreson and Robert Trumpbour

The Triple Asian Olympics
Asia Rising – the Pursuit of National Identity, International Recognition and Global Esteem
Edited by J.A. Mangan, Sandra Collins and Gwang Ok

The Triple Asian Olympics – Asia Ascendant
Media, Politics and Geopolitics
Edited by J. A. Mangan, Luo Qing and Sandra Collins

The Visual in Sport
Edited by Mike Huggins and Mike O'Mahony

What is the Future of Sport History in Academia?
Edited by Duncan Stone, John Hughson and Rob Ellis

Women, Sport, Society
Further Reflections, Reaffirming Mary Wollstonecraft
Edited by Roberta Park and Patricia Vertinsky

Games and Sporting Events in History

Organisations, performances and impact

Edited by
Annette R. Hofmann, Gerald Gems and Maureen Smith

Routledge
Taylor & Francis Group

LONDON AND NEW YORK

First published 2017
by Routledge
2 Park Square, Milton Park, Abingdon, Oxon, OX14 4RN, UK

and by Routledge
711 Third Avenue, New York, NY 10017, USA

Routledge is an imprint of the Taylor & Francis Group, an informa business

British Library Cataloguing in Publication Data
A catalogue record for this book is available from the British Library

ISBN 13: 978-1-138-68223-8

Typeset in Times New Roman
by RefineCatch Limited, Bungay, Suffolk

Publisher's Note
The publisher accepts responsibility for any inconsistencies that may have
arisen during the conversion of this book from journal articles to book chapters,
namely the possible inclusion of journal terminology.

Disclaimer
Every effort has been made to contact copyright holders for their permission to
reprint material in this book. The publishers would be grateful to hear from any
copyright holder who is not here acknowledged and will undertake to rectify
any errors or omissions in future editions of this book.

Contents

Series Editors' Foreword   ix
Citation Information   xi
Notes on Contributors   xiii

1. Revisiting (and Revising?) Sports Boycotts: From Rugby against South Africa
   to Soccer in Israel   1
   Malcolm MacLean

2. Re-Entering the Sporting World: China's Sponsorship of the 1963 Games of
   the New Emerging Forces (GANEFO)   21
   Russell Field

3. Opening a Window on Early Twentieth-Century School Sport in Cape
   Town Society   37
   Francois J. Cleophas

4. On the Margins: Therapeutic Massage, Physical Education and Physical
   Therapy Defining a Profession   51
   Alison Wrynn

5. Discourses on the Production of the Athletic Lean Body in Central Europe
   around 1900   65
   Rudolf Müllner

6. Women Boxers: Actresses to Athletes – The Role of Vaudeville in Early
   Women's Boxing in the USA   78
   Gerald Gems and Gertrud Pfister

7. British Cultural Influence and Japan: Elizabeth Phillips Hughes's Visit for
   Educational Research in 1901–1902   94
   Keiko Ikeda

Index   109

Series Editors' Foreword

On January 1, 2010 *Sport in the Global Society*, created by Professor J.A. Mangan in 1997, was divided into two parts: *Historical Perspectives* and *Contemporary Perspectives*. These new categories involve predominant rather than exclusive emphases. The past is part of the present and the present is part of the past. The Editors of *Historical Perspectives* are Mark Dyreson and Thierry Terret.

The reasons for the division are straightforward. *SGS* has expanded rapidly since its creation with over one hundred publications in some twelve years. Its editorial teams will now benefit from sectional specialist interests and expertise. *Historical Perspectives* draws on *The International Journal of the History of Sport* monograph reviews, themed collections and conference/workshop collections. It is, of course, international in content.

Historical Perspectives continues the tradition established by the original incarnation of *Sport in the Global Society* by promoting the academic study of one of the most significant and dynamic forces in shaping the historical landscapes of human cultures. Sport spans the contemporary globe. It captivates vast audiences. It defines, alters, and reinforces identities for individuals, communities, nations, empires, and the world. Sport organises memories and perceptions, arouses passions and tensions, and reveals harmonies and cleavages. It builds and blurs social boundaries, animating discourses about class, gender, race, and ethnicity. Sport opens new vistas on the history of human cultures, intersecting with politics and economics, ideologies and theologies. It reveals aesthetic tastes and energises consumer markets.

By the end of the twentieth century a critical mass of scholars recognised the importance of sport in their analyses of human experiences and *Sport in the Global Society* emerged to provide an international outlet for the world's leading investigators of the subject. As Professor Mangan contended in the original series foreword: "The story of modern sport is the story of the modern world—in microcosm; a modern global tapestry permanently being woven. Furthermore, nationalist and imperialist, philosopher and politician, radical and conservative have all sought in sport a manifestation of national identity, status and superiority. Finally for countless millions sport is the personal pursuit of ambition, assertion, well-being and enjoyment."

Sport in the Global Society: Historical Perspectives continues the project, building on previous work in the series and excavating new terrain. It remains a consistent and coherent response to the attention the academic community demands for the serious study of sport.

Mark Dyreson
Thierry Terret

Citation Information

The chapters in this book were originally published in *The International Journal of the History of Sport*, volume 31, issue 15 (September 2014). When citing this material, please use the original page numbering for each article, as follows:

Chapter 1

Revisiting (and Revising?) Sports Boycotts: From Rugby against South Africa to Soccer in Israel
Malcolm MacLean
The International Journal of the History of Sport, volume 31, issue 15 (September 2014)
pp. 1832–1851

Chapter 2

Re-Entering the Sporting World: China's Sponsorship of the 1963 Games of the New Emerging Forces (GANEFO)
Russell Field
The International Journal of the History of Sport, volume 31, issue 15 (September 2014)
pp. 1852–1867

Chapter 3

Opening a Window on Early Twentieth-Century School Sport in Cape Town Society
Francois J. Cleophas
The International Journal of the History of Sport, volume 31, issue 15 (September 2014)
pp. 1868–1881

Chapter 4

On the Margins: Therapeutic Massage, Physical Education and Physical Therapy Defining a Profession
Alison Wrynn
The International Journal of the History of Sport, volume 31, issue 15 (September 2014)
pp. 1882–1895

Chapter 5

Discourses on the Production of the Athletic Lean Body in Central Europe around 1900
Rudolf Müllner
The International Journal of the History of Sport, volume 31, issue 15 (September 2014)
pp. 1896–1908

Chapter 6
Women Boxers: Actresses to Athletes – The Role of Vaudeville in Early Women's Boxing in the USA
Gerald Gems and Gertrud Pfister
The International Journal of the History of Sport, volume 31, issue 15 (September 2014)
pp. 1909–1924

Chapter 7
British Cultural Influence and Japan: Elizabeth Phillips Hughes's Visit for Educational Research in 1901–1902
Keiko Ikeda
The International Journal of the History of Sport, volume 31, issue 15 (September 2014)
pp. 1925–1938

For any permission-related enquiries please visit:
http://www.tandfonline.com/page/help/permissions

Notes on Contributors

Francois J. Cleophas is Senior Lecturer in Sport History at Stellenbosch University, South Africa. His focus area is South African sport and Physical Education History

Russell Field is Assistant Professor in the Faculty of Kinesiology and Recreation Management at the University of Manitoba, Canada.

Gerald Gems is Professor of Health and Physical Education at North Central College in Naperville, USA, and past president of the North American Society for Sport History (NASSH). He is currently vice-president of the International Society for the History of Physical Education and Sport (ISHPES).

Annette R. Hofmann is Professor of Sports Studies at Ludwigsburg University of Education, Germany, president of the International Society for the History of Sport and Physical Education (ISHPES) and Academic Editor, Europe, of *The International Journal of the History of Sport*. She has recently edited *Gertrud: Global Scholar – Global Spirit* (2015) and *License to Jump: A Story of Women's Ski Jumping* (2015).

Keiko Ikeda, PhD, is a Professor at the Faculty of Education at Yamaguchi University, Japan. Her research areas include Pre-Victorian British sport history, in particular, sport journalism, and Japanese sport history on imperialism, fascism and gender.

Malcolm MacLean is Reader in the Culture and History of Sport at the University of Gloucestershire, UK, and is a former Chair of the British Society of Sports History. His research focuses on sport in imperial, colonial and postcolonial settings, and, most recently, he co-edited *The Philosophy of Play* with Emily Ryall and Wendy Russell (Routledge, 2013) and edited 'The Sports Club in History: International Perspectives', in *The International Journal of the History of Sport*.

Rudolf Müllner is Professor of Sports Science at the Centre of Sport Science and University Sports in Vienna, Austria. He writes on social, cultural and historical issues of sport.

Gertrud Pfister is past president of the International Society for the History of Physical Education and Sport (ISHPES) and past President of the International Sport Sociology Association.

Maureen Smith is Professor in the Department of Kinesiology and Health Science at California State University, USA. Smith is an active member in the North American Society for the Sociology of Sport, a past president of the North American Society for

Sport History (NASSH) and a vice-president of the International Society for the History of Physical Education and Sport (ISHPES).

Alison Wrynn is a former member of the International Olympic Committee, Olympic Studies Centre, a Postgraduate Research Grant recipient, the current editor of the *Journal of Sport History* and a Fellow of the National Academy of Kinesiology, USA.

Revisiting (and Revising?) Sports Boycotts: From Rugby against South Africa to Soccer in Israel

Malcolm MacLean

School of Sport & Exercise, University of Gloucestershire, Gloucestershire, UK

For the first time in nearly 30 years, 2013 saw increasing public awareness of calls for a comprehensive boycott of and sanctions on a state based on questions of an 'entrenched system of racial discrimination'. The call to boycott South African sport emerged in the 1950s as the apartheid state was developing and refining its comprehensive and systematic legal form amid growing international pressure for decolonisation. This is a different social and political context than the call 50 years later by Palestinian civil society for boycott, divestment and sanctions (BDS) against Israel. This paper draws on analyses of international anti-apartheid movements' campaigns against sporting contact with South Africa and the BDS call for the isolation of the Israeli state to propose a theory of sports boycotts. It looks at the anti-apartheid campaigns to consider ways in which the BDS campaign has an impact on existing historical understandings of cultural boycotts as a tactical and strategic campaign tool.

Boycotts and related forms of political pressure have been a recurring element in the analyses of sport in international relations and international relations in sport. This paper does three things. First, it revisits the anti-apartheid sports campaign to consider its form and character. This will inform a wider discussion of boycotts, embargoes and sanctions as political tactics and explore what it is about the characteristics of international sport that makes sports sanctions distinctive. Finally, a nascent theory of sports boycotts will be assessed through the campaign targeting the 2013 UEFA U-21 tournament to explore the extent to which we need to review or revise our analyses of bilateral sports boycotts in particular and cultural boycotts more generally.

The focus in the sports boycotts literature on the Olympic boycotts of 1980 and 1984 emphasising multilateral sports boycotts obscures key aspects of sport in international relations, diverts attention away from the global distinctiveness of the International Olympic Committee (IOC) as a sports body and downplays the significance of differences between the organisation of Olympic Games and other forms of international sports events. The paradox of the Cold War focus on the 1980 and 1984 Olympic boycotts is that the 1976 Montreal boycott was part of the only time an international sports boycott was successful in achieving its long-term goals – the ending of South African apartheid. Although not the most significant factor in the collapse of apartheid, the sports boycott was responsible for a series of significant blows against the cultural security of apartheid's dominant groups. Analysis of the anti-apartheid boycott movement has tailed off in recent years, in part because there is only so much we can say about sports boycotts, in part because South African history is developing new areas of analysis focussing on the country's sporting past and physical culture, and in part because there have been other pressing issues to explore.

The relevance and significance of sports boycotts changed in 2012/2013 with the intensification of action in support of a 2011 call from within Palestinian civil society for the relocation of the 2013 UEFA Under-21 championships to be held in Israel. This campaign invoked as one of its predecessors the anti-apartheid campaign's call between the mid-1950s and 1992 for the isolation of South Africa. Other calls for sports and wider boycotts in the previous 20 years had been limited or, as we have seen in the recent call for LGBT athletes to boycott the Sochi Olympics over Russia's recent anti-gay legislation, centred on individual athletes rather than sport systems. Public discussion of boycotts and similar kinds of pressure on states has been dominated by state-sponsored comprehensive sanctions activity, such as those directed at Iraq and Iran, or the so-called smart or targeted sanctions directed at members of the political elites in places such as Zimbabwe and Syria. Unlike state-sponsored action, this recent call for a cultural boycott of the Israeli state was a campaign grounded in the civil society networks of those peoples who are the subject of close and restrictive state control. There seem to be significant parallels with the South African case. The explicit invocation of the anti-apartheid campaign and its role as the most high profile of the bilateral boycotts campaigns means that the time is right to begin to revisit and review our analyses of sports boycotts.

While many may feel uncomfortable with calls for a boycott of Israel and the application to Israel of the apartheid label[1] given the UN's 1973 definition of apartheid as 'inhuman acts for the purpose of establishing and maintaining domination by one racial group of persons over any other racial group and systematically oppressing them',[2] we must also be wary of falling into the trap of equating apartheid with the South African situation only or reifying the South African system. Israel's actions are contested in international law. The International Court of Justice in 2004 issued an Advisory Opinion that the Separation Wall Israel is building across the Occupied Palestinian Territories (OPT) is in violation of international law, while elsewhere it has been argued that Israel's support for the West Bank settlement building programme is also in violation.[3] Defenders of Israel point, in response, to alleged violations of international law by neighbouring states and assert Israel's compliance with UN resolutions. The issue is not the legitimacy of either stance; the situation is hotly contested and advocates of the boycott can point to important critiques of the situation they are seeking to address. These questions of the validity of charges against Israel are secondary to the fact of the Campaign for Boycott, Divestment and Sanctions (BDS) and the focus of this paper: how we might make sense of bilateral and multilateral sports, and by implication cultural, boycotts in the light of this 2013 campaign.

Boycotting (South African) Apartheid Sport

The boycott campaign was one of the principal tools that the anti-apartheid movement had in its toolkit to dismantle the White South African government's systematic racial classification and oppression. In discussions of anti-apartheid campaigns, it is common to identify 1959 as the year that the boycott movement came together into coordinated international activism. There had been boycott events before 1959; the All Africa People's Conference in 1958 called for a boycott of South African goods and during the mid-1950s the White governing body of table tennis had been expelled from the international federation (IF). It was the formation of the Boycott Movement Committee drawing together representatives of anti-apartheid groups from South Africa and the UK in London in December 1959 that marked a significant new level of coordination in the campaign coinciding with an emerging activist campaign in New Zealand focussing on the 1960 rugby tour of South Africa under the slogan 'No Maoris, No Tour'. This campaign laid the base for one of the most sustained elements of the sports boycott – the movement to stop rugby union and other sports contact between New Zealand and South Africa that lasted until the mid-1980s.[4]

The situation of South African sport under apartheid was complex. Although it was possible to point to systematic racial discrimination in South Africa from the time of earliest colonisation and the emergence of social practices from around the time of World War I that embedded that discrimination in legal and quasi-legal practice, the situation changed with the election in 1948 of a government led by the conservative Reformed National Party, replacing the more liberal New Democratic Party. Liberal is a relative term here; Jan Smuts, the Party's leader defeated in the 1948 election, actively supported segregation, arguing in 1929 that:

> The old practice mixed up black with white in the same institutions, and nothing else was possible after the native institutions and traditions had been carelessly or deliberately destroyed. But in the new plan there will be what is called in South Africa 'segregation'; two separate institutions for the two elements of the population living in their own separate areas. Separate institutions involve territorial segregation of the white and black. If they live mixed together it is not practicable to sort them out under separate institutions of their own. Institutional segregation carries with it territorial segregation.[5]

Where Smuts' government differed significantly from the incoming government was its support for the view that Black South Africans should be considered and treated as permanent residents of a White-dominated South Africa, not as guest workers whose real home lay in the reserves. Although this difference anticipated the political distinctions to emerge with the formalisation of the Bantustan policy, the basic legal and therefore systemic elements of apartheid developed in the first few years of National Party rule; alongside key legislation including the Population Registration Act (1950) that required all residents to be registered as one of four racial groups, the various Pass Laws Acts (1952 and thereafter), the Prohibition of Mixed Marriages Act (1949) and the Immorality Act (1950) and the Bantu Education Act (1953), the principal laws affecting sport were the Group Areas Act (1950) and the Reservation of Separate Amenities Act (1953).

These latter two pieces of legislation and the regulations and case law that flowed from them, along with several other Acts of Parliament including the Coloured Persons Communal Reserves Act (1961), divided the country into regions designated for occupation and use by the four identified 'racial' groups – White, Black, Indian and Coloured, where Coloured encapsulated most non-Indian Asians, people of mixed race descent and otherwise acted as a 'miscellaneous' category. This division overwhelmingly favoured the White group, 24% of the population who controlled 86% of the land, and the best land at that. Despite being popularly seen, externally, as a National Party programme, this legislation formalised the practice of territorial segregation Smuts had envisaged in 1929. By 1954 this separation then was both spatial – the Group Areas Act – and could be enforced in relation to individual structures, services and related facilities – the Reservation of Separate Amenities Act.

The effect of these developments on sport was profound, preventing informal or 'pick-up' games, while allowing 'interracial' sport between members of organised teams and leagues where a permit had been issued. At times this legislation led to moments of absurdity if they were not so offensive, such as the awards ceremony at the 1963 Natal Open golf championship, which was won by the Indian Sewsunker 'Papwa' Sewgolum.

Sewgolum had been allowed to play, but the permit did not allow him access to the club house; the trophy was handed to him through a window and the South African Broadcasting Corporation suspended its news reporting of the tournament because its rules did not allow it to cover 'mixed' sport.

In the initial stages of the post-war era as organised international opposition began to emerge, the focus was on these exclusionary mechanisms that prevented 'mixed sport'.[6] Visiting sports teams habitually excluded athletes of colour from their teams, hence the campaign in New Zealand in 1960 around the slogan 'No Maoris, No Tour', while it was the controversy over the selection of the former South African 'Coloured' Basil D'Olivera as a member of the MCC (English) cricket team to tour South Africa in 1968 that was one of the crucial factors in South Africa's isolation from international cricket.[7] The international campaign for a sports boycott operated on two principal fronts, one focussed on multilateral sports settings with an emphasis on the Olympic Games and the second centred on bilateral sports contacts. While the initial emphasis of the campaign, as seen for instance in New Zealand in 1960, was to oppose discriminatory sports practices, towards the latter half of the 1960s this position shifted to one where anti-apartheid groups opposed the apartheid system, not just its effects on sport, invoking Hassan Howa's (who became leader in the late 1970s of the South African Council on Sport) statement that there could be 'no normal sport in an abnormal society'.[8]

Olympic Boycotts

The campaign aimed at Olympic participation scored early successes with the suspension of South Africa from the 1968 Mexico Games, although that has been overshadowed in Olympic memory by the Smith–Carlos salute and the Tlatelolco massacre that resulted in the deaths of 28 student protestors and wounding of several hundred of the their fellow activists in the Plaza de las Tres Culturas in the lead up to the Games. Without wishing to understate the effect of the Tlatelolco massacre on Mexican politics, or arguably the study of sports history in Mexico, the decision by the IOC, under pressure from a threatened boycott by 50 nations as well as Black members of the USA team, to withdraw its invitation to South Africa had a profound effect on the boycott narrative. Although South Africa had not been invited to the 1964 Tokyo Olympics, the IOC had sidelined demands to explore claims that the South African National Olympic Committee (SANOC) violated the Olympic Charter by practising racial discrimination – an allegation made to the IOC by the South African Sports Association in 1960. Debates in Mexico City forced the IOC to act. The IOC's fact-finding mission to South Africa in 1967 had been instructed to address only whether SANOC complied with Olympic regulations, not to judge apartheid; this instruction to limit the focus came after repeated accommodation of and adaptation to the structure of apartheid sport alongside denunciation of but no action against government interference in sport. The South African Government insisted that SANOC comply with South Africa's 'customary' separation of sport along racial lines. This requirement along with increasing membership of the IOC from Third World and Eastern bloc states that resulted in a shift in the IOC's power balance meant that in 1970 the IOC voted to expel South Africa. The vote was close at 35 to 28 with three abstentions, and may have been that a provocative and inflammatory speech by SANOC leader Frank Braun as well as the use of Olympic symbols during the 1969 and 1970 'South African Games', devised as compensation for the expulsion from the Mexico Games, caused some IOC members to vote for expulsion instead of a less harsh penalty.[9] Thereafter, as seen in Montreal in 1976, the focus of anti-apartheid boycott activity at the Olympics was directed at third party links, those states such as New Zealand, that maintained high-level sporting relations, although the focus on rugby union and cricket has constrained analyses of the sport–apartheid nexus.[10]

While these changing geopolitical conditions had a significant impact on the direction and effectiveness of the boycott campaign targeting South African sport in the 1960s, they must not be allowed to blind us to the other major factor in the process: the presence of a credible internal non-racial sports movement.[11] Most sports had four officially sanctioned 'national' governing bodies, one for each 'racial' group – White, Black, Asian and Coloured. In many cases there was also a fifth non-racial governing body that, in being non-racial, rejected the confines and provisions of the apartheid structures. In addition, there were also representative campaigning bodies such as South African Sports Association and the South African Council on Sport. These non-racial sports bodies gave the international anti-apartheid movement and the boycott campaign institutions and groups they could identify as legitimate anti-apartheid voices in sport politics. For many in the international solidarity campaign, the voice of non-racial sport was the South African Non-Racial Olympic Committee. An aspect of the debate, therefore, was over the credibility of various voices and the legitimacy both of apartheid and of the sovereign authority of South Africa to determine its own policies. While the international sports world debated these questions and while the South African government during the 1960s made adjustments to their sports policies and the rules governing visiting teams in particular, the geopolitical shift associated with 1950s and 1960s decolonisation and with the growing presence of Eastern bloc and Third World states in global cultural politics contributed to a shift in the political demands concerning apartheid sport. Whereas at the beginning of the 1960s debates around apartheid sport focussed on who was allowed to represent South Africa and limits placed on membership of touring teams, by the latter half of the decade the focus was on the apartheid state itself.[12]

This change in the political demands was more obviously seen in the single-sport campaigns that tended to be localised and focus on the participation by South African athletes in specific events or competitions but were often accompanied by successful campaigns to expel South African federations from international sports governing bodies. These campaigns saw South Africa expelled from or have its membership cancelled or suspended by a wide range of international sports bodies by the end of the 1970s, including men's cricket, netball, football, basketball, amateur cycling and swimming. In two cases, table tennis and darts, the international governing body recognised a non-racial federation.[13] Much of this was the consequence of behind-the-scenes lobbying and pressure developed through national governing bodies, while a key factor in some cases was the pressure seen in the IOC's debates from Third World states and those aligned to the Soviet Union and People's Republic of China – early, if in some cases pragmatic, supporters of boycotts and sanctions.

Bilateral Contact

The vital role that governments, especially those in sub-Saharan Africa, played should not be underestimated. This was not, however, a factor in the handful of sports that carried the greatest cultural weight in White South Africa, most especially cricket and rugby union – although it was rugby union that mattered most, being both a vital marker of national dynamism and power and essential to the integrity of Afrikaner masculinity as the epitome of national vigour.[14] Given the global distribution of rugby union and its dominant teams, its cultural significance in South Africa meant the most important sporting contacts were with the UK, Australia and New Zealand. During the 1960s, these three national governments were committed to 'bridge building' or a policy of 'constructive engagement'; a change in outlook in Australia during the early 1970s and a temporary shift in New Zealand between 1973 and 1975 weakened that consensus, but for most of the period of the organised boycott campaign, the governments of both the UK, especially during the Conservative Government of Margaret Thatcher, and New Zealand between 1975 and 1984 maintained a policy of engagement with the apartheid state. The demand for the sports boycott in all three countries, therefore, lay with civil society campaign groups such as Stop the 'Seventy Tour and the Anti-Apartheid Movement in the UK and Halt All Racist Tours and the National Anti-Apartheid Council (later, HART: NZAAM) in Aotearoa/New Zealand. Each of these organisations maintained close links with the network of non-racial sports bodies within South Africa; in the case of HART: NZAAM, there were also close working relationships with the South African liberation movements such as the African National Congress (ANC), Pan-Africanist Congress of Azania (PAC), Black Consciousness Movement of Azania (BCM(A)) and the South West African People's Organisation (SWAPO).[15]

The cultural politics of South Africa and the significance of rugby union in Afrikaner masculine cultures meant that, in terms of the sports boycott after 1970, the national governing bodies for rugby in the UK, Australia and New Zealand had a disproportionate influence. After the early 1970s when cricket ties were cut and the rugby unions in the UK and Australia suspended competition with South Africa, the most important recalcitrant group breaching the sports boycott was the New Zealand Rugby Football Union (NZRFU). While other sports breached the boycott such as Masters athletics and other governing bodies held out such as the French rugby union, in South Africa it was the NZRFU that mattered. This was seen, for instance, as early as 1970 when Maori and Pacific Islander members of the national rugby team, the All Blacks, were given 'honorary White' status for the duration of the team's tour – although the South Africans asked that any Polynesians in the team not be 'too dark'.[16]

The Global Sports System

The final factor contributing to the cultural impact of the sports boycott in South Africa was the global sports system that sustained international tours. Maintaining the focus on rugby union as the most important international sports contact to the regime of power in apartheid South Africa and, in terms of the sports boycott, the most recalcitrant, South Africa's sporting isolation lasted at most only six years: South Africa was readmitted to full international competition in 1992. The last notable rugby tour, a 'rebel' tour of a close to full strength New Zealand national team, was in 1986 (the 1989 'international' tour had only limited significance and included no New Zealanders, widely seen as South Africa's predominant rival to global rugby supremacy). Cricket, the other sport of significance in White South Africa, maintained a programme of 'rebel' tours until the late 1980s.[17]

Official tours were organised by the IF, in rugby union's case the International Rugby Board (IRB), following a tightly planned programme known several years in advance; the only way for a match to be an official international 'test' was if it was sanctioned by the IRB. Timing, scheduling, rules, officiating, locations, eligibility and anything else to do with touring programmes all had to be endorsed by the IRB and were rigorously policed by national governing bodies. Other than national-level competition, such as in rugby union national provincial-level leagues during the amateur era, these international tours were the only opportunity most people had to see elite competition. The tours also tended to be of a long duration. For instance, the South African rugby tour of New Zealand in 1981 lasted

56 days, plus travel time and two weeks of matches in the USA. Even the unofficial, 'rebel', New Zealand tour of South Africa in 1986 lasted six weeks and included 11 matches. These events were rare, had a high profile and were of great cultural significance.

The anti-apartheid sports boycott, focussing on South Africa, had six distinctive features that were more obvious where the campaign focussed on single sport settings than the multi-sport context of the Olympic Games, but that are also distinctive in that the Olympic issue was resolved relatively early in the boycott era. The first feature was that sport mattered in that it was a major factor of White South African culture, but that some sports mattered more than others for reasons specific to the South African cultural order. The second distinctive feature is that the boycott call came from oppressed groups within South Africa. The third is that these oppressed groups and anti-apartheid allies within the country had, during the apartheid era, built credible internal alternatives to the apartheid-based sports governance system in the form of non-racial bodies. Fourth, the campaign gained strength during 1960s with decolonisation, the power of the Third World project and growing significance of Eastern bloc states. Fifth, during its first 10 years the boycott campaign shifted emphasis from narrowly sport-focussed to anti-apartheid in general as the wider anti-apartheid movement and its related boycott campaigns matured. Finally, the campaign confronted an internationally regulated sports system where, for international purposes, the IF governed relations with many aspects of management delegated to national governing bodies.

These six characteristics influence the analytical fit with how the wider literature on boycotts can help shape explanations of this cultural boycott. This literature is limited. For the most part, discussion of boycotts focuses on two things: economic boycotts and, to a lesser extent, third party boycotts such as industrial or political action in support of another group's boycott activity. The national focus of these debates means that this discussion is limited by the characteristics of specific jurisdictions. The following discussion will therefore draw on the economics-based literature centred on international economic and relations questions to propose a theory of sports boycotts in the context of a wider set of cultural boycotts. The starting point is that boycotts are only ever tactical or at best strategic; they are never an end in themselves but always a means to an end.

The Boycott as a Tactic

The international relations and economics literature tends to conflate sanctions, embargoes and boycotts. Debates about the use of sanctions as a policy tool often assume a simple and direct relationship between political power and economic strength, whereas it is often the case that boycotts are imposed by the relatively powerless – as seen in the US Civil Rights Movement's Alabama Bus Boycott in 1954. Even with the presumption of power, the consensus in the literature is that economic sanctions work by attrition, are ineffective as a singular policy response and are more likely to be effective when invoked as a part of a broader strategy including diplomatic and other non-economic pressure.

Drawing on this literature produces an interpretation of boycotts, embargoes and sanctions shaped by a focus on formal state actions and measures of economic consequences. As a result, we can define sanctions as

> actions initiated by one or more international actors (the 'senders') against one or more others (the 'targets') with either of two purposes: to punish the targets by depriving them of some value and/or make the targets comply with certain norms the senders deem important.[18]

We need also to consider legal and political theory to distinguish between three seemingly synonymous terms. Although 'sanction' also acts as a generic term, for the purposes of the remainder of this discussion, sanctions are penalties attached to transgression and breach of international law. Embargoes are a prohibition by one country or a group of countries of certain kinds of economic or other relations as a reprisal action designed to coerce political policy shifts or to injure a target nation taking a certain political stand. Finally, the boycott is the cessation or curtailment of contact or relations with a target nation on account of political differences, so as to punish a nation for a political position adopted or to coerce it into abandoning it.[19] Given these distinctions, the campaign to isolate South African sport during the apartheid era was enforcing a boycott of South African sport in response to a call for an embargo of apartheid. When it comes to the recent actions focussed on Israel, this distinction is important.

The debate about sanctions faded after the early 1980s as scholars turned their attention to other issues of international economic relations and with the emerging neo-liberal dominance. By 1980 a consensus had been reached regarding sanctions, embargoes and boycotts. Scholarly debate of the issue since then has operated within the parameters of that consensus; there has been no significant reconceptualisation of these models. The discussion embedded embargoes and boycotts within a general focus on sanctions. This is unreasonable in the case of sporting and other cultural boycotts. The use of sanctions as a policy tool relies on the assumption of a direct relationship between political power and economic strength. Although there is usually a simple reason for the invocation of sanctions, there are always complex factors in any state's decision to use them. These factors are often as much about relations with other third-party states as those with the target state. The crucial limitation in cultural policy on the applicability of this literature focussing on state actions in economic policy is that boycotts are often a tool of the relatively powerless.

While noting this limitation, the economics literature suggests that it is possible to draw some common conclusions from the application of sports embargoes and boycotts and of economic sanctions. Sanctions, and by implication boycotts or embargoes, can achieve their intended outcome. This outcome is possible because sanctions can maintain the perception that damage has been inflicted, can express a sense of morality and justice, can signify disapproval and displeasure, can satisfy the emotional needs of the sanctioner to be seen to be acting, can help maintain the sanctioner's positive image and reputation, can relieve domestic pressure on the sanctioner, especially if there is a broad popular movement, and can inflict symbolic vengeance on the target. Debates in the UK in 2011 and the USA intermittently since 2003 over the calls for an academic boycott of Israeli higher education institutions show just how intense and fraught the perceived impact of boycotts, embargoes and sanctions can be. Furthermore, if there is no short-term solution or compromise, there is ongoing inconvenience, target states become examples, and the sanctioner's self-image and self-confidence can be restored.

The effectiveness of sports boycotts and embargoes relies on several distinctive features. The most important of these is product substitution. Just as the impact of economic sanctions needs to be seen in the light of access to other sources of or substitutes for goods being denied, consideration needs to be given to access to additional or alternative sports events.[20] The organisation of international sport means that the product being denied could not be acquired from elsewhere, even if there are close alternatives. International sport is often described as a monopoly, that is where a single 'seller' dominates the international sport 'market'. For instance, the Commonwealth Games Association can be seen as providing a sports event similar to that provided by the IOC in that the Commonwealth Games and other similar events such as the Francophone or Pan-African Games emulate but do not seek to replace the Olympic Games. The Games of the

New Emerging Forces (GANEFO) in Indonesia in 1963 was an international multi-sport festival event emulating the Olympic Games and largely funded by the People's Republic of China as an alternative to the Olympics, where the IOC had recognised Taiwan (Republic of China) as its Chinese member; GANEFO may be seen as an attempt at product substitution.[21] As in this case, very few attempts at product substitution have been successful, although some, notably in cricket, rugby union and rugby league, have had significant effects. This dominance of Olympic-centred analysis means that international sport is often described as a monopoly, that is where a single 'seller' dominates the international sport 'market'. This approach overstates the agency of international sports organisations. Monopsony exists where there are several sellers but only one purchaser – it is the inversion of monopoly where a single seller has multiple purchasers, and markedly shifts the balance of market power and relations.

While the argument that international sports governing bodies are monopolistic is correct in that they monopolise international sports provision, the full significance of analyses derived from international economics in relation to sports boycotts may only be seen if bodies such as the IRB and the IOC are understood as cartels with *either* monopolistic *or* monopsonistic characteristics.[22] Doing so requires a shift in emphasis in analysis of what can be seen as an international sports market away from a focus on the international body to focus on the national governing body (NGB). The tendency to focus on control by the international body belies an ideological dominance of Olympic studies where the IOC is, historically and currently, a top-down governance regime – the IOC predated National Olympic Committees. Seeing the IOC as a monopolistic cartel – that is as a single seller – is correct, although the now-defunct Friendship Games show that there are limits to that monopoly. This is not the case in most sports where IFs – the IRB, FIFA, the IAAF, FINA and so forth – were at their moment of formation confederations of pre-existing national bodies meaning that they should be understood as monopsonistic cartels.

Effective analysis of non-Olympic sports boycotts requires that sport specific IFs are understood as cartels with monopsonistic characteristics. In the case of international competition by nationally representative teams, these international sports bodies are the only purchaser, in part because they have devised and organised the 'market' in international sports competition. Devising and organising international sport is part of what these IFs, as confederations of pre-existing NGBs, were set up to do, along with determining agreed rules of play and organising national competition. Furthermore, they are monopsonistic cartels of monopsonistic bodies: their market control as the single purchaser exists at both international and national level. Their effectiveness as a monopsonistic cartel relies on their ability to prevent the development of viable substitutes, which is in part why the creation of 'rebel' leagues in cricket in 1977, rugby union in 1995 and rugby league in 1996 had such a profound impact on the structure and organisation of each of those sports.

For reasons of space, further discussion of a detailed analysis of boycotts, embargoes and sanctions must be deferred. Issues essential to this more detailed analysis include the extent to which target states have access to close alternatives, for example the 'rebel' tours of South Africa, as well as other counter leverages such as an increasing cultural emphasis on the significance of national-level competition, for instance the status accorded cricket's Currie Cup in apartheid era South Africa once the boycotts began to take effect. Further analysis is needed of the extent to which the boycott campaigns can be seen to be effective, which will require a longer term view than that often taken by critics of the approach who seem to expect immediate or short-term results. The existing literature that points to the place of boycotts, sanctions and embargoes as part of a wider suite of policy instruments and as attritional is crucial here.

There are several elements where common conclusions about economic and cultural boycotts do not exist. First, unlike economic sanctions, hinting at cultural and sporting boycotts is not more effective than imposing them. Second, there is little evidence that the imposition of sporting and cultural boycotts imposes costs on sender states other than to the organising body.[23] Third, other than in the case of some aspects of multilateral sports events, third parties seldom experience any costs or losses associated with sporting and cultural boycotts. Fourth, it is unlikely that sports-related sanctions will undermine the credibility of the sanctioner leading to them being seen as an unreliable supplier – in large part because international sport is monopsonistic – although the 'unreliable supplier' issue may limit action by individual NGBs, depending on the organisational reach of IFs.

There are two general points where common ground exists. First, the sanctioner needs to be fully aware of the potential costs. In analyses of economic sanctions, these are relatively straightforward and direct costs may be comparatively accurately calculated.[24] In sporting and cultural boycotts, there is a far greater number of factors to consider, ranging from the domestic political response to the effect on the cultural standing of particular activities or sports. Second, the target's responses may lead to new sources of supply being discovered, the stimulation of conservation to reduce demand or development of substitutes – in the South African sports case, these responses include the 'rebel' tours and the strenuous efforts on the part of the South African government and key elements of its civil society to circumvent the boycott.[25]

Additional common conclusions may be drawn about the effectiveness of sanctions, embargoes or boycotts applied by international or multinational bodies.[26] These tend to carry more moral power than action taken by individual countries but contain the potential to weaken the international body by causing withdrawals or attacks by powerful target states. The nature of multinational and international sport means that it is important to consider the compatibility of sports' structures with the objectives of the campaign. Conclusions derived from consideration of Olympic boycotts, particularly Moscow in 1980 and Los Angeles in 1984, do not fit the isolation of South African sport. By dealing with individual sports and a single national organising body as well as having a focus on governments through domestic political pressures, the campaign developed a form different from the Olympic boycotts. It could be presented as a response to a call from within South Africa and as directly linked to South Africa's conditions. The same could not be said for the Olympic boycott campaigns organised by the USA and the USSR. However, the idealist sentiment asserting a supra-political status of sport was still powerful and able to be utilised by governments in South Africa and elsewhere to oppose the anti-apartheid movements. This indicates that the issues on which to focus in considering the isolation of apartheid sport are the political structures of the protest movement as well as those of single sporting bodies and governments, the existence of a popular protest movement leading the call for a boycott and the use of the apolitical sports argument and the anti-apartheid movement's ability to counter that through the significance of rugby and cricket and the politicisation of South African sport.

The basic lesson to be learned from the economic sanctions literature is that sanctions, embargoes and boycotts may not achieve all their intended goals, but can still have a profound impact. As Daoudi and Dajani argue, 'they have the power to cut fresh inroads, impose heavy sacrifices on the target, and inflict deep internal cleavages in the political fabric of the target regime – cleavages hard for the untrained eye to see on initial impact'.[27] It is likely that only superpowers are able to bear the economic strain or impact of being a target in the short run, although there are many states which remain convinced of their 'rightness' when faced with challenges to their resilience as cultural isolation grows with non-economic sanctions. In the South African case, there were changes in the boycott strategy following limited sporting integration in the late 1980s with the support of the ANC, which, in turn, held out the promise of return to international competition. Had the isolation of rugby union been more complete and in effect earlier, there is little doubt that White South Africa would have lost a major aspect of its cultural strength.

The economics and international relations literature helps us fill out some conceptual gaps in discussing the South African sports boycotts, and leads to a three-part model proposing that sanctions, embargoes and boycotts:

(1) are effective only as part of broader suite of isolating activities;
(2) operate in a market determined by monopsonistic cartels, so analyses of likely and actual effectiveness must address:
    (a) access to alternatives in sender states,
    (b) access to alternatives in target states;
(3) have an effect that tends to be cultural and to do with national psychological well-being, and determined by the significance of the sport in question.

In addition, the anti-apartheid campaign suggests that sports boycotts gain legitimacy and therefore solidarity/support from:

(1) being in support of an indigenous call;
(2) being able to point to alternative representative sports bodies.

Noting that the anti-apartheid campaign on which this model is based was played out in a global environment that, 20 years ago, was markedly different from the current one, the opposition to the UEFA Under-21 championships held in Israel in 2013, including a boycott call, provides an opportunity to revisit this analysis. Comparing one campaign – and so far the only time sport has been a significant factor in the BDS campaign currently targeting Israel – with developments over a 30-year movement is not a good basis for meaningful evaluation, so this discussion is tentative, exploratory and cautious in its conclusions.

Israel, the BDS Campaign and Soccer

The June 22, 2011, appeal to UEFA by 42 Palestinian football clubs, a further 18 players and managers, and 19 other leading Palestinian sport figures to reverse its decision to hold its 2013 under-21 championship in Israel marked a shift in the Palestinian BDS campaign. The call appears to be the first coordinated BDS attempt to address a multilateral sports event; the dispersed character of the BDS campaign means being any more definitive is unwise. The call for the tournament to be moved from Israel echoed the principal elements of the BDS campaign, charging Israel with practising 'a unique combination of occupation, colonization and apartheid against the indigenous Palestinian population'.[28] Noting the definitions earlier, this should be seen as call for a sporting sanction to be imposed on Israel in response to a call for an embargo on the grounds that it is held to violate international law and Palestinian human rights in its 'occupation, colonization and apartheid'.

The 2011 letter highlights football-related evidence to support its charge of 'occupation, colonization and apartheid'. The 'occupation' charge is sustained by reference to two factors: the destruction of large section of the Gaza Strip in 2008/2009 during Operation Cast Lead including the destruction of the Rafah National Stadium, an action defended by Israel as targeting militants launching rockets, and the related deaths of footballers among the 1400 dead in Gaza. The call also identifies the proximity of the Separation Wall, ruled illegal in 2004 by the International Court of Justice, to the Faisal Al Hussein Stadium in Al-Ram and the detention 'without trial or ... public explanation' of the Palestinian National Team member Mahmoud Kamel Al-Sarsak.

The 'colonization' charge is sustained by the reference to the siting of Ramat Gan Stadium, designated host of some games, on land seized from the Palestinian villages of Jarisha and al-Jammasin al Sharqi under the Absentee Property Law, 5710-1950, labelled in the call as the Absentee Property Owners Law (1950). The law, at Art 1(b), defined as absentee every Palestinian or resident in Palestine who left their usual place of residence in Palestine for any place inside or outside the country after the United Nations resolution agreeing to the partition of Palestine[29]; this means anyone, including those non-combatants fleeing conflict in 1948, who left their property for anywhere else inside or outside pre-partition Palestine was designated absentee and their property liable to seizure by the state.

The 'apartheid' charge is the one that often jars with wider public opinion, given the close association of apartheid with the era of National Party rule in South Africa from 1948 to 1994. As noted earlier, in 1973 the UN defined apartheid as 'inhuman acts for the purpose of establishing and maintaining domination by one racial group of persons over any other racial group and systematically oppressing them'; legal scholars and others continue to debate the application of this definition to Israeli domestic law. The call to UEFA, however, identifies the Israeli permit system, seen as parallel to the South African Pass Laws, as placing limitations on Palestinian freedom of movement that denies footballers access to tournaments and other matches and to the opportunity to practise.[30]

The call to rescind the opportunity for Israel to host this tournament takes a form that links closely to the 2005 BDS call, and must be understood in that light. The BDS call is a right's based call for action to build pressure on Israel 'to respect fundamental human rights and to end its occupation and oppression of the people of Palestine'.[31] The call, being rights based, does not envisage a specific political structure, but calls for action to address key issues for the three sections of Palestinian society – refugees, the occupied and Palestinian citizens of Israel. It therefore calls on its supporters to pressure Israel to recognise and act on its international obligations by:

(1) ending its occupation and colonisation of all Arab lands and dismantling the Wall;
(2) recognising the fundamental rights of the Arab-Palestinian citizens of Israel to full equality; and
(3) respecting, protecting and promoting the rights of Palestinian refugees to return to their homes and properties as stipulated in UN resolution 194.

The three aspects of sports' call to UEFA, occupation, colonisation and apartheid, parallel these three aspects of the 2005 declaration.

A Broad Suite of Isolating Activities

An accurate reading of the sports organisations' letter to UEFA requires that it be placed in the BDS context. To do so means that there are two other key factors to consider; the first relates to the genesis of the BDS campaign, the second to the detail of the BDS call. The genesis of the call directs attention to the history of Israel and Palestine. For much of the twentieth century, the politics of the region have been presented as one of national liberation, both in the form of the Zionist project of settlement and state-building, and the Palestinian resistance to occupation by and expulsion from that state. A Palestinian politics of national liberation may be seen in the federation of organisations that became the Palestine Liberation Organisation. Changes in geopolitical relations and in Palestinian society meant that during the last quarter of the twentieth century there were significant changes in Palestinian politics, including heightened military control in the OPT (Gaza and the West Bank) and the emergence of new forms of civil society including social clubs, welfare and educational organisations. The era also reveals changes in political organisation, with a shift away from accommodation with the settler state through mechanisms such as the *mukhtar* (headman) system.[32]

Increasing frustration at limited change for the better for Palestinians within the Green Line, marking Israel's borders, and in the OPT saw an outburst of resistance in 1987, now known as the First Intifada.[33] This Intifada saw active resistance to Israeli policy and practice from Palestinian citizens and those living under occupation in a way that Israel had not experienced before, and the consistent but not always successful efforts that the Palestinians made to avoid armed conflict unsettled Israeli police and the Israeli Defence Force in a way that meant some of the Israeli responses seemed to be excessive, at significant public image costs. In an effort to control the Intifada, and after considerable international pressure, Israel and the PLO entered negotiations leading to the Oslo accords of 1993 and the creation of the Palestinian Authority (PA) with jurisdiction over a range of social, security and civil issues in the OPT. The notable omission from the PA was many of the civil society institutions that had filled an important need on the ground during that earlier era of armed national liberation struggle. This exclusion as well as with the problematic role of the PA as an agent of development under conditions determined by the occupation and therefore as an agent of the occupation led to a widespread Palestinian view that the PA was a corrupt organisation. The result was shifts in the political balance of forces in Palestinian society opening space for more active civil society[34]; it was 171 organisations comprising a major part of this civil society that issued the BDS call in 2005. This is the first significant difference from the South African case: the groups calling for BDS are not national liberation movements similar to those in South Africa but civil society institutions that are often critical of the 'official' national liberation groups, now dominated by those gathered around Fatah and around Hamas.

The second key aspect of the BDS call that is relevant to this exploration of the 2013 UEFA U-21 championship is its target. Although the 2005 call, and much of the discussion since, invokes the South African precedent, the terms of the call are different. Whereas the call for the total isolation of South Africa meant that there should be no contact of any form other than with the liberation movements, the Palestinian call is for BDS aimed at the State of Israel, not the total isolation of Israelis; this is clear in the inclusion of the invitation to 'conscientious Israelis to support this call, for the sake of justice and genuine peace'. The sports organisations' call sits alongside efforts to organise other cultural boycotts, an academic boycott and economic boycotts of Israeli business as well as companies investing in and sustaining the occupation.[35] The economic and cultural boycotts have been more successful than academic and sports boycotts. BDS advocates are clear, time and again, that the focus is the state of Israel, not individual Israelis. Hence, the 2011 call was consistent with the broader BDS campaign in calling on UEFA to withdraw the championships from Israel; the target was not Israeli players in European leagues. In this sense there is a fundamental difference with the South African-focussed campaign.

This background to the U-21 championship campaign suggests that this case is consistent with the first element of the model. There has been a call for widespread BDS activity that has seen attempted and successful action in a range of economic sectors – transport, education, culture and others. The BDS campaign itself admits that it 'had been slow to promote a sporting boycott'[36] although there has been some BDS-related sport-focussed protest activity, such as during the 2009 Israel–Sweden Davis Cup match,[37] sport-related BDS activity has been only a very small part of the campaign. This is likely to be a result of the 'boycott Israel, not Israelis' stance. There is a second strand related to the boycott call as part of a wider sphere of action linked to UEFA's anti-racism work. UEFA, as is the case with most of its constituents, actively supports anti-racism campaigns; these campaigns, although designed to focus on structural racism as well as more overt racist acts, tend to gain most attention when addressing overt racism. Based on this focus and alongside the campaign against holding the tournament in Israel, critics also drew attention to manifestations of overt racism in Israeli football. Much of the criticism centred on the Jerusalem-based club Beitar, officials of which have been criticised within Israel for what seems to be reluctance to confront some of the more overt and ostentatious displays of anti-Palestinian, anti-Arab and anti-Islamic views among the club's supporters, highlighting in particular the actions of a fan group targeting two Chechen players signed by the team early in 2013 – its first Muslim players. Others have argued that this is a minority of fans, although minorities combined with club inaction has not stopped UEFA or national federation anti-racism activity in other settings. This UEFA focussed anti-racism argument is best seen as in parallel to but not part of the principal boycott call. It has, however, seemed to have a profile that has overshadowed and distracted from the BDS aspects of the campaign.

International Football Tournaments

Considering international sport within a market determined by monopsonistic cartels means that analyses of the likely and actual effectiveness of boycotts must address both the access to sporting alternatives in sender states and the access to alternatives in target states. This requires a focus on access to and the status of elite youth football in both likely sender states and in Israel. It is on this point that the character of the international sports market as monopsonistic becomes important. UEFA, as the only 'purchaser', can determine both the character of exchange in the market and the participants in that market. This means that a unilateral decision by one or a minority of the participating national associations to boycott could have been extremely expensive in that they could have been seen as an unreliable supplier and possibly in violation of membership and competition rules. In this multilateral competitive context, the IF is not only the single purchaser but also organises the market, including determining the rules of market entry and participation; under these conditions member associations are unlikely to act unilaterally. In this situation where national governing bodies have a single 'purchaser' for international competitive events a decision by UEFA as that 'purchaser' to withdraw the tournament from Israel would have no significant effect on the senders' access to elite competitive sport; there would be no need to seek an alternative.

The effect on Israel, had UEFA acted on the BDS call, could have been significant, for the same reason that any other member association would be unlikely to act unilaterally. Israel would lose access to elite international youth football played at home. Furthermore, the control the IFs exercise over club football, such as the Champions League, would threaten access to all forms levels of elite football should a general football or sports boycott be successful. Given that the call was not for a comprehensive UEFA boycott but for the tournament to be hosted by another UEFA member, should UEFA have agreed the effect would have less severe but still significant. It is almost certain that Israel would not have participated in the tournament, and it would not have had access to an alternative form of competition at home. Under these circumstances, and noting the specific characteristics of international football governance including the control of elite club play, a decision by UEFA to relocate the tournament is likely to have been a major blow to Israeli football, leaving aside the political and psychological consequences of the move.

National Psychological Well-Being

The third element of the model, that the effect of any boycott tends to be cultural, related to national self-perception, confidence and well-being and determined by significance of the sport in question, in this case, is unanswerable; there was no boycott. That the tournament took place, however, is presented by representatives of the Israel Football Association (IFA) as a significant advance for and benefit to Israeli football. The tournament director, Ronen Hershco, presented it as a success in terms of legacy even though the Israeli team did not progress beyond the group stage.[38] It is reasonable to assume that had UEFA decided to shift the tournament the effect would have been significant, especially if there was no significant shift in the 'security situation', as the conflict is often euphemistically labelled. Given the counterfactual aspects of this proposition, it remains no more than an assumption although the combination of football's cultural significance in Israel combined with Israel's powerful desire to normalise its global position and role as seen in the government's 'Brand Israel' programme suggests that the assumption may be well founded.

Solidarity and Legitimacy

In addition to these three aspects of the model, success and international support for the boycott relies on the legitimacy of any boycott activity, which relates to matters 'on the ground' in the Israel–Palestine sporting and political nexus. The protest action targeting the UEFA competition is clearly in support of an indigenous call from the Palestinian sports community with the June 22, 2011, letter signed by 42 sports clubs and a further 37 individuals. This is a marked change from the initial 2005 BDS call where there are no obvious sports clubs among the 171 civil society signatory groups. In the sports case there is legitimacy granted to the BDS activity in that it is in support of a call by Palestinian sports groups.

The more difficult aspect of legitimacy concerns the presence of alternative representative sports bodies. It may be that this is distinctive to the South African setting and has less resonance in the case of Israel/Palestine. The question of sports federations in historic Palestine shows the presence of several groups claiming representative status. The Palestine Football Association, for instance, cited by FIFA as the predecessor of its member organisations for both Palestine and Israel was founded in 1928 and admitted to FIFA in 1929, yet the current information page for Palestine shows its membership of FIFA beginning in 1998.[39] The PFA initially had Arab members, in 1929 11 of its 69 teams were Arab teams, but after the mid-1930s until its transformation into the Israel Football Association it became increasingly Zionist group with only minimal membership of mandatory Palestine's Arab population. Parallel organisations emerged from the mid-1940s in the form of the Arab Palestine Sports Association, also known as General Palestinian Sports Association, and the Islamic Sports Club.[40] Palestine was only admitted to FIFA in 1998, 50 years after partition, in the wake of recognition of Palestine as a proto-state as part of the Oslo Accords and the emerging 'two state solution'. The effect is that while Israel and Palestine exist as separate political entities, BDS campaigners are not able to point to alternative representative sports bodies in Israel because the Palestinians exist in three distinct formations – refugees in neighbouring states and, more widely dispersed, residents of the OPT and citizens of Israel. In football terms, the latter are incorporated in the IFA while the PFA covers the OPT and some refugee camps. The distinction is based on the proto-state-like status of Palestine. Furthermore, while each remains identified as a distinct state/quasi-state the respective football associations are in different regional confederations – UEFA for Israel and the Asian Football Confederation for Palestine and the rest of region. The BDS call directed at UEFA was in the interests of groups that are not the concern of UEFA. The legitimacy of the campaign, therefore, relies on its status as an indigenous call for action.

BDS Summary

Returning to the model:

1. The first element is that sports boycotts are effective only as part of broader suite of boycott activities; the call on UEFA to withdraw the 2013 under-21 tournament from Israel is clearly part of a wider BDS campaign, and the first time the campaign had ventured into multilateral sport. In this sense, the call is consistent with the campaign's references to the South African focussed campaign and different from other boycott calls, such as the recent LGBT rights based call to boycott the Sochi Olympics which while based in LGBT activist groups remained distinct from either broader sport-oriented or civil rights focussed activism centred on Russia; that is, there is not a wider Russia- or sport-centred boycott activities in which the campaign could gain traction.

2. The monopsonistic cartel that controls football has more power than some other international governing bodies because of its influence over elite club play, including international club competition. This suggests that football's national governing bodies would be unlikely to act unilaterally but had UEFA acted the impact on 'sender' states would have been minimal in terms of access to alternatives while Israel would likely be excluded from access to any alternatives. There are two further factors to consider here, that also mark the campaign apart from its South African predecessor. The first is that changes in global geopolitics mean that individual state governments are unlikely to take action over a sports boycott. The second is that even in the case of sports boycott, the global sport media complex means that Israelis may lose access to live international sports events but not to televised or other mediated forms.

3. It is likely that action by UEFA to relocate the tournament would have had effects that were primarily cultural and detrimental to Israel's national self-image in part because of the significance of football but more so because of government efforts to normalise Israel's international image.

4. As with the South African campaigns, the 2013 campaign gained legitimacy among supporters from being in support of a call from within the Palestinian sport structure; that is, an indigenous call. Unlike the South African case campaigners are not able to point to alternative representative sports bodies, in part because of distinction between Israel and Palestine as states and proto-states.

The initial model is an argument based on a boycott tactic; in this case it can also be seen to be substantially appropriate in the case of an embargo – but more work and case study analysis is necessary to refine the elements related to the legitimacy question and the role of sport-specific IFs.

A significant challenge to the BDS campaign, when developing its sport aspect, lies in the organisation of sport in Israel and Palestine. Football presents the issues well. Noting the existence of the Islamic League in Israel, mainstream Israeli football is not explicitly or uniquely divided along ethno-nationalist lines, unlike much of the rest of Israeli society and politics. There is a compelling analysis by Tamir Sorek, that football is, in his words, an 'integrative enclave' which he notes is a combined product of the 'interests of the Hebrew sports media and state institutions ... and the Arab soccer fans, players and bureaucrats' while also limiting its integrative power because it acts as a site for 'the majority's interest in maintaining the status quo, and the need of a discriminated-against national minority to maintain active protest while at the same time preserving proper relations with the majority society'.[41] As with nearly every other site of social interaction in Israel/Palestine, football is layered, complex and wrapped in contested and disputed historical narratives and on the ground political power imbalances. This integrative element means that whereas, in many other respects, Israel might meet the UN's definition of an apartheid state[42] in the case of football at least that is a more difficult case to make. This weakness may be seen in the way some campaign supporters have had to rely on the liberal framing of football's official bodies' anti-racism campaigns that tend to focus on individual and overt racist acts rather than structural or contextual racism. Development of a sport-focussed strand in the BDS campaign therefore suffers from a weak sport-specific analysis in dealing with Palestinian citizens of Israel: the situation is different for the occupation mainly because of its illegal aspects. The June 22, 2011 call by the 42 clubs pointed to the three aspects of colonisation, occupation and apartheid highlighted in the BDS campaign, but in the absence of sport-specific issues, a sport-focussed campaign may find it difficult to gain traction.

Conclusion

This paper explores the politics of international sports relations by proposing a model for understanding sports boycotts based in global sport structures. This model is related to analyses of economic boycotts but is also based in an analysis of the way the structure of international sports governance creates and shapes the market in international competitive sport. The call by 42 Palestinian sports clubs for UEFA to relocate its 2013 under-21 tournament from Israel made in line with the wider BDS campaign targeting Israel allows exploration of the organisation and politics of sports boycotts, as a specific form of cultural boycott, in a new geopolitical context. The analysis poses further questions concerning the extent to which the distinctive features of sports organisation and governance in Israel/ Palestine influence the extent to which a sports boycott can be a meaningful tool in the BDS tactical repertoire. Football's role as an integrative enclave in Israel and the separate existence of internationally recognised Palestinian sports bodies suggests that previous tactical approaches to colonial and post-colonising analyses will be of limited use. Second, the embedding of neo-liberal ideologies and the dominant role of market organisation means that international and national governing bodies exercise much of their control in less direct means than a generation ago. Third, the changing shape of global geopolitics, the decline of a bipolar world and growing influence of corporate institutions in international relations lessens the likely role of national governments in any wider sports or cultural boycott movement; as a result, analysis will need to focus on non-state and civil society institutions as factors in global sport politics.

The major mistake any analysis could make would be to take the BDS campaign's statements that it is inspired by the South African anti-apartheid boycott to mean that it is the same as that boycott; this new campaign is focussed on relations with the state of Israel, not with Israelis – this means analysts and activists need to grasp the analytical distinctions between playing rugby *against* South Africa and playing soccer *in* Israel.

Notes

1. Tilley, *Beyond Occupation*.
2. International Convention on the Suppression and Punishment of the Crime of Apartheid. Adopted by the General Assembly of the United Nations on November 30, 1973. Article 1, https://treaties.un.org/doc/Publication/UNTS/Volume%201015/volume-1015-I-14861-English.pdf (accessed August 3, 2013).
3. International Court of Justice, Reports of Judgments, Advisory Opinions and Orders: Legal Consequences of the Construction of a Wall in the Occupied Palestinian Territory, Advisory Opinion of July 9, 2004. International Court of Justice, Reports of Judgments, Advisory Opinions and Orders, http://www.icj-cij.org/docket/files/131/1671.pdf (accessed August 3, 2013). Daniel Steiman, "The Settlements Are Illegal under International Law," *Jerusalem Post*, December 29, 2013, http://www.jpost.com/Opinion/Op-Ed-Contributors/Thesettl ements-are-illegal-under-international-law-336507 (accessed January 3, 2014); Al-Rayyes, *The Israeli Settlements*; UN Human Rights Council, "Report of the Independent International Fact-Finding Mission to Investigate the Implications of the Israeli Settlements on the Civil, Political, Economic, Social and Cultural Rights of the Palestinian People throughout the Occupied Palestinian Territory, Including East Jerusalem," http://www.ohchr.org/Documents/ HRBodies/HRCouncil/RegularSession/Session19/FFM/FFMSettlements.pdf (accessed January 3, 2014).
4. Fieldhouse, *Anti-Apartheid*, 1–20; Skinner, *The Foundations of Anti-Apartheid*, 162–70; Richards, *Dancing on Our Bones*, 21–7; Templeton, *Human Rights*, 31–7.
5. Cited in Cook, "Race Segregation," 228.
6. Archer and Bouillon, *The South African Game*, 104–5; Booth, *The Race Game*, 60–1.
7. Murray and Merritt, *Caught Behind*, 89–116; Gemmell, *The Politics*, 146–54.
8. Booth, *The Race Game*.
9. Lapchick, *The Politics of Race*, 139–40, 191–4.
10. Bolling and Bolsman, "Here Come 'Chelsea'."
11. Archer and Bouillon, *The South African Game*, 186–205; Nauright, *Sport, Cultures and Identities*, 135–8.
12. Gemmell, *The Politics*, 117–39.
13. Archer and Bouillon, *The South African Game*, 334–5.
14. Grundlingh, "Playing for Power?"
15. Richards, *Dancing on Our Bones*; Fieldhouse, *Anti-Apartheid*; O'Donnell and Simons, *Australians against Racism*, esp. 108–27.
16. Templeton, *Human Rights*, 50.
17. Gemmell, *The Politics*, 163–78.
18. Daoudi and Dajani, *Economic Sanctions*, 7.
19. Ibid., 8–9.
20. Barber and Spicer, "Sanctions against South Africa"; Hayes, *Economic Effects of Sanctions*; Jenkins, *The Effects of Sanctions*.
21. Connolly, "The Politics of the Games"; Field, *Re-Entering the Sporting World*.
22. Houlihan, *Sport and International Politics*.

23. This difference in the perception of economic significance may clearly be seen in the debate during late 2002 and early 2003 over an English World Cup cricket match against Zimbabwe in Zimbabwe where the England and Wales Cricket Board was faced with a £1 million fine. This became a major point of contention between the ECB and the British Government.

24. Although, as Jenkins, *Effects of Sanctions*, shows, this is not always so.

25. Ramsamy, *Apartheid*.

26. Hunter, "The United Nations."

27. Daoudi and Dajani, *Economic Sanctions*, 160.

28. "Palestinian Sports Community Appeal to UEFA – Red Card against Israel," *BDS Movement: Freedom, Justice, Equality*, http://www.bdsmovement.net/2011/letter-to-platini-7377 (accessed August 5, 2013).

29. Tilley, *Beyond Occupation*, 207; White, *Palestinians in Israel*, 22–5; White, *Israeli Apartheid*, 44–5; Rabinowitz and Abu-Baker, *Coffins on Our Shoulders*, 46–7.

30. Lippe, "Football, Masculinities and Health."

31. "Palestinian Civil Society Call for BDS," *BDS Movement: Freedom, Justice, Equality*, http://www.bdsmovement.net/call (accessed August 7, 2013).

32. Rabinowitz and Abu-Baker, *Coffins on Our Shoulders*.

33. Ibid., esp. 75–98.

34. Hever, *The Political Economy*, 14–7.

35. The growing profile of BDS economic action may be seen in the debates in early 2014 over the actor Scarlett Johansson's marketing relationship with the Israeli company SodaStream, which maintains factories in the Occupied Palestinian Territories, leading to the end of her work as an ambassador for the aid and development agency Oxfam.

36. Jonathan Cook, "Israeli Football, Racism and Politics: The Ugly Side of the Beautiful Game," *Scottish Palestine Solidarity Campaign*, http://www.scottishpsc.org.uk/index.php/solidarity/boycott/sports/football/1573-racismrampant-in-israeli-football-rewarded-by-uefa (accessed August 5, 2013).

37. "Anti-Israel Protest Staged at Sweden Tennis Match," http://www.reuters.com/article/2009/03/07/us-sweden-davis-protestsidUSTRE5261R220090307 (accessed August 7, 2013).

38. "Herscho Reflects on Israel's Under-21 Legacy," http://www.uefa.com/under21/news/news id= 1969771.html (accessed August 10, 2013).

39. FIFA, Palestine, http://www.fifa.com/associations/association=ple/index.html (accessed August 10, 2013); FIFA, Israel, http://www.fifa.com/associations/association=isr/index.html (accessed August 10, 2013).

40. Sorek, *Arab Soccer in Israel*, 17–30.

41. Ibid., 185–6.

42. Davis, *Apartheid Israel*; White, *Israeli Apartheid*; Tilley, *Beyond Occupation*.

References

Al-Rayyes, N. *The Israeli Settlements from the Perspective of International Law*. Ramallah: Al-Haq Institute, 2000.

Archer, R., and A. Bouillon. *The South African Game: Sport and Racism*. London: Zed Press, 1982.

Barber, J., and M. Spicer. "Sanctions against South Africa – Options for the West." *International Affairs* 55 (1979): 385–401.

Bolling, H., and C. Bolsman. "'Here Come "Chelsea" of Sweden': Djurgården Football Club on Tour in Apartheid South Africa." *Sport in History* 33, no. 3 (2013): 353–372.

Booth, D. *The Race Game: Sport and Politics in South Africa*. London: Frank Cass, 1998.

Connolly, C. "The Politics of the Games of the New Emerging Forces (GANEFO)." *The International Journal of the History of Sport* 29, no. 9 (2012): 1311–1324.

Cook, O. F. "Race Segregation in South Africa: New Policies and Factors in Race Relations." *The Journal of Heredity* 21 (1930): 225–233.

Daoudi, M. S., and M. S. Dajani. *Economic Sanctions: Ideals and Experience*. London: Routledge & Kegan Paul, 1983.

Davis, U. *Apartheid Israel: Possibilities for the Struggle Within*. London: Zed Books, 2004.

Field, R. "Re-Entering the Sporting World: China's Sponsorship of the 1963 Games of the New Emerging Forces." Games and Sporting Events in History: Organisation, Performances and Impacts: 14th ISHPES Congress, Taipei, Taiwan, August 18–22, 2013.

Fieldhouse, R. *Anti-Apartheid: A History of the Movement in Britain*. London: Merlin, 2005.
Gemmell, J. *The Politics of South African Cricket*. London: Routledge, 2004.
Grundlingh, A. "Playing for Power? Rugby, Afrikaner Nationalism and Masculinity in South Africa, c.1900-70." *The International Journal of the History of Sport* 11, no. 3 (1994): 408–430.
Hayes, J. P. *Economic Effects of Sanctions of Southern Africa*. London: Gower, 1987.
Hever, S. *The Political Economy of Israel's Occupation: Repression Beyond Exploitation*. London: Pluto, 2010.
Houlihan, B. *Sport and International Politics*. Hemel Hempstead: Harvester Wheatsheaf, 1994.
Hunter, M. G. "The United Nations and the Anti-Apartheid in Sport Movement." *Canadian Journal of the History of Sport* XI (1980): 19–35.
Jenkins, C. *The Effects of Sanctions on Formal Sector Employment in South Africa*. Brighton: Institute of Development Studies, University of Sussex, 1993.
Lapchick, R. *The Politics of Race and International Sport: The Case of South Africa*. Westport, CT: Greenwood Press, 1975.
Lippe, G. v. d. "Football, Masculinities and Health on the Gaza Strip." Forthcoming.
Murray, B., and C. Merritt. *Caught Behind: Race and Politics in Springbok Cricket*. Johannesburg: Wits University Press, 2004.
Nauright, J. *Sport, Cultures and Identities in South Africa*. London: Leicester University Press, 1997.
O'Donnell, P., and L. Simons. *Australians against Racism: Testimonies from the Antiapartheid Movement in Australia*. Sydney: Pluto, 1995.
Rabinowitz, D., and K. Abu-Baker. *Coffins on Our Shoulders: The Experience of the Palestinian Citizens of Israel*. Berkeley: University of California Press, 2005.
Ramsamy, S. *Apartheid: The Real Hurdle. Sport in South Africa and the International Boycott*. London: International Defence and Aid Fund for Southern Africa, 1982.
Richards, T. *Dancing on Our Bones: New Zealand, South Africa, Rugby and Racism*. Wellington: Bridget Williams Books, 1999.
Skinner, R. *The Foundations of Anti-Apartheid: Liberal Humanitarians and Transnational Activists in Britain and the United States, c. 1919–64*. Basingstoke: Palgrave, 2010.
Sorek, T. *Arab Soccer in Israel: The Integrative Enclave*. Cambridge: Cambridge University Press, 2005.
Templeton, M. *Human Rights and Sporting Contacts: New Zealand Attitudes to Race Relations in South Africa 1921–94*. Auckland: Auckland University Press, 1998.
Tilley, V., ed. *Beyond Occupation: Apartheid, Colonialism and International Law in the Occupied Territories*. London: Pluto, 2012.
White, B. *Israeli Apartheid: A Beginner's Guide*. London: Pluto, 2010.
White, B. *Palestinians in Israel: Segregation, Discrimination and Democracy*. London: Pluto, 2012.

Re-Entering the Sporting World: China's Sponsorship of the 1963 Games of the New Emerging Forces (GANEFO)

Russell Field

Faculty of Kinesiology and Recreation Management, University of Manitoba, Winnipeg, Manitoba, Canada

Prior to the 2008 Olympics, China's most sustained support of an international multi-sport event came in 1963 when it contributed significantly to the financing of and then dominated the medals table at the inaugural Games of the New Emerging Forces (GANEFO), held in Jakarta. GANEFO is a singular moment through which to understand politics and sport in the 1960s. This article is a consideration of China's role in GANEFO, and the West's response to China's involvement. It explores the ways in which China used the event to navigate issues of international and regional geopolitics, and considers the diplomatic and sporting corridors within which GANEFO resonated. GANEFO was a platform through which geopolitical tensions were revealed, and China engaged in propaganda campaigns directed at the West and positioned itself to win allies among the decolonising countries of Asia and Africa – astride the artificial boundary that separated the Second and Third Worlds. China's interest in and the West's response to GANEFO reflected the ways in which anti-communist Cold War politics were conflated with racialised, post-colonial discourses and tension between Second World powers.

When an outsider noted of a significant moment in Chinese sporting history that the world's most populous nation 'took her place in the international community of sports, and did so in a brilliant manner', it might be assumed that such praise came in the wake of the 2008 Beijing Olympic Games.[1] These comments, however, were made 45 years earlier, by an American observer of a little-remembered multi-sport event that took place in Jakarta, Indonesia. November 2013 marked the 50th anniversary of this contentious (at the time) moment in the history of decolonisation and international sport, one in which the People's Republic of China (hereafter, China) played a central role. Prior to the 2008 Olympics, China's most sustained support of an international multi-sport event came in 1963 when it contributed significantly to the financing of and then dominated the medals table at the inaugural Games of the New Emerging Forces (GANEFO), held in Jakarta.

GANEFO is a singular moment through which to understand politics and sport in the 1960s. This article is drawn from a larger work-in-progress that places GANEFO at the intersection of sport and politics in the 1960s and seeks to combine the diplomatic and archival record with oral history narratives to incorporate the history of this alternative multi-sport event within discourses of decolonisation and international sport. The present article is a consideration of China's role in GANEFO, which occurred at a time when China had withdrawn from the international Olympic movement over the issue of the recognition of Taiwan, the Republic of China. In examining China's relation to GANEFO, this article explores the ways in which China used the event to navigate issues of international and regional geopolitics, and considers the diplomatic and sporting corridors within which GANEFO resonated. In turn, the implications of China's interest in GANEFO for its relationship to the First, Second and Third Worlds are considered, while recognising that these geopolitical ties cannot be so easily separated.

China's interest in international sport and its contentious ties to sport's most prominent governing body, the International Olympic Committee (IOC), during this period are the point of departure. From the outset, GANEFO's organisers positioned themselves in opposition to the IOC leadership, which was framed – in particular by Indonesian and Chinese leaders – as firmly in the grip of the US and Western political interests. GANEFO was to be, as one Chinese summary of the Games recalled, 'an international sport event that is not controlled by imperialism and colonialism'.[2] In addition to Chinese-language sources such as this (*The New Flag in International Sports*) and propaganda texts (written and visual) prepared by the Chinese state in English for export, the analysis that follows also includes a number of contemporary Western interpretations of China's diplomatic and sporting aims.

This article seeks to understand China's central role in GANEFO – encouraging, financing and athletically dominating the event. As a Second World power, one which by 1963 was also experiencing diplomatic friction with the dominant socialist state, the USSR, China was a geopolitical adversary of the West in East and Southeast Asia. Despite the apparent straightforwardness of Cold War binaries, from the emergence of the non-aligned movement China had positioned itself discursively alongside decolonising Third World nations, straddling the line between the Second World and the non-Caucasian 'emerging forces'. GANEFO can be understood, at least rhetorically, as a realisation through sport of some of these geopolitical manoeuvrings and a site where China's relations with the First, Second and Third Worlds played out.

GANEFO and the Politics of International Sport

The Third World was not a place. It was a project. During the seemingly interminable battles against colonialism, the peoples of Africa, Asia, and Latin America dreamed of a new world. They longed for dignity above all else, but also the basic necessities of life (land, peace, and freedom). They assembled their grievances and aspirations into various kinds of organizations, where their leadership then formulated a platform of demands.[3]

If the Third World was, as Vijay Prashad contends, more a project than a place, GANEFO was a visible sporting manifestation of this project, an explicit attempt to link sport to the politics of anti-colonialism and tangible evidence of the Third World's ability to mobilise itself through sport. The event took shape at a preparatory conference in Jakarta in April 1963. The Indonesian hosts were joined by representatives from Cambodia, China, Guinea, Iraq, Mali, Pakistan, North Vietnam, the United Arab Republic and the USSR (Ceylon and Yugoslavia attended as observers). This meeting planned the multi-sport event and a subsequent conference intended to solidify the political unity of the new emerging forces, both of which were grounded in 'the Spirit of the Asian-African Conference in Bandung' and brought together peoples 'who are against imperialism, people who are against exploitation de l'homme par l'homme, against exploitation'.[4]

Seven months later, from November 10 to 22, 1963, roughly 3000 participants from – but not all officially representing – 48 nations met in the Indonesian capital and competed in 20 sports (virtually all Olympic and Western) and cultural festivities. Athletes hailed primarily from recently decolonised countries in Asia and Africa (as well as former colonies in Latin America), which were labelled the 'new emerging forces' by Indonesian President Sukarno, who created GANEFO as part of his attempts to situate his nation as a regional power.[5] Although, significantly, GANEFO's genesis was also related to diplomatic problems arising from Indonesia's hosting of the 1962 IVth Asian Games (discussed below).

The Games, whose opening ceremonies unfolded in front of a crowd of 100,000 in Jakarta's Bung Karno Stadium, included such symbols and rituals as a torch relay, a symbolic flame, a parade of athletes in front of the head of state, the raising of the specially designed flag of the GANEFO movement, opening and closing ceremonies, cultural exhibits and adjudicated competitive athletic events that resulted in the awarding of medals. Of all the teams that marched into Bung Karno Stadium past the presidential viewing stand, only the host nation's was larger than the Chinese team. And, by the time that GANEFO ended, no nation could rival the success of China, which topped the medals table with 137 total medals (55 gold, 46 silver and 36 bronze), with Chinese and North Korean athletes setting world records in archery, track and field, and weightlifting.[6] It is worth noting that not all of the athletes represented the best sporting talent that their respective nations had to offer, but China was chief among those countries that did send its most competitive representatives.

The Games, along with the subsequent political conference of GANEFO attendees, ensured that the event had geopolitical and sporting consequences, which drew the attention of foreign ministries in both the First and Second Worlds. Sukarno and his supporters in China and elsewhere intended GANEFO to be the sporting arm of a larger, eventually unrealised political movement, but except for an Asian GANEFO in Phnom Penh in 1966, the Games were never held again. While Sukarno publicly framed GANEFO as a quadrennial rival to the IOC Games, by 1965, he had been ousted, and the 1967 GANEFO originally planned for Cairo was subsequently moved to Beijing, before disappearing from the sport calendar altogether with the onset of the Cultural Revolution.

Despite its contemporary significance, GANEFO is largely absent from histories of Indonesia and the period of Sukarno's presidency.[7] The event, however, can be understood within the Indonesian leader's anti-colonial, nationalist and Third Worldist positions as well as his efforts to promote a homogenised sense of Indonesian identity in the face of ethnic and regional diversity, and criticisms of the Java-centrism of his government.[8] The Chinese historians who have considered GANEFO, such as Xu Guoqi, examine China's attempts to use sport, specifically GANEFO, as a political and propaganda tool 'to advance its international status'.[9] From this platform, China 'could champion developing countries and revolution on an international stage'.[10] At the same time, as Amanda Shuman asserts, GANEFO also served a domestic purpose for the Chinese state, indicating a 'commitment to using elite competitive sport for nation building' in a way that suggested a stronger, healthier, more vital populace.[11]

Until recently, GANEFO has received relatively little attention from historians of sport, obscured by higher profile (in the West) civil rights struggles connected to sport in the 1960s, including the suspension of South Africa's apartheid regime by the IOC[12] and the American 'black power' demonstration by US sprinters Tommie Smith and John Carlos at the 1968 Mexico City Olympics.[13] Most considerations of GANEFO have framed the event as an expression of Indonesia's independence and Sukarno's efforts to link politics and sport,[14] while GANEFO was also important in attempts to position Indonesia within the non-aligned world.[15] Accounts that consider the geopolitical implications of GANEFO, focus on China's financial support as evidence of GANEFO's implication within Cold War politics.[16] More recently, Chris Connolly has examined the ways in which internal tensions within the GANEFO federation contributed to the event's demise and Terry Gitersos has contrasted GANEFO with the 1965 Jeux d'Afrique to suggest that the Third World was a contested zone within international sport.[17] These analyses highlight that GANEFO was more than just a tool in Cold War-inspired joustings among international sport bodies. As this article argues – using China's support of GANEFO as the lens through which to view the event's geopolitical complexity – the threat from GANEFO as perceived in the West was never a homogenous amalgam of Second and Third World interests

A Threat to International Sport, an Opportunity for China

As an event rhetorically framed to contest the hegemony of Western sporting bodies, and one organised through governmental and diplomatic channels, GANEFO caused considerable consternation in the offices of the IOC and various international sport federations (IFs).[18] The event was threatening to sport's power structure, and IOC President Avery Brundage asserted that GANEFO 'is unquestionably the first move in a campaign to take over international sport'.[19] International sport officials were widely concerned over the mixing of politics and sport in the Cold War climate of 1963: NATO's Allied Travel Commission refused travel visas to many athletes from the Soviet bloc; there were debates about recognising two Germanys, two Chinas, two Koreas, and two Vietnams in international sport; and concern over how to deal with the racism of apartheid-based South African teams, countries with state-funded athletes, whose amateur status was contentious, and the newly decolonised countries, which had their own national sport organisations that wished to be recognised within the world of international sport. While Brundage wanted sport to be 'independent' of political influence, Indonesian Foreign Minister, Dr Subandrio, contended that 'sport cannot be separated from politics, and Indonesia uses sports as a political tool to foster solidarity and understanding between nations'.[20] Otto Schantz notes that for Sukarno 'sport was inextricably linked with politics, whereas Brundage regarded this standpoint as "an abnegation of one of the most fundamental and important principles of the Olympic Movement"'.[21]

With the Olympic Games scheduled for Tokyo in 1964, GANEFO was a rival attempt 'to reach out to the Asian sport world'.[22] The objections of the IOC and IFs to GANEFO were grounded in the involvement primarily of the China (who were not part of the Olympic movement at the time) and Indonesia, whose National Olympic Committee (NOC) had been suspended in the wake of the controversies at the IVth Asian Games a year earlier. The rules of international sport, created and administered by these bodies, precluded athletes from competing against sportspeople from countries not affiliated with the IOC or the relevant IF. So athletes and national sport leaders were threatened with suspensions that would impact their participation in the upcoming Tokyo Olympics if they competed in Jakarta.

The warnings from the IOC and IFs were, in part, responsible for the calibre of the teams that competed at GANEFO, few of which included their country's best athletes. China and North Korea were notable exceptions. One thousand Chinese athletes gathered in Beijing on September 14, 1963, to compete in 14 sports, from which 229 athletes, including 'national champions and national record holders', were chosen to compete at GANEFO. Along with officials, media, an acrobatic troupe from Shanghai and other cultural delegates, they comprised 'the biggest delegation to be sent abroad in Chinese sports history'.[23] As one British diplomat noted, China 'not being a member of the International Olympic Federation [sic], had nothing to lose by sending its best athletes'.[24]

China also contributed financially to GANEFO. While ostensibly instigated by Sukarno and organised by the Indonesian government as an explicit attempt to link sport to the politics of anti-imperialism, anti-colonialism and the emergence of the Third World, GANEFO was primarily financed by China. The latter saw in Indonesia an ideological and strategic ally. As Taomo Zhou argues, 'Sukarno's conceptualisation of "new emerging forces" of the formerly colonized world echoed Beijing's strategic thinking'.[25] It is also worth noting the 'domestic' interest that connected the two nations. The position of the approximately 2.5 million ethnic Chinese in Indonesia was a source of tension as they were 'an ethnic minority which had accumulated a disproportionately large share of wealth [and] were oftentimes regarded by other ethnic groups as a source of economic oppression'.[26] Yet, in the lead-up to November 1963, as a Canadian embassy communiqué from Jakarta noted: 'The public has been called on to make GANEFO a great success. It is doing this, rather involuntarily, through cash contributions. Local Chinese organizations lead the way by far in donations'.[27]

A meeting between Sukarno and Chinese President Liu Shaoqi, on the second anniversary of a friendship treaty between the two countries, concluded with a joint statement, in which China pledged to 'reaffirm to firmly support President Sukarno's advocacy to hold the Games of the New Emerging Forces'.[28] That this support was financial was clear to all Western observers – although confirming its extent was difficult to ascertain. The US embassy officials in Jakarta assumed that 'the first CHICOM offer of financial assistance was made' during a December 1962 meeting between Sukarno and the Chinese deputy minister of sport.[29] While '[t]here have been persistent rumors in Indonesian sports circles that the Red Chinese would foot the entire bill for GANEFO', other diplomatic sources (e.g., the Australian, British and Canadian embassies) were unable to confirm the precise nature of the Chinese financial contribution.[30] The British embassy was 'unable to obtain confirmation of the persistent rumour that the Communist Chinese Government were indirectly putting up the money for the fares in all cases', but the Western media reported that African delegations were sponsored by China, while the host Indonesians subsidised the participation of Asian and Latin American athletes.[31] As a *Sports Illustrated* article on GANEFO noted: 'China paid a part of the cost, importing the opponents from places like Mali in Africa, Albania and North Vietnam, and it also donated 50 tons of gymnastic equipment and 3,000 basketballs. But Indonesia bore the brunt of the expense'.[32]

The First World: Viewing China's Role in GANEFO through a Cold War Lens

On the eve of GANEFO's opening, with sportsmen and sportswomen from around the world facing possible suspension if they participated, the *Chicago Daily World* considered the position of these athletes:

> Which will they choose – ostracism from the Olympics and recognized international sports competition or a free ride at Jakarta? A choice for Red China and Indonesia could split the international sports movement into warring camps. That's what worries the Olympic sportsmen.[33]

The implications of such a rift are discussed below but, in diplomatic circles, concern was more focused on the geopolitical implications of China's participation than on the impact on international sport. GANEFO was portrayed in the West as a 'red' event because of Sukarno's ties to the Indonesian communist party (PKI) and the Games' sponsorship by China. 'The whole affair', observed one Canadian diplomatic official, 'has a distinctly "red" tinge'.[34] Caesar Torres and Mark Dyreson's characterisation of 'Indonesian strongman Achmed Sukarno, with support from Beijing and Moscow', founding GANEFO 'to counter the IOC's "bourgeois" control of world sport' and Guttmann's conclusion that the 'impetus for GANEFO may, in fact, have come from Beijing, where the Chinese Communists were eager to embarrass the IOC' suggests considering GANEFO in the terms of, what Tina Chen has called, 'the bipolar Cold War world'.[35]

As early as the 1955, Bandung conference, which is generally acknowledged as the genesis of the non-aligned movement, US officials worried over the perceived leftist leanings of non-aligned countries, with Sukarno of particular concern. But Cold War anxieties were pre-eminent, especially given the US interests in the region. The US embassy in Jakarta worried in November 1962 about a 'significant political consequence' in the aftermath of the Asian Games controversy: 'a chorus of voices from the extreme left has been raised here in favor of Indonesia taking the lead in organizing a new Afro-Asian-Latin American sports federation'.[36] As noted earlier, GANEFO was born out of the controversy that arose from Indonesia's hosting of the IVth Asian Games in August 1962, when entry was refused to the teams from the Republic of China (Taiwan) and Israel. The sporting consequence of the Asian Games was that the IOC suspended Indonesia (or, more specifically, the Indonesian NOC), which promptly withdrew from the IOC and set about planning GANEFO.

The US analysis of the events that transpired during the IVth Asian Games focused on 'communist' elements. In the riots that occurred in Jakarta, '[e]fforts were made by Communist elements in the mob, and subsequently, by the Communist press, to picture the United States as the driving force behind Sondhi', the Indian IOC member and putative head of the Asian Games committee, who was spearheading efforts to sanction Indonesia for excluding Taiwan and Israel.[37] Furthermore, one report noted that although 'the United States came through the Asian Games controversy relatively unscathed ... there is little doubt that had the Games been cancelled, the weight of Indonesian opinion would have held the United States responsible'.[38] Generally, the Asian Games incident was seen as a reflection of the influence of China and the United Arab Republic over Indonesian affairs, and consequently another sign of Sukarno's leftist leanings.[39]

Nearly a year later, the US State Department still had 'serious doubt' about 'Indonesia's willingness and ability to keep the communists from making a propaganda circus of GANEFO'.[40] So that, in September 1963, two months in advance of the event, the US embassy in Jakarta recommended to the State Department that 'it also might not be out of place to discreetly make known to our Asian and African friends the part to be played by Communist China in supporting GANEFO'.[41] In response, the State Department sent a communiqué, over the signature of Secretary of State Dean Rusk to the US embassies around the world that detailed US misgivings with recent Afro-Asian gatherings in Jakarta, 'which turned out to be little more than high-fidelity amplifiers for Chinese Communist propaganda'. The communiqué instructed diplomatic officials that: 'On balance, the disadvantages of GANEFO to the Free World far outweigh any discernible advantages'.[42]

China for its part maintained that the IOC and IFs had threatened athletic sanctions against potential GANEFO participants because these were 'the last trump' of 'American imperialists' and supported the Indonesian position that '[t]he new emerging forces should use revolutionary methods to destroy the organizations which are controlled by imperialists and colonialists'.[43] Chinese propaganda reflected such views. The Chinese delegation in Jakarta included journalists, photographers and filmmakers. The foreign-language export magazine, *China Sport*, produced a special issue on GANEFO, which was repackaged as a book, *GANEFO Opens New Era in World Sport*.[44] As one contemporary

American commentator noted, 'through GANEFO Communist China was able to project an attractive image to a vast international audience'. She went on to note that

> The propaganda benefits Communist China derived from GANEFO did not necessarily end when the Games did. The Film Bureau of the Chinese People's Republic, in cooperation with the Indonesian National Committee for GANEFO, produced an excellent full length color film of the Games, with English commentaries for overseas distribution in which the Chinese displayed mastery of subtle propaganda techniques. The Indonesian contributors to the film were always given precedence over their Chinese colleagues. Chinese achievements were not stridently advertised. The spectators were repeatedly made aware of the spirit of fraternal competition of the New Emerging Forces which the narrator contrasted with the alleged 'cut-throat' atmosphere of other athletic events.[45]

China, GANEFO and the Second World

In the nascent non-aligned movement, Prashad argues, 'Communism as an idea and the USSR as an inspiration held an important place in the imagination of the anticolonial movements from Indonesia to Cuba'.[46] In the 1960s, this was of particular concern in the West; so much so that the US State Department concluded that 'GANEFO, if held, will be heavily exploited by the communists'.[47] But 'exploited' by which communists and how exactly remained a point of some debate. By the time GANEFO was being proposed, 'China's association with the Soviet-led socialist camp weakened as the rift between Beijing and Moscow became more apparent'.[48] Geopolitically, China sought 'to more closely identify with formerly colonized countries, since the latter shared its grievances and anxieties in the struggle for political independence and economic development during the Cold War'.[49] Little attention has been paid to expanding the Cold War binary and considering the ways in which GANEFO reflected Sino–Soviet tensions in Southeast Asia alongside China's efforts to extend its geopolitical and social influence within the Third World.

With China sympathetic in the early 1960s to nationalist governments in Southeast Asia as an attempt to build its sphere of influence,[50] and outside the Olympic Movement over the recognition of Taiwan, it could openly support and finance Sukarno's efforts at hosting an alternative international sporting event. While GANEFO was China's re-entry into international sport, the USSR faced trickier diplomatic options. The latter had returned to the Olympic movement in 1951 and by the early 1960s had, in the person of Konstantin Andrianov, a member on the IOC's executive board, significant representation, given the importance of sport to Soviet foreign policy.[51] But GANEFO provided a new challenge, requiring the Soviets to balance their 'stance as the champion of the Newly Emerging Forces', as Alfred Senn has noted, 'without compromising their position within the IOC'.[52] In these terms, the US and USSR stood to lose ground if GANEFO was successful in creating a diplomatic architecture around which the interests of former Asian and African colonies could coalesce. The same communiqué from the US embassy in Jakarta that suggested GANEFO would be 'heavily exploited by the communists' also noted that 'The U.S. and the U.S.S.R. can only lose by the establishment of GANEFO as a true "colored Olympics" rather than simply another A-A [Afro-Asian] propaganda show. Conversely, the Chinese Communists can only gain by this situation'.[53]

The consideration GANEFO has received from Soviet historians focuses primarily upon the implications of participation for the USSR's relations with the IOC. As Jenifer Parks notes,

> Soviet leaders felt compelled to participate in this endeavor in order to maintain the Soviet presence in Asia, but rather than risk sanctions from the IOC or IFs, the Sports Committee recommended to send only teams 'not connected with the IOC or IFs'.[54]

Contemporary accounts, however, noted that GANEFO was also implicated in the Sino–Soviet struggles for influence in Southeast Asia. One Associated Press wire story in the US framed GANEFO in terms of the Sino–Soviet split:

> Russia's dilemma is Communist China's delight. The more trouble Red China can stir up in the Communistic world, some observers believe, the more status Russia will lose and the more China will gain in this athletic facade for political throat cutting.[55]

The Soviets were in an especially difficult position – wanting to dominate the Olympics but not wanting to cede GANEFO to China – and had to work hard in Southeast Asia 'to overcome the disadvantage of their Caucasian origin'.[56] By contrast, China through its financial patronage only stood to benefit from GANEFO.

Beyond access to international sporting opportunities for China and the USSR, GANEFO was a site where their Second World tensions played out. In the 1950s, while still a member of the IOC, the Chinese had looked for support from the Soviets on the 'two Chinas' issue, but their 'representatives increasingly felt belittled and ignored not just by the IOC but also by their Soviet comrades'.[57] In the wake of the subsequent Sino–Soviet split, China looked to extend its influence among the decolonising countries of Africa and Asia. Narratives of non-Caucasian, anti-colonial brotherhood run throughout the Chinese propaganda that emanated from GANEFO, produced both for domestic consumption and export.[58] But the USSR merits virtually no mention, let alone praise. Soviet GANEFO propaganda 'contrasts strikingly with that made by the Chinese' and was pitched at a domestic audience, eschewing efforts to curry favour with their Indonesian hosts: 'For instance, the Russian [GANEFO] film depicts Soviet boxers crushing their Indonesian opponents and plays up other Soviet victories. Whereas the Chinese cameraman included some very picturesque sights of Java, the Soviet cameraman inserted shots of the slums of Djakarta'.[59] For their part, Soviet officials contended that China was exerting undue control over the organisation of GANEFO, maintaining that the struggle for Afro-Asian influence was leading the Chinese to assert a 'racial hierarchy' by manoeuvring 'to exclude the Soviet Union and East European socialist countries from GANEFO and to allow membership only to countries of Asia and Africa'.[60] While these efforts were ultimately unsuccessful, 'the Chinese delegates in GANEFO continued to try to establish GANEFO as a rival organization to the IOC and existing IFs', a position wholly unacceptable to Soviet officials.[61]

Western diplomats and media, perhaps enmeshed in Cold War binaries, seemed especially attuned to the implications of GANEFO for Soviet interests. As the US embassy in Jakarta noted: 'The Soviet Union, caught between a desire to continue its good relations with Indonesia and its dislike for providing support to anything that would assist the CHICOMS, undoubtedly finds itself in an embarrassing position'.[62] The Soviets' interest in Southeast Asia made

> participation in GANEFO mandatory for them. They must, however, view with considerable chagrin the fact that this action, by adding to the success of GANEFO, also adds to CHICOM prestige, in Indonesian eyes at least, as Red China emerges as the wholehearted supporter of GANEFO.[63]

Observers were conscious of the ideological implications of the USSR's re-entry into international sport a decade earlier. 'The USSR faces the unpleasant prospect', noted one US diplomatic assessment, 'of having its second rate teams beaten by the Chicoms and losing face in Asia or losing its long cherished opportunity to vanquish the West at the Tokyo Olympics'.[64] Western media offered a similar assessment of this dilemma, as the *Chicago Daily Tribune* asked, 'Which will it be, competition at Jakarta and an end to his

[Khrushchev's] Olympic hopes, or loss of face with the Reds if he boycotts Sukarno's games?'[65] After China won the medals table in Jakarta, one American observer noted that the 'popularity of the Chinese must have been particularly embarrassing to the Soviets'.[66] The nature of Sino–Soviet relationship to Sukarno's event coloured post-GANEFO reports. A summary of international media coverage of GANEFO, commissioned by the American Central Intelligence Agency, concluded that

> the Chinese Communists, who are attempting to make GANEFO a major political, social, and propaganda tool, were outspoken in their views, as were those press organs in other Asian countries where there is strong pro-Chinese Communist sympathy or alignment. As for the Moscow-oriented areas, practically no comment could be found, and what there was of it generally displayed almost clinical objectivity and apparent unwillingness to be committed to any propaganda program outside the sphere of Soviet influence.[67]

A Battleground for Influence in the Third World

In September 1963, before such accounts had been written, GANEFO's star was still waxing, and, according to the US embassy in Jakarta, '[i]t is still too early to tell to what extent GANEFO will prove to be a new rallying point in the anti-white campaign'.[68] Such fears – that GANEFO might 'prove to be a focus for the split in the sports world along racial lines' – were spurred not only by events in Indonesia.[69] There was increasing anger, especially in sub-Saharan Africa, over the apartheid regime in Pretoria. As preparations for GANEFO were underway, the IOC was moving the 1963 IOC Session from Nairobi to Baden-Baden after it became clear that the Kenyan hosts would not be dissuaded from their opposition to representatives of South Africa's whites-only sport system being present at the meetings. In such a context, GANEFO could become 'an Olympic Games of the Colored Nations' and the 'Chinese Communists ... seem to have a great deal to gain'.[70]

It is through this lens – currying favour with recently decolonised nations – that Western observers viewed Chinese financial assistance to participants in GANEFO. While Sukarno was sympathetic to China during the Sino–Soviet rift in the late 1950s and early 1960s, African nations were thought to be in the Soviet camp.[71] So perhaps it is not surprising that one US embassy source in Jakarta 'stated Red China is committed to paying the cost of participation of African participants'.[72] Moreover, an Australian report noted:

> The Chinese have unquestionably been of the greatest help in arranging for the attendance of 'progressive' groups from countries not represented either by governments or by national institutions, as the case may be, almost always these have been drawn from communist groups and often have represented pro-Peking factions.[73]

After the fact, the Canadian diplomatic assessment was that China had 'scored effectively in making it possible through its financial assistance for many delegations from "black" Africa to feel that they were competing on equal footing with the major countries in the world'.[74]

When the First World did think of the Third, Prashad argues, it rarely left behind stereotypes of the colonial era, adding to those the belief that the 'darker peoples' were now even more likely, in his words, to be 'poor, overly fecund, profligate, and worthless' in the absence of their colonial masters.[75] If the 1955 'Bandung [Conference] provided the terrain to end China's isolation from world opinion and support', then, as Zhou argues, 'China's proclaimed solidarity with the Third World also served as a propaganda tool for winning the hearts and minds of the developing world, where the competition for influence among the Western powers and the Soviet Union intensified in the 1960s'.[76] Geopolitical allegiances and development initiatives were areas where Sino–Soviet tensions played out in the early 1960s. Chinese premier and foreign minister, Chen Yi, chastised the USSR in 1964 for 'not wholeheartedly helping to promote the development of the Afro-Asian countries', and 'adopting a chauvinist attitude in international affairs and within the international Communist movement'.[77] With China sympathetic in the early 1960s to nationalist governments in Southeast Asia as an attempt to build its sphere of influence, and outside the Olympic Movement over the recognition of Taiwan, it saw a benefit to supporting Sukarno's efforts at hosting an alternative international sporting event. At the GANEFO preparatory conference in April 1963, Chinese vice premier, He Long, observed that 'the Games of the New Emerging Forces was the outcome of the spirit of the Bandung Conference'.[78]

While some of the specific considerations of GANEFO have framed the event as an expression of Indonesia's independence and Sukarno's efforts to link politics and sport, GANEFO also needs to be considered within the role that international development played in sport and geopolitics in the 1960s. Dipesh Chakrabarty argues that economic development was central to decolonisation and anti-colonial projects.[79] So while China critiqued Soviet development policies, it is important not to overlook Indonesia's agency in these relationships. International development was prominent in post-colonial Indonesia[80] and the influence of First and Second World powers lent a development subtext to GANEFO. Sukarno advocated for an amicable resolution to the Sino–Soviet split in the Second World to advance Indonesia's position in this regard and accepted assistance from both sides of the Cold War divide, which was reflected during GANEFO. International athletes and guests, many financed by China, arrived in Jakarta and travelled along a highway paid for by the US, stayed (senior officials, at least) in the International Hotel constructed by Japanese investment and competed or spectated at the massive Bung Karno sports complex originally built by the Soviet Union for the IVth Asian Games in 1962.

Western observers, however, remained committed to a narrative in which GANEFO was a threat. If the event was a success, especially if African nations joined the cause, then GANEFO could overwhelm the IOC Games and offer a particularly racialised alternative. In such a context, China was taking advantage of the opportunities offered by Indonesia's willingness to host GANEFO:

> Peking must be delighted that Jakarta is so ready to make the running for it. No doubt the Indonesians are confident that they will be able to go on using the Chinese, but in the long term and assuming the status quo is upset in favour of Indonesia and China, the radical coloured nations are likely to look to China rather than Indonesia, if only because the latter will probably remain only a major regional power.[81]

The Aftermath of GANEFO

US concerns over GANEFO, especially where China was concerned, reflected their geopolitical interests in the region. While there was concern that GANEFO's 'very existence as a forum for Communist propaganda can exacerbate Indonesia-U.S. relations',[82] officials also worried over the strain placed upon the US allies in the region (Japan and the Philippines, in particular), who felt compelled by regional politics and economic interests to send athletes to Jakarta. Yet, it is in the Philippines that we find an important counter-balance to the Western narratives that colour China's interest in GANEFO. Ernesto T. Bitong, 'Sports Editor of the generally pro-American [Manila] *Evening News* and President of the Philippine Sport Writers Association',[83] challenged the dominant US characterisation of China's interest in GANEFO when he observed:

The trouble is when a country like Red China volunteers to help these new, small countries compete in the Djakarta games, the immediate conclusion in some local quarters is that the international competition is communist-inspired, that the meet is another forum for pro-commies. What would have been the reaction if it was Uncle Sam who asked to foot the bill of the athletes? Will it generate the same cries, the same enthusiasm?[84]

As GANEFO wrapped up, Western discourses shifted to a dismissal of the event on sporting terms. A British diplomat was not alone in noting that '[v]ery few of the teams were in any way representative of their country's real sporting ability'.[85] At the same time, the prominence of the Chinese team in Jakarta was also not lost on observers. The same British diplomat continued, 'it is not surprising that the Games were completely dominated by the team from China', so that the medals table 'must have created the impression that Peking is somewhat of a sports giant'.[86] Although the Thai ambassador to Indonesia, in speaking to Canadian officials, was dismissive – 'GANEFO of course is just a Chinese show' – others viewed China's non-sporting gains in Jakarta as significant.[87] 'The Chinese still appear to be the chief beneficiaries of GANEFO', wrote one US embassy official, while 'Italian observers have noted', according to a Canadian diplomatic communiqué, 'that from a wider political angle the games may have been more of a success for Communist China than for Indonesia'.[88]

There were incidents within competition that led some to suggest that the hosts were catering rather too much to Chinese athletes. Brazil, which also competed in yachting at GANEFO, sent a basketball team comprising male university students from Rio de Janeiro associated with the Confederação Brasileira de Desportos Universitários. They gained brief notoriety during their game against China, which Brazil lost 89–64. Feeling that the referees at the match were favouring the Chinese players, the Brazilians twice tried to abandon the game, only to be talked out of this course of action by their own team's officials. When it turned out that a Brazil–China rematch would decide the gold medal, the Brazilian players refused to appear, in protest over the refereeing. The Chinese took the floor, against no opponent, sunk one basket, and won the match 2–0. Similarly, another account contended that 'in one case at least the Indonesian judges deprived a Soviet woman gymnast of two obviously deserved gold medals in order to hand them to her nearest Chinese rival'.[89]

Sino–Soviet tensions would not only play out on the balance beam. Debate during the post-GANEFO conference, over the future of the event, found the two Second World powers on opposite sides. With China eager to formally establish GANEFO as a quadrennial competitor to the IOC Games, the Soviets, firm in their support for the IOC, 'opposed the holding of further such games, claiming that all "emerging" countries should combine their efforts in the Olympic Games'.[90] Sukarno, eager to consolidate GANEFO, brokered a compromise position, 'one of co-existence and even of co-operation with the Olympic movement'.[91] By October 1964, with negotiations between the IOC and Indonesian NOC having progressed to the point where the suspension of the latter was lifted in time for the Tokyo Olympics, the full impact of this rhetorical realignment of GANEFO was clear.

China, however, continued to support the idea of GANEFO, with GANEFO II briefly slated for Beijing in 1967, after the plan to hold the games in Cairo collapsed and Sukarno had been shunted aside by Suharto's military-led coup. In the meantime, China sponsored a second, Asian-only GANEFO. Revisiting the resistive rhetoric of its predecessor, the Asian GANEFO was held in Phnom Penh in December 1966 to intentionally coincide with the Asian Games that were taking place in Bangkok. As in Jakarta, there was a leader, Cambodia's Prince Sihanouk, who was 'very pro-Chinese'.[92] As in 1963, China 'had a large investment, financial and political, in the success of GANEFO', and 'built for Cambodia a splendid sports city', including a 100,000-seat stadium.[93] 'Without this munificent contribution', noted a Canadian diplomat in Phnom Penh, 'it is extremely doubtful that Cambodia could have played host for GANEFO'.[94]

Despite its subsequent disappearance from the sporting calendar, GANEFO was for a five-year period in the 1960s, China's entrée into international sport. Shuman notes the ways in which sporting success abroad was mobilised as a positive national self-image in China.[95] But GANEFO was also a platform through which geopolitical tensions were revealed, and China engaged in propaganda campaigns directed at the West and positioned itself to win allies among the decolonising countries of Asia and Africa – astride, as noted above, the artificial boundary that separated the Second and Third Worlds. It is in this context that GANEFO reveals that while, as Wested argues, 'the processes of decolonization and of superpower conflict may be seen as having separate origins, the history of the twentieth century cannot be understood without exploring the ties that bind them together'.[96] Although GANEFO was rhetorically framed as a project instigated by Sukarno for the sporting peoples of the non-aligned movement, it is instructive to recall Chen's call to 'think more about the intertwined histories and multiple legacies for contemporary political projects of Third Worldism and the Third World'.[97] And it is on these terms that China's interest in and the West's response to GANEFO reflected the ways in which anti-communist Cold War politics were conflated with racialised, post-colonial discourses and tension between Second World powers.

Notes

1. Pauker, "GANEFO I," 182.
2. Ren, *The New Flag*, 11. The author wishes to express appreciation to Dongwan He for her translation of the Chinese text.
3. Prashad, *The Darker Nations*, xv.
4. *GANEFO Opens New Era*; "Key-Note Address," 3. (The Bandung Conference took place in Indonesia in 1955).
5. See Majumdar and Mehta, *Olympics*.
6. Associated Press, undated Wire Story; and *GANEFO Opens New Era*.
7. See, for example, Brown, *A Short History*; and Gelman Taylor, *Indonesia: People and Histories*. Legge, *Sukarno*, makes brief mention of the event.
8. See, for example, Hadiz, "The Left"; and Roosa, "President Sukarno."
9. Xu, *Olympic Dreams*, 51.
10. Ibid., 53.
11. Shuman, "Elite Competitive Sport," 278.
12. See, for example, Booth, "Hitting Apartheid for Six."
13. See, for example, Hartmann, *Race, Culture*.
14. Lutan and Hong, "The Politicization of Sport"; and Sie, "Sports and Politics."
15. Adams, "Pancasila"; and Majumdar and Mehta, *Olympics*.
16. Torres and Dyreson, "The Cold War Games"; and Guttmann, *The Olympics*.
17. Connolly, "A Politics"; and Gitersos, "The Sporting Scramble."
18. Field, "The Olympic Movement's Response."
19. Brundage, November 9, 1963.
20. Cited in IOC Circular Letter, no. 279.
21. Schantz, "The Presidency of Avery," 130.
22. Senn, *Power, Politics*, 130–1.

23. Ren, *The New Flag*, 30.
24. Gilchrist et al., December 20, 1963, 2.
25. Zhou, "Ambivalent Alliance," 7.
26. Ibid., 11.
27. Canadian Embassy, November 9, 1963, 2.
28. Ren, *The New Flag*, 18.
29. American Embassy, September 4, 1963, 5. "CHICOM" refers to the People's Republic of China.
30. Ibid.; Canadian Embassy, Nov 16, 1963, 1: "It is public knowledge that China is helping with the costs but to what extent is difficult to ascertain".
31. Gilchrist, December 20, 1963, 3; Associated Press, undated: China "has offered to pay expenses of invited African states to the GANEFO Games".
32. Ross, "Sukarno's Lavish GANEFO."
33. "Trouble on Olympus," November 12, 1963.
34. Canadian Embassy, November 16, 1963, 2.
35. Torres and Dyreson, "The Cold War Games," 73; Guttmann, *The Olympics*, 109; Chen, "Third World Possibilities," 427.
36. American Embassy, November 28, 1962, 15.
37. Ibid., 3.
38. Ibid., 12.
39. Ibid., 5.
40. Department of State, September 16, 1963, 1.
41. American Embassy, September 4, 1963, 9.
42. See note 40 above.
43. Ren, *The New Flag*, 14, 16
44. "GANEFO's Splendid Achievements"; and *GANEFO Opens New Era*.
45. Pauker, "GANEFO I," 181. Despite Pauker's claims regarding an English soundtrack, the two copies of this film that I have viewed, in different repositories in Beijing, both have Chinese narration.
46. Prashad, *The Darker Nations*, 9.
47. Department of State, September 16, 1963, 4.
48. Zhou, "Ambivalent Alliance," 5; see also Lüthi, *The Sino-Soviet Split*.
49. Zhou, "Ambivalent Alliance," 5.
50. See, for example, Qiang, "China and the Cambodian"; and Harding, "China and the Third World."
51. Parks, "Red Sport, Red Tape"; Riordan, "Rewriting Soviet Sports History."
52. Senn, *Power, Politics*, 132.
53. American Embassy, September 4, 1963, 9.
54. Parks, "Red Sport, Red Tape," 180.
55. Associated Press, undated.
56. See note 53 above.
57. Shuman, "Elite Competitive Sport," 262.
58. See, for example, Ren, *The New Flag*; *GANEFO Opens New Era*; and "GANEFO's Splendid Achievements."
59. Pauker, "GANEFO I," 183.
60. Parks, "Red Sport, Red Tape," 185.
61. Ibid.
62. American Embassy, September 4, 1963, 2.
63. Ibid., 9.
64. American Embassy, October 9, 1963, 1.
65. See note 33 above.
66. Pauker, "GANEFO I," 181.
67. Central Intelligence Agency, December 13, 1963, 1.
68. American Embassy, September 4, 1963, 2.
69. Ibid.
70. Ibid.
71. Lüthi, *The Sino-Soviet Split*.
72. American Embassy, September 4, 1963, 5.

73. Department of Foreign Affairs, January 16, 1964, 6.
74. Under-Secretary of State, March 3, 1964, 2.
75. Prashad, *The Darker Nations*, 8.
76. Ibid., 37; Zhou, "Ambivalent Alliance," 6.
77. Cited in Zhou, "Ambivalent Alliance," 6.
78. Ren, *The New Flag*, 29.
79. Chakrabarty, "The Legacies of Bandung," 46.
80. Li, *The Will to Improve*.
81. Department of Foreign Affairs, January 16, 1964, 6.
82. American Embassy, September 4, 1963, 9.
83. American Embassy, October 3, 1963, 7.
84. Cited in Ibid.
85. Gilchrist, December 20, 1963, 1.
86. Ibid.; Canadian Embassy, March 3, 1964, 1.
87. Canadian Embassy, November 13, 1963, 2.
88. American Embassy, October 9, 1963, 1; Canadian Embassy, March 3, 1964, 2.
89. Gilchrist, December 20, 1963, 3.
90. Under-Secretary of State, March 3, 1964, 2.
91. Ibid.
92. Canadian Delegation, December 20, 1966, 2.
93. Ibid., 1
94. Ibid.
95. Shuman, "Elite Competitive Sport," 278.
96. Wested, *The Global Cold War*, 74.
97. Chen, "Third World Possibilities," 423.

References

Archival Sources

American Embassy, Djakarta. to Department of State, Washington. "The Asian Games Controversy." November 28, 1962. RG 59, Box 3244, EDU 15 INDON. National Archives, College Park, MD.

American Embassy, Djakarta. to Department of State, Washington. "Indonesian Sports, Politics and GANEFO." September 4, 1963. RG 59, Box 3244, EDU 15 INDON. National Archives, College Park, MD.

American Embassy, Djakarta. to Department of State, Washington. "Preparations for the 'Games of the New Emerging Forces' (GANEFO)." October 9, 1963. RG 59, Box 3244, EDU 15 INDON. National Archives, College Park, MD.

American Embassy, Manila, to Department of State, Washington. "Philippine Reactions to GANEFO Invitation." October 3, 1963. RG 59, Box 3244, EDU 15 INDON. National Archives, College Park, MD.

Associated Press. Wire Story (GANEFO medal standings), November 19, 1963. Box 201, Avery Brundage Collection, University of Illinois Archives.

Associated Press. Untitled and Undated Wire Story. Box 201, Avery Brundage Collection, University of Illinois Archives.

Brundage, Avery to Otto Mayer. November 9, 1963. CIO-PT-BRUND-CORR/7063, Sous-dossier 3: Correspondence, Septembre–Decembre 1963. Olympic Studies Centre, Lausanne.

Canadian Embassy, Djakarta, to Under-Secretary of State for External Affairs, Ottawa. "GANEFO." November 9, 1963. RG 25, vol. 5554, file 12671-CH-40. Library and Archives Canada, Ottawa.

Canadian Delegation to I.C.S.C., Phnom Penh, to Under-Secretary of State for External Affairs, Ottawa. "Asian Games for New Emerging Forces (GANEFO)." December 20, 1966. RG 25, vol. 10919, file 55-26-GANEFO, vol. 1. Library and Archives Canada, Ottawa.

Canadian Embassy, Djakarta, to Under-Secretary of State for External Affairs, Ottawa. "GANEFO Opening Ceremony – November 10." November 13, 1963. RG 25, vol. 5554, file 12671-CH-40. Library and Archives Canada, Ottawa.

Canadian Embassy, Djakarta, to Under-Secretary of State for External Affairs, Ottawa. "GANEFO." November 16, 1963. RG 25, vol. 5554, file 12671-CH-40. Library and Archives Canada, Ottawa.

Central Intelligence Agency, Washington. "Survey of Editorial Comment on GANEFO." December 13, 1963. RG 25, vol. 5554, file 12671-CH-40. Library and Archives Canada, Ottawa.

Department of Foreign Affairs (Australia), Canberra. "GANEFO and CONEFO." January 16, 1964. RG 25, vol. 5554, file 12671-CH-40. Library and Archives Canada, Ottawa.

Department of State, Washington, to All Diplomatic Posts [except Eastern Europe]. "Indonesian Sponsorship of GANEFO." September 16, 1963. RG 59, Box 3244, EDU 15 INDON. National Archives, College Park, MD.

"GANEFO's Splendid Achievements.", *China Sport*, No. 1, 1964. Box 201, Avery Brundage Collection, University of Illinois Archives.

Gilchrist, A.G., Djakarta, to R.A. Butler. Foreign Office and Whitehall Distribution, London. "The Games of the New Emerging Forces." December 20, 1963. RG 25, vol. 5554, file 12671-CH-40. Library and Archives Canada, Ottawa.

IOC Circular Letter, no. 279. 1965. File: B-1003-FI/021: Reunion de la CE avec les FI à Lausanne le 12 avril 1965, Sous-dossier 4: Correspondance, 1965. Olympic Studies Centre, Lausanne.

"Key-Note Address of H.E. Dr. Sukarno." *GANEFO Bulletin*, no. 1, (1963, July). RG 59, Box 3244, EDU 15 INDON. National Archives, College Park, MD.

"Trouble on Olympus." Chicago Daily Tribune, November 12, 1963. Clipping. Box 201, Avery Brundage Collection, University of Illinois Archives.

Under-Secretary of State for External Affairs, Ottawa, to Canadian Embassy, Djakarta. "GANEFO." March 3, 1964. RG 25, vol. 10919, file 55-26-GANEFO, vol. 1. Library and Archives Canada, Ottawa.

Literature

Adams, Iain. "Pancasila: Sport and the building of Indonesia – Ambitions and Obstacles." *The International Journal of the History of Sport* 19, nos 2/3 (2002): 295–318.

Booth, Douglas. "Hitting Apartheid for Six? The Politics of the South African Sports Boycott." *Journal of Contemporary History* 38, no. 3 (2003): 477–493.

Brown, Colin. *A Short History of Indonesia: The Unlikely Nation?* Crow's Nest: Allen & Unwin, 2003.

Chakrabarty, Dipesh. "The Legacies of Bandung: Decolonization and the Politics of Culture." In *Making a World after Empire: The Bandung Moment and its Political Afterlives*, edited by Christopher J. Lee, 45–68. Athens: Ohio University Press, 2010.

Chen, Tina Mai. "Third World Possibilities and Problematic: Historical Connections and Critical Frameworks." In *New World Coming: The Sixties and the Shaping of Global Consciousness*, edited by Karen Dubinsky, Catherine Krull, Susan Lord, Sean Mills, and Scott Rutherford, 421–430. Toronto: Between the Lines, 2009.

Connolly, Chris A. "A Politics of the Games of the New Emerging Forces (GANEFO)." *The International Journal of the History of Sport* 29, no. 9 (2012): 1311–1324.

Field, Russell. *The Olympic Movement's Response to the Challenge of Emerging Nationalism in Sport: An Historical Reconsideration of GANEFO*. Lausanne: http://doc.rero.ch/record/24926 IOC Library, 2011.

GANEFO Opens New Era in World Sports: Chinese Sports Delegation in Djakarta. Beijing: People's Sports Press, 1964.

Gelman Taylor, Jean. *Indonesia: People and Histories*. New Haven, CT: Yale University Press, 2003.

Gitersos, Terry Vaios. "The Sporting Scramble for Africa: GANEFO, the IOC and the 1965 African Games." *Sport in Society* 14, no. 5 (2011): 645–659.

Guttmann, Allen. *The Olympics: A History of the Modern Olympic Games*. Urbana: University of Illinois Press, 1992.

Hadiz, Vedi R. "The Left and Indonesia's 1960s: The Politics of Remembering and Forgetting." *Inter-Asia Cultural Studies* 7, no. 4 (2006): 554–569.

Harding, Harry. "China and the Third World: From Revolution to Containment." In *The China Factor: Sino-American Relations and the Global Scene*, edited by Richard H. Solomon, 257–295. Englewood Cliffs, NJ: Prentice-Hall, 1981.

Hartmann, Douglas. *Race, Culture, and the Revolt of the Black Athlete: The 1968 Olympic Protests and Their Aftermath*. Chicago: University of Chicago Press, 2003.

Legge, J. D. *Sukarno: A Political Biography*. Sydney: Allen & Unwin, 1972.

Li, Tania Murray. *The Will to Improve: Governmentality, Development, and the Practice of Politics*. Durham, NC: Duke University Press, 2007.

Lutan, Rusli, and Fan Hong. "The Politicization of Sport: GANEFO – A Case Study." *Sport in Society* 8, no. 3 (2005): 425–439.

Lüthi, Lorenz M. *The Sino-Soviet Split: Cold War in the Communist World*. Princeton, NJ: Princeton University Press, 2008.

Majumdar, Boria, and Nalin Mehta. *Olympics: The India Story*. New Delhi: Harper Collins, 2008.

Parks, Jenifer. "Red Sport, Red Tape: The Olympic Games, the Soviet Sports Bureaucracy, and the Cold War, 1952–1980." PhD diss., University of North Carolina 2009.

Pauker, Ewa T. "GANEFO I: Sports and Politics in Djakarta." *Asian Survey* 5, no. 4 (1965): 171–185, Originally published as: Pauker, Ewa T. "GANEFO I: Sports and Politics in Djakarta". RAND Corporation report, P-2935, 1964.

Prashad, Vijay. *The Darker Nations: A People's History of the Third World*. New York: The New Press, 2007.

Qiang, Zhai. "China and the Cambodian Conflict, 1970–1975." In *Behind the Bamboo Curtain: China, Vietnam, and the World Beyond Asia*, edited by Priscilla Roberts, 369–404. Washington, DC: Woodrow Wilson Center Press, 2006.

Ren, Dao. *The New Flag in International Sports: The Games of the New Emerging Forces*. Beijing: People's Sports Press, 1965.

Riordan, James. "Rewriting Soviet Sports History." *Journal of Sport History* 20, no. 3 (1993): 247–258.

Roosa, John. "President Sukarno and the September 30th Movement." *Critical Asian Studies* 40, no. 1 (2008): 143–159.

Ross, T. Peter. "Sukarno's Lavish GANEFO Was Mostly Snafu." *Sports Illustrated* 19, no. 23 (1963, December 2). http://sportsillustrated.cnn.com/vault/article/magazine/MAG1075439/index.htm

Schantz, Otto. "The Presidency of Avery Brundage (1952–1972)." In *The International Olympic Committee – One Hundred Year: The Idea, The Presidents, The Achievements*, edited by O. Schantz, and K. Lennartz. Lausanne: International Olympic Committee, 1997.

Senn, Alfred Erich. *Power, Politics, and the Olympic Games*. Champaign, IL: Human Kinetics, 1999.

Shuman, Amanda. "Elite Competitive Sport in the People's Republic of China, 1958–1966: The Games of the New Emerging Forces." *Journal of Sport History* 40, no. 2 (2013): 258–283.

Sie, Swanpo. "Sports and Politics: The Case of the Asian Games and the Ganefo." In *Sport and International Relations*, edited by Benjamin Lowe, David B. Kanin, and Andrew Strenk, 279–296. Champaign, IL: Stipes, 1978.

Torres, Cesar R., and Mark Dyreson. "The Cold War Games." In *Global Olympics: Historical and Sociological Studies of the Modern Games*, edited by Kevin Young, and Kevin B. Wamsley, 59–82. Amsterdam: Elsevier, 2005.

Wested, Odd Arne. *The Global Cold War: Third World Interventions and the Making of Our Times*. Cambridge: Cambridge University Press, 2005.

Xu, Guoqi. *Olympic Dreams: China and Sports, 1895–2008*. Cambridge, MA,: Harvard University Press, 2008.

Zhou, Taomo. "Ambivalent Alliance: Chinese Policy towards Indonesia, 1960–1965." Working Paper # 67. Washington, DC: Woodrow Wilson International Center for Scholars 2013.

Opening a Window on Early Twentieth-Century School Sport in Cape Town Society

Francois J. Cleophas

Department of Sport Science, University of Stellenbosch, Matieland, Stellenbosch, Republic of South Africa

An attempt was made at recording structured sport in non-White schools in Cape Town, South Africa, prior to 1956. The study was introduced with a historical presentation of sport at mission schools. It was shown how these schools inherited a legacy of deprivation and neglect that impacted upon sport participation. Yet, champion sportspersons at these schools gained some recognition in a racist and hostile society. This was possible due to the efforts of a few Teachers' League of South Africa (TLSA) campaigners who saw sport development as part of their mission of uplifting children in their charge. The TLSA attempted organising athletic meetings from 1916 onwards. Teachers belonging to this organisation were instrumental in establishing the first mass-based school sport organisation in Cape Town in 1928, the Central School Sports Union (CSU). This organisation was the only avenue of meaningful sport participation for most of Cape Town's marginalised children. A study of the CSU enables historians to open a window not only on social and political complexities of school sport but also on the broader early twentieth-century Cape society.

Introduction

Recent works reported on the history of Physical Education at mission schools in Cape Town, South Africa, but neglected sport.[1] This study attempts a sport-historical review of sport at mission schools in Cape Town until 1955, with emphasis on the Coloured[2] community. These were church schools in village centres or rural districts. Sometimes these were infant schools, sometimes industrial schools, sometimes partly school, partly churches. They were generally attended by Coloured children and often also by the poorer classes of White children.[3] Although the curriculum of mission and public schools were the same, the latter was supported financially by the state with the taxes of all citizens, while the former was financially dependant on churches.[4] Until 1955 school sport organisations in South Africa acquiesced to official state policies and seldom overtly challenged segregation and racism in society. State racism intensified after the First World War and climaxed in 1948, with the brutal implementation of Apartheid when the National Party was voted into power. After the removal of Coloured people from the voters roll and closure of their schools that were in White residential areas, school sport organisations had no option but to radicalise.

This study hones in on the Central School Sports Union (CSU)[5] that operated within the milieu of political acquiescence. The period of review, terminating in 1955, was chosen because the year 1956 marked the start of the Western Province Senior School Sport Union that ushered in a new era of radical school sport history in Cape Town. The major aim of this study was to utilise sport history as a vehicle for understanding broader Cape society. Therefore, this study was guided by the research question: 'How did the CSU reflect social and political developments in Cape Town, South Africa?' A research tool, reconstructionism, was used to provide the theoretical framework for investigation. Reconstructionists believe that erasing the dividing line between evidence and its interpretation ultimately opens the door to accepting any interpretation.[6] Therefore, this research relied heavily on sources that relate directly to the CSU.

The establishment of the CSU in 1928 marked an introduction of mass-based school sport in urban Cape Town. Mass-based sport referred to a single organisation that provided multi-code participation opportunities for many schools. The CSU therefore catered for athletics, cricket, rugby, netball and soccer for pupils who mainly come from indigent homes in the Cape Peninsula.[7] The late 1920s and 1930s was a time period that witnessed the emergence of mass-based school sport in South Africa. The Coloured Primary School Union of the Transvaal[8] was established in 1926 and provided rugby, soccer and basketball for learners.[9] During the 1930s, the Pinetown and Suburban Indian Schools' Sports Association was established in Natal.[10] A mass-based school sport organisation for Coloured children was also established in the rural town of Bredasdorp, Cape Province, in 1936 with the assistance of the Teachers' League of South Africa (TLSA) branch and provided athletics, netball and rugby for school learners.[11] In Cape Town, mass-based school sport was organised by individuals who were involved in a variety of organisations. An example of this is the case of Dr Ishmael Abdurahman. In 1938, it was reported that this Dr Abdurahman announced an interschool boxing and wrestling union, independent from the provincial boxing body, that was to link up with the inter-schools athletics union.[12] Abdurahman was a supporter of the Coloured political organisation, the Afrikaanse Nasionale Bond (Afrikaans National Organisation) that canvassed for the ruling National Party amongst Coloured voters.[13]

Mission Schooling in Twentieth-Century Cape Town

After the 1905 School Board Act made public education compulsory for White children only, mission schools became the mainstay of Coloured and African children. They were usually day schools where parents sent their children for a better education that their immediate surroundings offered them. These schools inherited a legacy of neglect and deprivation, and the churches could not afford to provide elaborate sport fields as did the elite White Boys and Girls schools of the early twentieth century. Mohamed Adhikari, a historian who focussed on issues relating to racial identity, remarked that 'few went beyond grade six and by 1913 fully sixty-five per cent of all pupils in mission schools were in the sub-standards and ninety-nine per cent below grade eight'.[14] In 1917, General Jan Smuts, the South African Prime Minister, stated that 'to apply the same institutions on an equal basis to White and Black alike does not lead to the best results'.[15] Consequently, the Superintendent-General of the Cape Education Department (CED) announced in 1918 that 'separate education systems are necessary for the two main sections (Coloured and African) of the non-European population'.[16] The result was that, by 1938, it was reported that 70% of non-White children in South Africa were not attending school.[17]

Since the nineteenth century, missionaries promoted a moralistic education layered with paternalism as is evident in a South African Colleges award-winning essay of A.F. Caldecott in 1884: '... for the present our chief aim must be to discipline them (Africans) into habits of obedience, self-control and order'.[18] Sport became a suitable means for achieving these objectives. Mission schools were also influenced by a moralistic ideology of athleticism that had relevance for both dominance and deference.[19] African athletes of international standing, elsewhere on the continent, recognised the role of schools in the awakening of an athletic consciousness in their childhood. In Kenya, Arere Anentia, who competed in the 1956 Olympic Games, was one of the first Africans of the Gusii Nation to attend school.[20] Kipchoge Keino, Africa's first sub four-minute miler, admitted that Anentia was 'the hero of his school days'.[21] In South Africa, the South African Olympic and British Empire Games Association officially denied people of colour access to international participation.[22] In the absence of access to international participation, the Black South African author, Ezekiel Mphahlele, remembers 'the manner in which certain boys' names lingered in a school a few years after they have left, like your all-rounder, your sprinter and miler and high jumper …'.[23] Similarly, some post-independence African leaders are remembered for their athletic prowess at university. The anti-Apartheid activist, Dennis Brutus, recalled how the Botswana president, Seretse Khama, 'was the best high jumper in South Africa [while at Fort Hare University] but was not allowed to compete against White athletes'.[24]

Sport in Cape Town Mission Schools Prior to the Establishment of the Central School Sport Union

Organised sport at mission schools grew out of the TLSA that was established on June 24, 1913, with a small membership of 45[25] and whose main concern was improved teacher salaries, not the development of school sport. However, sport was not neglected completely and its official organ, the *Educational Journal* (*EJ*), carried two sport reports in 1916. One was an anonymous writer who wrote about the value of swimming.[26] Another was about Fred Ingram, a White man, who took a team of 20 lads from the poorer section of the village in Newlands to stage a gymnastic display on trapeze, parallel bars and 5-foot-high vaulting horse to the patients at Robben Island.[27] These were children drawn from the St Andrew's Mission School in Newlands. Prior to the 1930s, little if any provision was made for girls' participation. Richard Dudley, a Marxist and radical thinker, who attended the St Andrew's Mission School at that time, stated that this was so because of a Victorian attitude of 'girls must play some musical instrument … while boys could grow up as barbarians …'.[28]

The TLSA planned an athletic meeting in 1916, the Alexander Cup Sports Competition (possibly named after a White Cape Town liberal-minded lawyer, Morris Alexander), at the Green Point Track in Cape Town, but too few schools entered and it had to be cancelled.[29] Only once the TLSA was on a relatively firm footing, members at grass-roots level began raising the issue of organised school sport. Cricket was their favoured sport, possibly because of its strong British moral character. In 1918, a writer in the *EJ* wrote:

> Why should we as a Teachers League not have an article on sport in the columns of our organ once in a while? Why should not local teams of different schools vie against each other as school teams? What would the King of Sport – Cricket – and such not make even better men of us …?[30]

Later that year, an article dealing with English cricket history appeared in the same journal.[31] The first call for an organised school sports body came in 1922 when a writer, Quex, wrote about a need for an association to encourage friendly rivalry between mission schools by means of soccer matches because no such body existed in Cape Town.[32]

The same year, a woodwork teacher, D.B. van Niekerk,[33] the TLSA president of 1919,[34] delivered a paper, 'Sport and the Development of Character', at the TLSA national conference.[35] However, education was seen as an academic enterprise and sport a peripheral issue. Unlike the common belief that the Battle of Waterloo was won on the playing fields of Eton, David van der Ross, a senior TLSA official, said: ' ... the Coloured boy has to learn that his battle will not be won on any football ground'.[36] The *Sun* was more specific and stated in an editorial column that the inordinate fondness for sport displayed by Coloured people leads them to place the things that matter in a subordinate position.[37]

Sport at mission schools proceeded on a friendly basis at public venues. In 1920, for example, the Dock Area School[38] played a friendly cricket match against St Paul's Mission School at the Sea Point Cricket Club's ground at Green Point Common.[39] While cricket was being promoted by a few mission schools, some attention, at times unsuccessful, was given to athletics. The response for the Alexander Cup Competition was so poor in 1916 that it had to be cancelled.[40] A more successful meeting was held on October 1, 1917, at the Green Point Track. This meeting formed part of the Weiner's Day Holiday celebrations, and according to a media report, it was attended by close to 5000 spectators.[41] This meeting, however, revealed a male bias of early twentieth-century school athletics, the dominance of short distance running events and the majority of age groups being in the junior division. The last point confirms a previous statement that the bulk of mission schools provided education up to Grade Six only.[42] A further characteristic of this athletic meeting was that it had an urban bias and catered for schools with a 'status'[43] amongst the Coloured population. The participating schools were St Stephen's from Paarl (the winners), Albertus Street Primary,[44] Zonnebloem[45] and Trafalgar High School[46] from Cape Town.[47] Previous research reported how these schools had Physical Training as part of their cultural ethos.[48] It could not be ascertained if the Alexander Shield Competition continued, but a suggestion was made in the press that a school football (soccer) competition could be organised on the same lines as the Alexander Shield.[49] A final characteristic of the Alexander Cup Sports Competition was that organised sport was practised with a sense of social responsibility. Not surprisingly, therefore, the proceeds of the competition were donated to the Cape Corps Gifts and Comforts Fund.[50] This was a fund that assisted families of the Coloured division of the South African army, known as the Cape Corps. It was against this backdrop of community involvement that the CSU was established.

Central School Sports Union (CSU)

The CSU was established in 1928 and became the parent body of all Coloured school sport bodies in Cape Town and beyond.[51] When the CSU became too unwieldy, other unions were established. In 1933, a Northern Schools Union was established to provide sport for mission schools in the Maitland–Durbanville area. This Union provided rugby, soccer and netball for school pupils.[52] In 1939, the Athlone School Sports Union was established by the founding schools of the CSU and provided rugby, soccer, cricket and tennikoit for boys, netball for girls and athletics for both genders.[53] In 1945 a Salt River and District School Sports Union was established that initially provided soccer for under-13 boys.[54]

Ernest Moses, a TLSA member, announced in 1929 that it was not generally known (by TLSA members and the broader public) that some teachers met in the Wesleyan School at Mowbray and established the CSU in June the previous year.[55] Under the direction of Dan Abrahams, Ned Doman, Gilbert Little, Percy Biggs and Captain Mozley, the activities of the CSU expanded beyond Cape Town as far as Paarl.[56] The CSU was supported by the Perseverance and California rugby clubs[57] who donated trophies. Because the bulk of children in schools affiliated to the CSU were in the primary standards, competition was only offered in the under-14 and under-16 age divisions in 1929. The mayor presented the trophies in the Mowbray Town Hall on November 12.[58]

The CSU was affected negatively by a poor state of schooling provision for Coloured people and therefore continued a tradition of social responsibility, driven by school teachers with a self-sacrificing attitude. Moses wrote that the CSU was intended for principals and teachers who were imbued with a spirit of self-sacrifice. The columnist, in 'From my Tower', expressed the following view in 1938:

> [T]he sports masters and mistresses should be given a word of thanks for giving much of their time to encourage the youngsters to take a real interest in athletics. There is much self-denial in the job, long distances to travel home from Mowbray every Wednesday.[59]

In 1938, Johnnie Kay, who presented prizes at a CSU meeting, said parents and children owe a debt of gratitude to the teachers for what they are doing for the future men and women of the country.[60]

School sport was also influenced by notions of Muscular Christianity. Initially, the CSU catered only for rugby and cricket, the manly sports, although Moses reported that 'it was hoped that girls under the supervision of lady teachers will have enjoyable hockey matches'.[61] The CSU also promoted participation for enjoyment and not for seeking external rewards.[62] The columnist, Uncle Jim, stated that the 'game is the main thing, but the aim to win and the perseverance of the whole team must eventually bear fruit'.[63] Uncle Jim was George Manuel, a liberal-minded journalist and an opinion maker in the Coloured community. However, mission school managers, who were in all cases clergymen, wielded absolute authority over schools under their jurisdiction and expected teachers to conform to particular religious and political beliefs.[64] A general idea held by these managers, who were usually conservative, was that sport hampers the growth of church and school. A striking example of this thinking was the statement made by Reverend C.R. Heywood, an Anglican minister from Malmesbury, before the Cape Coloured Commission of Enquiry in 1935:

> ... the personal jealousies to which the progress of the church, school, football club, everything is liable to be sacrificed at any moment – the immediate interest in all matters relating to sex ... indicate that a profound psychological change has to be brought about before the Coloured people can discharge a full sense of responsibility in their duties toward the country as a whole.[65]

Besides the attitudinal obstacles from dominant religious societies, a lack of athletic facilities at schools was also a stumbling block for progress. The CSU therefore affiliated to the Playing Fields Association (PFA) due to a lack of sport facilities and meagre finances for sport organisation.[66]

School Sport Facilities and Finances

The *EJ* referred to mission school buildings as 'death traps'.[67] The few mission schools that had decent teaching facilities had no comparable sport fields. Therefore, when the Zonnebloem College had its sports day with 900 competitors, the Green Point Track had to be used.[68] In capitalist societies, ruling classes viewed games at urban schools as a measure to divert attention of communities from these conditions, to suppress industrial unrest, anarchy and war in adult life and to prepare the child for religious life as an adult.[69]

Many Coloured people in Cape Town were conservative and the most important political party looking after their interests, the African People's Organisation (APO), was led by a group with no aggressiveness.[70] Because of this moderate approach, the CSU, which was in effect a Coloured school sport organisation, attracted support from liberal organisations such as the PFA.

The PFA was launched on July 9, 1925, in the famous Albert Hall, Great Britain, from the midst of ruling-class circles.[71] A PFA branch was launched in Cape Town on May 3, 1939, with a governing and policy-forming body 'consisting of nine members, one of whom, [a White clergyman] Rev. Arthur Green, rector of St Marks in District Six,[72] was chosen because of his knowledge and interest in the non-Europeans'.[73] These developments affected the organisation of the CSU because most schools in Cape Town operated within a milieu of poverty and neglect. Facilities were neglected because churches, controlling these learning institutions, did not have resources to build proper schools, a situation which was worsened by a haphazard government policy that was obsessed with addressing poverty on the basis of racial considerations.[74] In some cases, classrooms were unknown and single rooms in which several classes and teachers shouted one another down were the order of the day.[75] Sport facilities at these schools were not any better. Ernest Moses reported in his article that the City and Suburban Rugby Union (CSRU) permitted the CSU to use their grounds at Mowbray for cricket and rugby free of charge in 1929. A CSU athletic meeting was held there on November 2 on a track covered with long grass.[76] From the 1940s onwards, land that was used for sport by the CSU was gradually being appropriated by the state. Therefore, venues such as the Rondebosch and parts of the Green Common became inaccessible for school sport. The only school for Coloured learners that had a soccer field was Zonnebloem.[77] Agitation for decent sport facilities by the CSU proceeded along a political path of moderation by appealing to the goodwill of influential Whites, such as the PFA.

Principles, Practices and Programme of Action of the CSU

After a 1943 TLSA conference in Kimberley, a distinction emerged between moderate and radical sections in Cape Town's teaching fraternity. From then on, school sport administrators in Cape Town gradually linked their political agendas with sport. The Workers Party of South Africa was established in January 1935 and grew out of the Lenin Club.[78] One member, Richard Dudley, said in an informal interview in 2007 that some teachers in Cape Town, during the 1940s, assisted rural schools by organising athletic meetings and used it as an opportunity to discuss political matters. A political consciousness was visible with the first organised athletic sports day of the Somerset West School Sports Union (SWSSU). Victor February, a Coloured man and chairman of the SWSSU, used the occasion to remind those present, including N.E. Lambrechts, a White Chief Inspector in the CED,[79] about the importance of free compulsory education for all children, irrespective of race. Nevertheless, the CSU pursued a politically moderate course and continued its programme of soliciting support from sympathetic Whites. A few Whites responded positively to this programme of action because school sport remained a 'jolly affair' and never threatened the *status quo*. Uncle Jim reported on a gala day at the CSRU Grounds as follows:

> ... one of the largest gatherings of school children who had come to see their respective teams compete in the finals and also have a jolly time themselves ... The weather was fine ... some of the wildest naturally gave the usual bit of anxiety but that can well be expected when there are nearly 3 000 young bloods let loose for a day.[80]

Amongst the patrons of the CSU were White Municipal Councillors: Willenburg, Dr George Sacks, Abe Bloomberg and G. Ferry.[81] These individuals were also visible in other areas of Coloured community affairs and often expected political support during elections. For many years, TLSA teachers opposed racism by pursuing a liberal path and by working and being visible in a host of organisations.

When school sport events were organised in Cape Town, it was nearly always done so by teachers belonging to the TLSA. This was so when a swimming gala was organised by three Cape Town schools at the Trafalgar Park Baths in 1942. Besides swimming, about 800 children displayed mass drilling and agility. The organisers were Benjamin Kies, H. Abrahams, George Golding and Paul Heneke, all TLSA members.[82] The profits went towards the Trafalgar High School Bursary Fund. Kies was president of a radical discussion group, the New Era Fellowship that criticised the moderate programme of action of the TLSA and was a forum where issues affecting Blacks 'could be discussed by the more advanced members of the community, for the benefit of the less mature'.[83] In 1940 he along with two other radicals, Allie Fataar and Willem van Schoor, entered the executive of the TLSA and shattered the moderate image of the TLSA.[84]

In 1938, D.B. van Niekerk, the former TLSA president, played cricket for Foresters Cricket Club in the Paarl–Wellington Cricket Union.[85] A.F. Pietersen was a selector for the Coloured Springbok rugby team.[86] He served as a committee member, since at least 1926, on the national executive of the TLSA, representing the Paarl branch.[87] He was president of the TLSA in 1943.[88] This feature of social involvement continued when the CSU grew and divided into sub-unions. Ernest Moses provided the names of three CSU executive officials in his 1929 article in the *EJ*. All were visible in the TLSA and other community efforts. Samuel Dudley (Chairman, St Andrews' School, Newlands), a non-active TLSA member who promoted the playing of sport at his school,[89] I(M)nyombolo (Vice-chairman, Independent School, Athlone), an African teacher, who was associated with the Athlone branch of the TLSA,[90] and Dan J. Abrahams (Secretary)[91] were three early officials. Abrahams, an old Zonnebloem College student, was also a member of the Athlone branch of the TLSA, Excelsior Tennis Club, the Free Gardeners (Scottish Order), the Mowbray branch of the Cape Corps Welfare Committee and principal of the Mowbray Primary Methodist School.[92] Elsewhere it was reported that he was a member of the Cape Peninsula Homing Union (Coloured Section).[93]

Gilbert Samuel Little was a founding member of the CSU and was also visible in organisations outside school sport. In 1944, he was the chairman of the newly established Achilles Athletic Club.[94] One newspaper highlighted his contribution to school sport as being 'particularly outstanding ... in his coaching ability'. The *T.E.P.A*[95] reported on the death of Charles Sassman, 'a prime mover of the C.S.U.'.[96] He was also a soccer administrator, serving as treasurer of the Western Province Football Association (Coloured).[97] There was also Ernest Steenveld, the assistant secretary of the CSU in 1941, who was an active member of the TLSA and was the president of that association in 1994 when he was in his 80s.[98] A further media survey found that two socially and politically visible Coloured teachers, Ned Doman and George Golding, were school sport administrators with extensive community networks, worthy of historical inquiry.

E.J. (Ned) Doman was principal of the Athlone Primary School and the TLSA president in 1933.[99] He was a well-known tennis player who won the singles title in the first official South African (Coloured) tennis championship in 1937.[100] In 1934 he represented the provincial side, Western Province, against an all-India soccer touring team.[101] The same year he won the Goliath Cup in the Cape and District Tennis Union (CDTU) and two years later he was the president of that Union.[102] The CDTU was an organisation where school teachers played a leading role. Therefore, this union reflected the sense of social welfare amongst TLSA members. A typical social action of this Union was the interracial tennis tournament, organised by George Golding, to raise funds for equipment at the Groote Schuur Hospital.[103] The following players, who were prominent teachers in Cape society, were invited to this tournament: Eddie Smith, Ned Doman, George Golding, Leslie Kleinveldt and Alfie Jacobs. Smith was a teacher at Trafalgar High School and distinguished himself as a fly-half for the Universals Rugby Club that was affiliated to the CSRU. He was also secretary of the CSRU.[104] The most prominent amongst them was George Golding.

Golding was immersed in collaborationist politics during the 1930s until his death in the 1960s. However, the Black liberal press presented him as an eminent and influential sport person in the community. Golding thus overshadowed many other TLSA sport administrators in the media. In 1932 he argued that Coloured sportspersons be given more publicity.[105] Much of this publicity he called for, however, tended to focus on himself. Even after his death, the CSU was presented with a George Golding Memorial Trophy by his wife.[106] Due to his collaborationist politics, his patronage of the South African Soccer Board (Coloured) was regarded by community leaders as highly controversial.[107] An occasional political colleague of his, Richard van der Ross, a prominent Coloured personality with an avowed liberal outlook, described him as 'a flamboyant person, given to eye-catching personal habits of dress and bearing who achieved prominence as a tennis player and as a participant in conferences'.[108] He was therefore occasionally in the forefront of a few local sport developments. One development was that he and H. Abrahams made films of the annual physical culture demonstrations held at the Rosebank Showgrounds in Cape Town. These films aimed at recording the most important events in the life of the Coloured community.[109] In 1935 and 1937, he and Eddie Smith were the Western Province and South African (Coloured) men's doubles champions.[110] In the absence of a national organisation, he was crowned the South African (Coloured) lawn tennis champion at Trafalgar Park, Cape Town, in 1933.[111] Three years later, representing the Walmer Club, he was the winner of the prestigious Goliath Cup of the CDTU.[112] Golding was also a long-term sport administrator and was secretary of the South African Tennis Board of Control.[113] He was vice-president of the CDTU in 1932.[114] His involvement with the game of organised dominoes was also referred to occasionally. He was president of the local Universals Domino Club in Cape Town and president of the regional Western Province Domino Association (WPDA).[115] Golding's conservative political nature can be gauged from the fact that the WPDA had a religious clause in 1954 that prevented Muslims from participating in its activities.[116] He assisted with the formation of the Ashley Table Tennis Club at the Ashley Street Primary School in District Six, Cape Town.[117] This club became important in the development of the game in Cape Town and won every senior title in the Western Cape in 1949.[118] The individuals mentioned thus far, as a collective, shaped the CSU into a multi-coded school sport organisation as part of a web of community, social and political network very often along politically conservative lines.

Conclusion

This study introduced a historical overview of school sport for Coloured children in Cape Town, prior to 1956. The 1905 School Board Act introduced legislated segregation that officially discriminated between Coloured and White children. It was shown how organised school sport, amongst mission schools, was introduced by the TLSA in 1916.

The TLSA started as a politically moderate teachers organisation and internalised dominant White attitudes towards race and class. From 1928 onwards, teachers, affiliated to the TLSA, started organising school sport under the CSU. These teachers formed part of an intricate network of sport and community involvement but also organised school sport without overtly challenging the *status quo*. The CSU was, however, affected negatively by a poor state of schooling for Coloured people, and instead of confrontation, directed its energies into instilling in its members a tradition of social responsibility accompanied by a self-sacrificing attitude. The growth of sport at mission schools, the main source of education for Cape Town's Coloured children, was hampered by the poor state of the infrastructure and institutional racism at the time. The CSU proceeded by cajoling sympathetic and influential Whites for support. There were no difference between the political motives of Coloureds, seeking advancement in society and liberal Whites, using them for voter support during elections. Consequently, Coloured teachers used the CSU as a tool to move closer to White culture by accepting symbols and practices of the latter. School sport organised by the CSU never threatened the racist *status quo* of the state. The CSU could therefore not change the conditions of poverty and neglect that impacted on mission schools and sport, worsened by a haphazard and misguided government policy obsessed with addressing poverty on the basis of racial considerations. At the same time, many TLSA officials regarded academic prowess more important than school sport. This was partly motivated by the TLSA's leadership belief that 'refined' practices constituted a critical distinction between 'civilized' and 'barbarous' peoples.[119] In fact, many learners and teachers at Black schools during the nineteenth and early twentieth centuries were intent on disproving social Darwinist ideas that caricatured them as muscular beings. These social Darwinist ideas were found in official education circles, and in 1904 the Superintendent-General of Education, Thomas Muir, suggested:

> If you compare a White boy and a Coloured boy from the ages of 12 onwards, you will find that a White boy goes on growing mentally, whereas a Coloured boy seems for a while to stop. I believe there are physiological reasons given for it.[120]

That year an anonymous writer in the *Zonnebloem College Magazine* complained bitterly about the habit of 'stewing or loafing amongst the bigger fellows, i.e. pouring over a book or lolling in a classroom or at the foot of a tree in recreation hours, always with a schoolbook'.[121] However, as elsewhere in twentieth-century Africa, schools played a pivotal role in the sport consciousness of children and teachers. This consciousness was revealed in this study through a historical investigation of the CSU that opened a window on early twentieth-century school sport in Cape Town society. A further study will show how a new generation of political conscious school sport administrators emerged after the Second World War. These administrators were imbued with ideas of non-racialism and claimed to have made a complete break with the past.

Notes

1. Cleophas and Van der Merwe, "Physical Education"; Cleophas, "A Historical Exploration."
2. During the twentieth and twenty-first centuries, ruling parties in South Africa classified four major 'race' groups: African, Coloured, Indian and White. The researcher rejects notions of 'race' as a scientific category but uses these descriptions nevertheless for the sake of common

understanding. People who spoke Bantu languages were referred to as African, while persons who were the products of miscegenation between colonial Whites and other groups were labelled Coloured.

3.   Malherbe, *Education in South Africa*, 88.
4.   "Mission Schools or Public Schools?" *The Educational Journal,* no. 3 (1917): 4.
5.   The CSU was organized by Coloured teachers, and in a few exceptions, Africans played minor roles.
6.   Booth, *The Field*, 42.
7.   "The Student Sports Union," *Sun*, August 26, 1932; "Sport in Schools," *Cape Standard*, April 3, 1945.
8.   The Transvaal was one of the four provinces in South Africa during the period under review. The other were Cape Province, Natal and Orange Free State.
9.   "Sport in the Schools," *Sun*, October 21, 1932.
10. Cleophas, "Contexting," 23.
11. "School Sports," *Sun*, November 13, 1936; "Bredasdorp Sports Meeting," *Sun*, April 24, 1936.
12. "Wesley Wrestling & Boxing Tournament," *Cape Standard*, September 6, 1938.
13. Van der Ross, *The Rise and Decline*, 80, 86.
14. Adhikari, *Let Us Live*, 29.
15. Motlhabi, *The Theory and Practice*, 7.
16. Department of Public Education, Cape of Good Hope, *Report of the Superintendent-General*, 15.
17. "Appalling Conditions of Coloureds," *Cape Standard*, January 4, 1938.
18. Caldecott, *The Government and Civilization*, 30.
19. Ndee, "Sport, Culture and Society," 198.
20. Racing Past, "The History."
21. Noronha, *Kipchoge of Kenya*, 35.
22. South African Olympic and British Empire Games Association, *Minutes of the Meeting*, 2.
23. Mphalele, *Down Second Avenue*, 129.
24. Thomas, *Time with Dennis Brutus*, 7.
25. February, *From the Arsenal*, 196.
26. "The Value of Swimming," *The Educational Journal,* no. 2 (1916): 2.
27. "Gymnasium Display on Robben Island," *The Educational Journal*, no. 2 (1916): 12.
28. Wieder, *Teacher and Comrade*, 22.
29. "Roll Up, Schools!" *The Educational Journal*, no. 3 (1917): 2.
30. "Sports at School," *The Educational Journal*, no. 3 (1918): 3.
31. "Cricket," *The Educational Journal*, no. 3 (1918): 8.
32. "Inter-School Soccer," *The Educational Journal*, no. 5 (1922): 3.
33. All TLSA members with the exception of a few Africans were classified Coloured. The presidents of the TLSA were, without exception, moderate in political outlook.
34. Adhikari, *Let Us Live*, 185.
35. "The 1922 Conference," *The Educational Journal*, no. 5 (1922): 5.
36. "Our Childrens' Future," *The Educational Journal*, no.7 (1926): 3.
37. "Sport and Work," *The Sun*, December 2, 1932.
38. According to Sigi Howes from the Centre of Conservation, Western Cape Education Department, the Dock District Public School came about in 1895 when the St Andrew's Mission School (est. 1841) amalgamated with the Harbour Works EC Mission School (est. 1861). It catered for the dock workers' children, White and Coloured. By 1920, it was a school providing education for Coloured children only.
39. "Friendly Fixture," *The Clarion*, February 21, 1920.
40. "Roll Up, Schools!" *The Educational Journal*, no. 3 (1917): 2.
41. "Sports at Green Point Track," *Cape Times*, October 2, 1917.
42. Adhikari, *Let Us Live*, 52.
43. Although these schools carried status in the Coloured community, they were in poor condition compared to White schools. Adhikari, *Let Us Live*, 29. The *A.P.O.* commented on February 22, 1913, that the one public school set aside for higher learning for Coloured children, Trafalgar High School, was a 'miserable hovel and much inferior to many mission schools'. The *EJ* of October–December 1925 reported on a public school, to be opened for Coloured students the following year. This was Livingstone High School and became a highly respected

institution. Wieder, *Teacher and Comrade*, 1. This school was, however, described in the *Sun* of March 19, 1937, as one with less than 100 pupils and served the whole of the southern suburbs in Cape Town as the only public school.

44. This was a Public School and was a prestigious institution in the Coloured community. Adhikari, *Let Us Live*, 45.
45. Zonnebloem College was started as an elitist institution for the sons of African chiefs in the nineteenth century. During the twentieth century, it became a Coloured institution with a tradition of athletics. Cleophas, "Running a History Programme."
46. This was a public high school for Coloured children but was described by Dr Abdurhaman, the most influential political leader at the time, as a 'miserable hovel'. Adhikari, *Let Us Live*, 29.
47. "Inter-School Sports," *The Educational Journal*, no. 3 (1917): 8.
48. See Cleophas and Van der Merwe, "Exercising 'Race'."
49. "Schools and Sport," *Clarion*, April 5, 1919.
50. "Sports at Green Point Track," *Cape Times*, October 2, 1917.
51. "Schoolmasters Sponsor Sports," *Cape Standard*, May 1, 1945.
52. "Sport in Our Schools," *Sun*, September 1, 1933.
53. "Athlone and District Sports Union," *The Sun*, April 28, 1939.
54. "Schoolmasters Sponsor Sports," *Cape Standard*, May 1, 1945.
55. "The Schools' Sports Union," *The Educational Journal*, no. 7 (1929): 5.
56. "Death of Mr. D.J. Abrahams," *Cape Standard*, February 9, 1943.
57. The Perserverance Rugby Club was established in 1889 amongst the Coloured community in the old Raapenberg area in Mowbray, Cape Town. Booley, *Forgotten Heroes*, 163.
58. "The Schools' Sports Union," *The Educational Journal*, no. 7 (1929): 5.
59. "From My Tower," *Cape Standard*, March 8, 1938.
60. "Uncle Jim Writes About Football and Netball at Mowbray," *Cape Standard*, October 4, 1938.
61. "The Schools' Sports Union," *The Educational Journal*, no. 7 (1929): 5.
62. "The Students' Sports Union," *Sun*, August 26, 1932.
63. "Uncle Jim Writes of Men and Women in the Making," *Cape Standard*, September 13, 1938.
64. Adhikari, *Let Us Live*, 30.
65. Ibid., 135.
66. "Sport in Schools," *Cape Standard*, April 3, 1945.
67. "Coloured Education," *The Educational Journal*, no. 7 (1925): 3.
68. "Zonnebloem College Annual Sports," *Sun*, June 8, 1934.
69. Law, "Why Playing Fields?"
70. Bickford-Smith, van Heyningen and Worden, *Cape Town*, 81; Edgar, *An African American*, 76.
71. House of Lords, "Provision of Playing Fields"; Law, "Why Playing Fields?"
72. District Six was an inner-city living quarters in Cape Town whose inhabitants, largely Coloured, was described by one author, quoting from a Coloured Commission of Enquiry of 1937, as 'creatures of conditions in the same way as are the slum and criminal elements in all the great cities of the world'. Hatfield and Manuel, *District Six* (see "Foreword").
73. Law, "Playing Fields Associations," 14.
74. Van der Poel, "The Present Position," 44.
75. Dalehoudt, "Sir Thomas Muir," 227.
76. "Schools' Sports Union," *Sun*, November 11, 1932.
77. "Sport in Schools," *Cape Standard*, April 3, 1945.
78. Hirson, "The Trotskyist Groups," 30, 40.
79. Borman, *The Cape Education Department*, 241.
80. "Uncle Jim Writes About Football and Netball at Mowbray," *Cape Standard*, October 4, 1938.
81. "Schoolmasters Sponsor Sports," *The Cape Standard*, May 1, 1945.
82. "Schools' Swimming Gala," *Cape Standard*, February 17, 1942. Kies and Abrahams associated themselves with radical political elements, while Heneke and Golding moved in moderate circles. Adhikari, *Let Us Live*, 70, 78.
83. Lewis, *Between the Wire*, 181.
84. Adhikari, *Let Us Live*, 70.
85. "Paarl-Wellington Prolific Cricket Union," *The Sun*, December 11, 1936.
86. Booley, *Forgotten Heroes*, 15.
87. "Kimberley Conference Arrangements," *The Educational Journal*, no. 7 (1926): 12.

88. Van der Ross, *The Rise and Decline*, 180.
89. Wieder, *Teacher and Comrade*, 22–3.
90. Adhikari, *Let Us Live*, 97.
91. "School Sports Union," *Sun*, February 12, 1937.
92. "Death of Mr D.J. Abrahams," *Cape Standard*, February 9, 1943; "Cape Town Schools Hold Athletic Meet," *Cape Herald*, April 9, 1966.
93. "Pigeon Racing," *The Sun*, September 17, 1937.
94. "The Achilles Athletic Club," *Cape Standard*, March 14, 1944.
95. The *T.E.P.A.* was the official organ of the Teachers' Educational Professional Association (TEPA) was a breakaway body from the TLSA. The TEPA had a more politically moderate programme of action than the TLSA.
96. "Obituary. C.D. Sassman," *TEPA. Organ of the Teachers' Educational and Professional Association*, no. 4 (1950): 6.
97. "The Western Province Coloured Football Association," *The Clarion*, April 26, 1919. According to the *A.P.O., Official Organ of the African Political Organisation* of April 23, 1910, the WPFA (Coloured) was established in 1904.
98. Hendricks, "A Principled Engagement?" 154; "Central Schools' Sports Union Officials," *Cape Standard*, February 18, 1941.
99. Adhikari, *Let Us Live*, 185.
100. "South African Tennis Championships," *Sun*, January 8, 1937.
101. "Visit of All-India Soccer Team," *Sun*, June 29, 1934.
102. "Cape and District Tennis Union," *Sun*, June 8, 1934; "Cape and District Tennis Union," *Sun*, October 2, 1936.
103. "Outstanding Tennis Tourney," *Sun*, March 13, 1936.
104. Greyvenstein, *The Bennie Osler Story*, 23.
105. "Backwardness of Non-European Sport," *Sun*, October 14, 1932.
106. "Cape Town Schools Hold Athletic Meet," *Cape Herald*, April 9, 1966.
107. "The S.A. Soccer Board Executive in Happy Mood," *Sun*, June 18, 1948; "C.A.C. Golding in Disfavour with Footballers," *Torch*, July 19, 1948. The controversy centred around Golding's involvement with the Coloured Affairs Advisory Council (CAC). The CAC was a statutory body made up of Coloured people who had powers to advise the government on matters affecting that community. Radical teachers viewed the CAC as a racist, puppet institution. Adhikari, *Let Us Live*, 71.
108. Van der Ross, *The Rise and Decline*, 206.
109. "Film of Physical Display," *Cape Standard*, November 19, 1940.
110. "Western Province Tennis Tournament," *Sun*, January 11, 1935; "South African Tennis Championships," *Sun*, January 8, 1937.
111. "To What I Attribute My Success," *Sun*, January 13, 1933.
112. "Tennis Competition Ends," *Sun*, April 24, 1936.
113. "South African Board of Control," *Sun*, January 1, 1937.
114. "Backwardness of Non-European Sport," *Sun*, November 11, 1932.
115. "Sports News in Brief," *Sun*, March 25, 1950.
116. "Inclusion of Moslem Players," *Sun*, January 22, 1954.
117. "Cape Town Open Championships," *Sun*, June 18, 1948; "Ashley Table Tennis Club," *The Sun*, August 20, 1948.
118. "Western Province Open Table Tennis Championships," *Sun*, July 15, 1949.
119. Adhikari, *Let Us Live*, 166.
120. Cape of Good Hope, *Report of the Select Committee*, 43–4.
121. *Zonnebloem College Magazine*, "More Play Needed," 13.

References

Adhikari, Mohammed. *Let Us Live for Our Children: The Teachers League of South Africa, 1913–1940*. Cape Town: Buchu Books, 1993.
Bickford-Smith, Vivan, Elizabeth van Heyningen, and Nigel Worden. *Cape Town in the Twentieth Century: An Illustrated Social History*. Claremont: David Philip, 1999.
Booley, Abduragman. *Forgotten Heroes: A History of Black Rugby*. Cape Town: Manie Booley, 1998.

Booth, Douglas. *The Field. Truth and Fiction in Sport History*. New York: Routledge, 2005.

Borman, Martie. *The Cape Education Department. 1839–1989*. Cape Town: Cape Education Department, 1989.

Caldecott, A. F. *The Government and Civilization of the Native Races of South Africa*. Cape Town: Saul Solomon, 1884.

Cape of Good Hope. *Report of the Select Committee on Native Education*. Cape Town: Cape Times, 1908.

Cleophas, Francois Johannes. "Contexting an Ad Hoc Athletics Unity in Natal, 1945–48." *South African Journal for Research in Sport, Physical Education and Recreation* 35, no. 2 (2013): 15–35.

Cleophas, Francois Johannes. "A Historical Exploration of Physical Education (Males) and Physical Culture at Wesley School, Cape Town (1915–1966)." *South African Review of Education* 19, no. 1 (2013): 38–58.

Cleophas, Francois Johannes. "Running a History Programme Outside the Classroom: A Case Study of Athletics at Zonnebloem College." *Yesterday & Today* 8 (March 8, 2013): 63–87.

Cleophas, Francois Johannes, and Van der Merwe Floris Johannes Gerhardus. "Exercising 'Race' through the Coronation Physical Training Competition." *South African Journal for Research in Sport, Physical Education and Recreation* 34, no. 1 (2012): 43–56.

Cleophas, Francois Johannes, and Van der Merwe, Floris Johannes Gerhardus. "Physical Education and Physical Culture in the Coloured Community of the Western Cape: A Review." *African Journal for Physical, Health Education, Recreation and Dance (AJPHERD)* 15, no. 2 (June 2009): 235–256.

Dalehoudt, Herman. "Sir Thomas Muir – Die Onderwys in Kaapland tydens sy Bestuur as Superintendent-Generaal van Onderwys, 1892–1915 [Sir Thomas Muir – The Education in the Cape during His Management as Superintendent-General of Education, 1892–1915]." Unpublished DEd diss., Stellenbosch University, Stellenbosch, 1942.

Department of Public Education, Cape of Good Hope. *Report of the Superintendent-General of Education for the Year Ending 1918*. Cape Town: Cape Education Department, 1918.

Edgar, Robert, ed. *An African American in South Africa: The Travel Notes of Ralph J. Bunche, 28 September 1937–1 January, 1938*. Johannesburg: Witwatersrand University, 1992.

February, Vernon, ed. *From the Arsenal: Articles from the Teachers' League of South Africa. A Documentary Study of "Coloured" Attitudes between 1913–1980*. Leiden: African Studies Centre, c. 1983.

Greyvenstein, Chris. *The Bennie Osler Story*. Cape Town: Howard Timmins, 1970.

Hatfield, Dennis, and George Manuel. *District Six*. Cape Town: Longmans, 1967.

Hendricks, Paul Ross. "A Principled Engagement? Non-Collaboration and the Teachers' League of South Africa in the Western Cape." Unpublished PhD diss., University of Cape Town, Cape Town, 2010.

Hirson, Baruch. "The Trotskyist Groups in South Africa." *Revolutionary History* 4, no. 4 (1993): 25–56.

House of Lords, "The Provision of Playing Fields." *Hansard* 197 (May 29, 1956): cc552–cc580.

Law, W. H. "Playing Fields Associations in South Africa." *Vigor* 6, no. 2 (1953): 14–16.

Law, W. H. "Why Playing Fields?" *Vigor* 1, no. 5 (1948): 6–8.

Lewis, Gavin. *Between the Wire and the Wall: A History of South African 'Coloured' Politics*. New York: St Martin's, 1987.

Malherbe, Ernest. *Education in South Africa*, Vol. 1. Cape Town: Juta, 1925.

Motlhabi, Mokgethi. *The Theory and Practice of Black Resistance to Apartheid: A Social-Ethical Analysis*. Johannesburg: Skotaville, 1984.

Mphalele, Ezekiel. *Down Second Avenue*. London: Faber and Faber, 1959.

Ndee, Hamad. "Sport, Culture and Society from an African Perspective: A Study in Historical Revisionism." *The International Journal of the History of Sport* 13, no. 2 (1996): 192–202.

Noronha, Francis. *Kipchoge of Kenya*. Nakuru: Elimu, 1970.

Racing Past. "The History of Middle and Long Distance Running." Accessed November 15, 2013. http://www.racingpast.ca/john_contents.php?id=166

South African Olympic and British Empire Games Association. Minutes of the Meeting of the Executive Committee of the South African Olympic and British Empire Games Association held in the Carlton Hotel at 8 p.m. on Monday, 13 January 1947.

Thomas, Cornelius. *Time with Dennis Brutus: Conversations, Quotations and Snapshots 2005–2009.* Selbourne: Wendy's Book Lounge, 2012.

Van der Poel, Jean. "The Present Position of Coloured Education in the Cape Province." *The Cape Coloured People Today* (Reprinted from *Race Relations*) 9, no. 1 (1942): 42–46.

Van der Ross, Richard Ernest. *The Rise and Decline of Apartheid: A Study of Political Movements among the Coloured People of South Africa, 1880–1985.* Cape Town: Tafelberg, 1986.

Wieder, Alan. *Teacher and Comrade: Richard Dudley and the Fight for Democracy in South Africa.* New York: State University of New York, 2008.

Zonnebloem College Magazine, "More Play Needed." *Quarterly Magazine and Journal of the Association of St. John Baptist* 2, no. 8 (1904): 13–14.

On the Margins: Therapeutic Massage, Physical Education and Physical Therapy Defining a Profession

Alison Wrynn

Department of Kinesiology, California State University, Long Beach, CA, USA

The American physical therapy profession emerged during and following the First World War as a result of the need for trained providers of therapeutic exercise – who practised under the supervision of a physician – for the rehabilitation of injured soldiers. Most of these pioneer physical therapists came to the profession with a background in corrective exercise developed in women's physical education programmes at a variety of colleges and universities throughout the country. A number of scholars have examined the therapeutic exercise components of physical education that migrated their way into physical therapy practice but less focus has been placed on the use of massage as a therapeutic tool in physical therapy's earliest years. Recently, Danish historian Per Jorgensen began to analyse the connections among massage practice, physical therapy and chiropractic in Denmark from 1900 to 1930. My central question focuses on an analysis of how the practice of massage was used in physical therapy, and the ways in which massage practitioners and physical therapists interacted and established their respective scope of practice in the first half of the twentieth century in the USA.

Kinesiology Today as a Support for Physical Therapy

We have more than 1200 students in our undergraduate programme in Kinesiology at CSU, Long Beach. Our neighbour campuses – CSU Fullerton and CSU Northridge – have close to 2700 students combined. So at three campuses, located within a one-hour drive of one another, we have approximately 4000 students majoring in Kinesiology. The vast majority of them have the intent of entering a graduate programme in Physical Therapy. They are facing a lot of competition!

Why are all these students descending upon Kinesiology programmes to prepare for Physical Therapy? Physical Therapy is considered to be one of the most 'recession proof' careers today. From 2004 to 2009 applications to PT graduate programmes increased 110%. Student enrolments increased more than 45% in that same time period.[1] As of 2016, the American Physical Therapy Association (APTA) (which at various times in its history was also called the American Physiotherapy Association; so I will use the two names of the organisation interchangeably)[2] will require the Doctorate as the entry-level degree for the Physical Therapy profession; most recently it was a Master's degree. APTA is also proposing that by 2020 physical therapists will not need to work under the direct supervision of a physician either through a referral or consultation, thus leading to greater professional autonomy.[3]

My students have asked me what the difference is now that a doctorate is required for entry-level physical therapist. Is there a lot more knowledge to be imparted in that extra year of study? Although I am sure that there is a great deal more clinical practice that these students undergo, one of the primary reasons for creating a higher standard for new physical therapists goes back to my opening numbers – so many students want to become PTs that there will soon be a glut of trained practitioners – all competing for jobs, and many of those currently in the profession, whether they admit it or not, do not view that as a good thing. As many professional groups have realised over the course of their history, if they make it more challenging to get a degree, the number of people who wish to seek entry into the physical therapy profession may diminish (this could, however, have just the opposite effect and make the profession even more attractive to candidates as it will confer the title of 'Dr' on its practitioners now).

Kinesiology departments in many locations across the USA are quickly becoming beholden to the interests of undergraduate students who only want the prerequisite course work necessary for entrance into physical therapy doctoral programmes, something that Kinesiology, as it has for almost a century, provides. Nearly 100 years ago it was the newly emerging profession of physical therapy that was looking to the established profession of women's physical education – with its strong grounding in Swedish gymnastics – to provide academic substance and training to the 'Reconstruction Aides' (RA) who would be needed in the Great War.

In previous works, I have explored the history of rehabilitation, and a fascinating, complex web emerged that connected a variety of 'allied health fields' – such as Athletic Training, Kinesiotherapy, PT, Therapeutic Recreation, Adapted Physical Education and Occupational Therapy – that today argue they are all distinct professions.[4] All of these professions claim Swedish gymnastics as a starting point in their history. The basic definition of the work of a physical therapist is ' . . . [one who] employ[s] physical agents such as heat, water, and light in treatment routines, and perform[s] tests to determine nerve, muscle, and skin condition and reaction'.[5] In addition, PTs use exercise and massage in their treatment. This article will focus only on the treatment modality of massage and the part it played in the professionalisation of physical therapy.

Although most people around the world are familiar with therapeutic massage, little research has been conducted on its effectiveness as a mode of treatment. For example, in the USA, by the late 1990s, more than 10% of Americans used massage on a regular basis. However, the National Institute for Health invests very little to study the efficacy of massage as a treatment. Far more research money has been spent on studying botanicals, acupuncture, meditation and chiropractic as therapeutic modalities than on massage.[6]

Massage practice has been around for many centuries. Most scholars agree that by 3000 BC it was being employed as a therapeutic measure in China. In the west, Hippocrates, around 460 BC, wrote about massage and the Romans continued its use.[7] Some researchers contend that therapeutic massage has encountered difficulties in becoming a part of the treatment regimen of the medical establishment due to its historical connection to folk remedies. Per Henrik Ling, the founder of Swedish gymnastics, which included a significant component of therapeutic massage, was not medically trained, and thus his treatments were opposed by most physicians. However, his results soon convinced the medical community to become more supportive of his work.[8]

Therapeutic massage came to America through the work of physicians Lewis Sayre, Weir Mitchell and others in the 1880s, although its use did not become widespread among the medical profession. Finding someone to assist physicians who wanted to utilise massage treatment was the problem that emerged. According to Hartvig Nissen, whom leading physical educator Amy Morris Homans of the Boston Normal School of Gymnastics contended was among the first to teach Swedish gymnastics in America,[9]

> Much harm has been done both to patients and to the reputation of 'massage', because physicians have been too quick to accept the[ir] card ... without looking up their record. I know of several instances where good-looking women ... have obtained work, although they did not know the first principles of massage, while others, who were first-class masseuses, but not perhaps as attractive looking nor as smooth spoken as their sisters, did not receive any patients.[10]

In his *Practical Massage and Corrective Exercises*, first published in 1889 and in its fifth edition by 1929, Nissen continued to argue that 'massage" was a misunderstood term. It was '... a handling and manipulating of the flesh ... for therapeutic purposes'.[11] Nissen also believed that massage should be used in conjunction with gymnastic exercise for the best effect.[12] Massage entered the curriculum of American physical education programmes (particularly for women) through Swedish gymnastics. As the twentieth century dawned, the question arose that how could massage practitioners best be trained so that they could provide services for physicians who wished to utilise massage?

Where Do Professions Come From? What Is Women's Place in the Allied Health Professions?

Historian Michael Goldstein argues that the notions of professionalisation and medicalisation have a shared attraction for one another. As groups sought to professionalise, '... many occupational groups explicitly or implicitly set out to associate themselves with physicians, who are usually taken as epitomizing a fully professional group'.[13] Physical education emerged as a profession in the late nineteenth century in response to a number of social, pedagogical and quasi-medical concerns. Its antecedents, however, were located in a variety of antebellum beliefs and practices regarding health, fitness, exercise and physical training. And many of its earliest leaders, both male and female, were drawn from the ranks of physicians.[14]

As Roberta Park has contended, at the end of the nineteenth century, physical education was in much the same position as medicine with a need to take hold of its strong beginnings and move forward into the twentieth century.[15] The early alliance with medicine seemed an ideal connection for physical education. Medicine was moving towards a model of attempting to cure those who were already ill; public health, and physical education, would be left with the job of preventing outbreaks of illness and maintaining health. However, by the 1920s, physical education had more closely aligned itself with the public school educational system in the USA, and teacher training programmes focused almost exclusively on sports and games in the preparation of teachers for the next several decades.[16]

Physical therapy, which would emerge almost four decades after physical education organised as a profession, chose a different path. It may have drawn its earliest practitioners from the field of physical education but it very quickly allied itself with the profession of medicine, moving away from its roots in corrective physical education. The desire to align with the well-established and well-respected field of medicine was paramount to the pioneers in physical therapy. Female physical educators had for decades been well trained in the Swedish form of gymnastics; many of these exercises became a part of corrective physical training and later physical therapy. Among those who knew the most about corrective exercises were physical educators at some of the better colleges.[17] Following the First World War, and into the late 1920s, physical therapy began to emerge as a valid career path for women physical educators, and physiotherapists aligned themselves with the American Medical Association (AMA).[18]

From its inception, PT has been dominated by women. In its earliest years, it considered calling its professional organisation the American Women's Physical Therapy Association before realising that there might be some men who were interested in entering the profession. Historian Cynthia Fuchs Epstein maintained that women who chose to participate in what she calls the 'prestige professions' (i.e. medicine, law, academia and science) were viewed with as much suspicion in 1968 as they had been in 1898.[19] The percentage of women who worked in such fields remained relatively static from 1900 to 1960, and in some instances it declined. The percentage of women physicians was documented as being 6% in 1910, and dropped to 4% by 1930.[20]

Physical therapy, like nursing, began as an allied health profession that was subservient to the virtually all-male medical establishment. Both professions were almost exclusively female at their inception. Today, PT remains largely female with 68.1% of physical therapists who are members of the APTA being female.[21] The numbers of male physical therapists began to climb following the Second World War when returning veterans utilised their GI Benefits to attend physical therapy schools. Within a decade of the war's end, men made up 20% of the membership of the APTA.[22]

I do not have space in this work to examine the racial issues within this profession but it is clearly a topic that needs more extensive analysis. Today, more than 93% of the members of the APTA are white.[23] The reasons for this racial divide include the fact that there were no physical therapy schools open to African-Americans in the southern part of the USA prior to 1963; a very small number of African-American women did find ways to enter the profession in the 1940s and 1950s. This did not mean, however, that they were unfettered in their participation in APTA. For example, when the APTA chose to hold its convention in a southern state in 1953 (Dallas, Texas), six African-American women members of APTA were refused housing at the segregated conference hotel. To its credit the APTA responded and moved their next conference from Florida to Los Angeles, California, so the women would not have to face this problem again.[24]

A pattern of gender segregation in science has also been studied by historian Margaret Rossiter, who contends that although women have been encouraged to study science and medicine, they were not provided the opportunity to move up the career ladder in any substantial way once they completed their training. Rather, they continued to be utilised as part of the lower ranking workers, notably among those needed in the era of big science that followed the Second World War.[25] Physical therapists were (and still are) required to practise under the supervision of a physician. Historically, the majority of these medical supervisors, Physical Medicine and Rehabilitation physicians (who call themselves physiatrists), have been male.[26]

Even before the demands of the First World War led to the need for trained RA, some women and men were already planning on expanding their training in physical education and corrective exercise into some form of training for physical therapy. In 1907, physical educators realised that exercise would be an ideal tool for rehabilitating injured individuals. Springfield College's James Huff McCurdy claimed 'Gymnastic training must be employed as a therapeutic agent ...'.[27] The Rehabilitation section of the American Physical Education Association was formed at the turn of the twentieth century and was led by Swedish gymnastic innovators such as Baron Nils Posse, his wife Rose, Hartvig Nissen and others, as well as physician physical educators such as R. Tait McKenzie.

When the women's only Boston Normal School of Gymnastics closed in 1909, and became the Department of Physical Education at Wellesley College, not all faculty moved to the new institution. A small group of women who would later become physical therapy pioneers – led by Marjorie Bouve and Marguerite Sanderson – created the Boston School of Physical Education (BSPE). They took this step after consulting with orthopaedic physicians Dr Joel Goldwaithe and Dr Elliot Brackett. Sanderson soon left to form the RA at the start of the First World War; Bouve remained at the school and reorganised the curriculum to allow for additional training for advanced students in physical therapy.[28]

Sanderson and the other founding faculty at the BSPE (Bessie Barnes, Caroline Baxter, Marjorie Bouve, Grace Shepardson, Mary Florence Stratton and Miriam Tobey) wanted to continue the tradition they had experienced at the Boston Normal School of Gymnastics of a two-year curriculum for teacher training and therapeutic exercise, instead of the four-year degree that would be required of students at the reorganised Department of Physical Education at Wellesley College. BSPE rapidly incorporated physical therapy into its curriculum as a result of founder Sanderson's experience as Director of the RA. By 1925 a physical therapy department had been established.[29]

Emergence of PT in WWI and the Use of Massage

Miriam Sweeney, who before the war had been a director of the orthopaedic clinics at the Children's Hospital of Boston, claimed that in the years leading up to the First World War 'The average masseuse [was] usually a strong healthy robust woman, of the illiterate type, often not even a high school graduate'[30]; thus, she declared that it would be the scientific application of practices such as massage that would demonstrate the worth of physical therapy to the medical community.

> Physical therapeutics has never had such an opportunity to be placed upon a scientific basis as at present. Massage, manipulations and orthopedic movements have been given in many places by persons who, often, have had only a three months' course in massage, and enough anatomy to cover the course superficially. ... Superficial training and knowledge is positively dangerous – more harm can be done by manipulations and muscle reeducation given in a faulty way than can be estimated. We must be prepared to qualify on a high plane, and thus protect not only the soldier patient but the reputation of the profession. We must emphasize the vital importance of knowing what is to be done and how to do it.[31]

The use of exercise and massage as rehabilitative measures took on added impetus during the First World War as the result of the vast number of combat-related injuries.[32] The need to return soldiers to a productive status was at first seen as a necessity of war – every man was needed on the front lines. In the years following the war, it was understood that these men needed to become economically productive, no matter what their ability level might be.[33]

In her 1918 American Physical Education Association Convention presentation, Marguerite Sanderson presented the case for the important role that women would fill as RA. According to Sanderson

> Teachers of [women's] physical education who have specialized in corrective work and who have had experience with pathological cases in a hospital or in the private practice of an orthopedic surgeon offer the best foundation for the work of reconstruction aides.[34]

As the USA prepared to enter the First World War, the US Army Medical Department realised that they would need personnel trained in '... massage [and] mechanical hydrotherapy ...'; however, there were no official programmes to train PTs until the Mayo Clinic programme began in 1918.[35] Within a year almost four dozen hospitals had PT facilities and had hired over 700 RA.[36] These Aides came primarily from physical education and received special courses that focused on massage and other aspects of PT such as hydrotherapy, electrotherapy and mechanotherapy. It was, however, believed to be most important that they be well versed in massage in order to be successful as an Aide.[37] R. Tait McKenzie, whose work with injured soldiers during the First World War established a strong connection between rehabilitation and physical education, contended that 'If only one means of treatment was possible, I would choose massage before any other …'.[38] Despite McKenzie's assertion, as the war began, not all physicians were enthusiastic about the use of massage in the treatment of injured soldiers; they were concerned that massage was being provided by untrained practitioners who were not under the direct supervision of a physician.[39]

At this point, let me briefly describe what men were contributing to the reconstruction effort. Dr Charles A. Prosser, Director of the Federal Board of Vocational Education, declared that '… men and women, experts [in rehabilitation], devoted their whole time to the problem of taking care of the unfortunate soldiers who found their way into the hospitals'.[40] Male physical educators, and former athletic coaches, were involved in the remedial gymnastics work provided to recovering soldiers. At one overseas rehabilitation hospital, under the supervision of Captain Charles Palmer, a group of 2 medical officers and 20 men supervised the remedial exercise department for between 400 and 600 men. The massage department, however, was left to the women. Palmer believed that massage was a critical part of the recovery process that he hoped would soon be even more closely linked with the gymnastic department.[41]

By war's end, 815 RA in Physiotherapy had been trained, and according to one source 95% '… of the Aides were either graduates of normal schools of physical education, or were college graduates who had majored in physical education'.[42]

Post-First World War

Following the war, physical medicine physician Harold Corbusier recommended that the RA form a national organisation. He believed that this would 'elevate and standardize the work, and place it on a more substantial basis'.[43] Dorothea Beck, who would become a President of the American Physiotherapy Association, agreed, stating that

> There must be preparation [in order to raise the standards of PT education]. … What we are going to do is to give to the medical profession a band of trained women whose ideals, whose personality and whose technical training are all that the physicians and surgeons of the American Medical Association … can wish.[44]

The Great War had demonstrated the value of physical therapy on a large scale. It established that a smaller group of physicians of physical medicine could supervise a large cadre of 'technicians' trained in physical therapy techniques to carry out their medical orders. This expansion of individuals who could contribute to the reconstruction of injured soldiers was a vital step in the creation of a profession of physical therapy.[45]

As a first step, in 1923, the AMA decided to '… recognize the increasing importance of special medical activities, such as radiology, physiotherapy and occupational therapy'.[46] In 1925 the Council on Physical Therapy of the AMA fully recognised physical therapy as a profession. In the 1930s the Council on Medical Education of the AMA was charged with reviewing the existing training programmes in PT and approving those that met the standards.[47] The title that these new physical therapists would use was very important to them. The women of the newly formed American Physiotherapy Association agreed on the need to work under the supervision of physicians, '… but some of the mature, cultured, and highly trained women who started the American Physiotherapy Association were unwilling to be classed only as technicians'.[48]

Their primary concern was competition from physical therapy technicians who practised independently and were virtually untrained. One of the early goals of the American Physiotherapy Association was to urge Physical Medicine physicians to stop using these independent technicians. Eventually, the PT technicians would be brought into the fold by creating methods to standardise their training and control entry into their profession.[49] The American Physiotherapy Association

> ... pledged to work with the American Medical Association to establish standards of education for physical therapists; to encourage the regulation of physical therapy practice by law; and to cooperate with, or under the direction of, the medical profession to provide a central registry for physical therapists.

Why was there such great concern on the part of these women that they be recognised by the medical profession as a part of the allied health team? On one hand, they wanted to create standards to restrict entry into the profession. In addition, they wanted to be recognised as professionals within the health care system. Part of the problem was that in the years following the First World War, most physicians were focusing on the newly emerging forms of medicine that utilised pharmaceuticals and surgery to care for illness and injury rather than using various physical agents – such as hydrotherapy, electrotherapy and massage. Thus, they left the door open to '... charlatans [who] attempted to fill this void by the unethical and often improper use of physical agents. This engendered even greater distrust, on the part of ethical physicians, of those who employed physical agents for treatments'.[50] This was the landscape that these women in the newly formed profession of PT faced. And although the use of electricity as a form of treatment attracted a fair number of frauds, the practice of massage was particularly problematic for female physical therapists as it was linked in many places to issues of vice and immorality.

Massage Parlours and Physical Therapy: The Case of Los Angeles, California

The Great War brought with it the kind of social dislocation that all conflicts do. Men moved in large numbers across the country as the USA rapidly deployed soldiers and sailors to Europe. Concerns about the behaviour of these large groups of socially isolated men focused not only on them but also on women. It was believed that 'delinquent' women and girls were travelling to the military camps and presenting the soldiers and sailors with ready access to prostitutes.[51] This was the social milieu that female RA had to face. There was a real concern that women who were interested in being near the military only had immoral objectives.

Despite these concerns about immorality, some institutions stepped to the forefront to train the RA who would be needed. Reed College (where one of the larger PT training programmes would be established during the war) was a leader in the 'social hygiene' and eugenics movement. The President of Reed College, William Trufant Foster, published the edited volume *The Social Emergency: Studies in Sex Hygiene and Morals* in 1913.[52] However, it was Foster, a prominent economist and President of the Pacific Coast Federation for Sex Hygiene, who committed the resources of Reed College to vocational training – including physical therapy – at the inception of the First World War.[53]

Today, massage has a legitimate place in therapeutic practice; however, it also has an illicit side. This has been a part of the history of massage since the beginning of its use as a treatment for injury and disease.[54] Physical Therapy historians Nicholls and Holmes contend that physical therapy fought so hard to establish itself as a profession due to its reliance on the potentially sensual and sometimes illicit practice of massage.[55] This argument has been supported by research on the history of the legitimatisation of massage practice in Great Britain in the late 1800s. The creation of a professional Society of Trained Masseuses led to the establishment of a group that could liaison with medical societies and the government and control the care of a segment of the population distinct from what other professional groups were doing up to that point in time. Members of the Society of Trained Masseuses agreed that therapeutic massage could only be practised under the supervision of a physician and the profession was limited to women (with a few exceptions).[56]

The use of therapeutic exercise became increasingly important (alongside massage, hydrotherapy and other practices) because it allowed the body to be viewed from the perspective of science as a machine. This dispassionate view of the body allowed massage practitioners within physical therapy to touch the body without fear of the practice being sensualised.[57]

The connections between American physical therapy and massage as both a therapeutic and illicit practice have not yet been examined in depth. To what lengths did the leaders of the APA go to assert their legitimacy as a part of the medical rehabilitation team? What did the public believe that these women who claimed to provide therapeutic massage services were really doing? In most parts of the country there were no laws that dealt with the legal status of therapeutic massage practitioners. In one city, a female physiotherapist was given the choice of licensing herself as a masseuse, barber or cosmetician if she wanted to practise physical therapy – she chose cosmetician.[58] Concerns about massage parlours in Los Angeles as the USA entered the First World War were illustrated by the fact that in the spring of 1917 the city decided to stop issuing any licences for massage businesses to quell the tide of what the *Los Angeles Times* called establishments that had as their goal 'perverted use'. This editorial did acknowledge the therapeutic uses of massage, claiming it was a 'recognized branch of health attainment' with practitioners who worked in conjunction with 'bona fide medical men'. The *Los Angeles Times* also commented that it was inappropriate for the city to lump all massage practitioners in together as it was fairly easy to tell the difference between a qualified nurse who wished to utilise massage in a treatment setting versus a 'notorious woman … connected with public scandal' who was clearly unqualified to provide therapeutic massage.[59]

Concerns did not diminish as the USA entered the war and in March 1919 an article in the *Los Angeles Times* suggested what to do with women who were running illicit massage parlours. Although the article entitled 'Lady Rubbers to the Front'[60] does not mention that women should work in therapeutic massage as RA, it clearly ties together the massage parlour technician and the trained RA.

The practice of Swedish massage, which was a part of the armamentaria of the physical therapist, was presented to the public as a valid therapeutic tool that could also serve as a cover for banned activities. The *Los Angeles Times* noted in February 1923 that

> Women posing as Swedish masseurs and manicurists, but whose names have appeared before on the police blotter as vagrants and violators of the rooming house ordinance, began a hurried exodus from their massage parlors when news was flashed over the underground wires that a drive had been launched against them by the police … the Purity Squad [and] the Morals Efficiency Commission.[61]

Unfortunately, it appears that the governmental officials and organisations in Los Angeles that were created to stem the tide of these illicit businesses, despite their highly moral sounding titles, were not above unethical behaviours themselves. In March 1925, the application of Safrona Joyner, a nurse, and her colleague physician Dr D.C. Ragland to open a physiotherapy practice was at first rejected (due to a claim that there were too many similar business establishments in the city) before being accepted by the Police Commission. The attorney for Joyner and Ragland, Griffith Jones, claimed that the only reason that the permit was issued was due to a bribe of $250 being paid by his clients. Why would there be such a commotion over the establishment of a physiotherapy clinic? Certainly, there might have been a misunderstanding over the nature of this newly established profession. In fact, the newspaper referred to this particular physiotherapy clinic first as a 'beauty parlor' and later as a 'massage parlor'.[62]

The women leaders of physical therapy were concerned about these issues – although, they did not acknowledge the connection between prostitution and massage in a direct way in the pages of the *PT Review* – their main professional journal. Instead, they alluded to the upright and moral stance of the well-trained physical therapists asserting that

> Doctors are realizing more and more the benefits derived from the intelligent use of [physiotherapy]. They are also learning that the American Physiotherapy Association is a professional body who is just as anxious as they are to keep the unqualified and the fakes out of the field.[63]

The members of the APA did understand, however, that 'Rubbing and massaging may be the same to the lay mind but in practice how different. … Specific knowledge is needed by the technician to perform … massage'.[64]

The Northern California Association of Physiotherapists maintained that the members of their organisation were the 'logical solution of the long and somewhat bitter struggle between legitimate medicine and osteopaths, chiropractors and quacks. We feel, therefore, that it is more than ever important to do all we can to uphold the ethics of our profession'.[65] These physiotherapists were concerned that the public believed 'A physiotherapist is the same as a masseuse … who gives treatments … like they give where [women] have [their] hair done'.[66]

The scrutiny of massage parlours continued following the war. There was a need to continue to licence these establishments, and frequent inspections, in order to 'eliminate those places using the name "massage parlor" merely for a screen'.[67] Those legitimate businesses that wanted to provide therapeutic massages found a difficult time in advertising their services. The *Los Angeles Times*, for example, refused to accept classified ads for 'Bath and Massage Parlors', and, according to police officials ' … fully 75 percent of the "parlors" advertised [were] nothing more nor less than poorly disguised houses of ill fame'.[68]

Conclusion: Status Today of Physical Therapy and Massage

Well before the First World War, Kurre Ostrum in his 1902 text *Massage and the Original Swedish Movements* stated his belief that in America ' … There is no medical agency that has been much abused as massage'.[69] He found it difficult to believe that massage schools were not better regulated, as they were in countries like Germany. Attempts to regulate massage schools continued in the years leading up to the Second World War in the USA. The city of Los Angeles attempted to regulate the massage schools as trade schools and thus established standards. The concern was that the State had yet to set standards for the massage profession.[70]

When discussing therapeutic massage at the outset of the First World War, physician David Lyman claimed 'There is no question but that we have neglected this important branch of therapy in our work in America'.[71] However, the medical profession was now looking past massage to new technological innovations to assist with their extensive rehabilitation challenges.[72] This included ultraviolet light by the 1920s, hydrotherapy in the 1930s and the Second World War 'strong exercises'. Following the war, proprioceptive neuromuscular facilitation and new technical discoveries such as ultrasound and microwave became popular. Historian Leonard Goldstone argues that massage began to be viewed as 'old fashioned' in the face of technological innovation.[73]

The rapid expansion of the role of physical therapists between the two World Wars, which in those years had as their particular focus issues regarding childhood paralysis, frequently related to polio, and during the Second World War, led to a call for increased training opportunities for physical therapists. But it also led the American Physiotherapy Association to express concern about the scope of practice of others who were ' . . . closely concerned in the physical restoration phase of rehabilitation [such as] . . . occupational therapists, physical education and recreational workers and nurses'.[74] There was a need to define each group's activities in order to reduce overlap in training and treatment.

Today, we continue to hear concerns that massage parlours are being used in many places around the world for illicit practices.[75] And, although physical therapists are not trained as much in massage as they once were, it is still a part of their treatment regimen. Whether it was in 1900, 1925, 1950 or today, there is still a concern that massage needs more research conducted on it to establish it as a valid medical treatment. As I stated in the Introduction to this paper, very little research money has been spent in recent years to determine that there is more to the efficacy of massage other than 'it feels good'.[76] An editorial in the *Archives of Physical Medicine* proclaimed the necessity for such research more than 60 years ago arguing that

> Sufficient sound clinical research and enough basic scientific investigations will eventually aid in evaluating [massage as a] physical agent. From such work much of the empiricism will be removed. It will then be prescribed rationally and specifically because of its proved effects on various pathologic and psychologic processes. No longer will such a quotation be possible as the following from the pamphlet issued several years ago by the Council of Physical Therapy of the American Medical Association on Massage: 'There is probably no other measure of equal known value in the entire armamentarium of medicine which is so inadequately understood and utilized by the profession as a whole.'[77]

Notes

1. *Today's Physical Therapist.*
2. Initially the women of the APTA wanted to call themselves physical therapists but the physicians who worked in rehabilitation were against this title as they were called physical medicine physicians and thought that such a close name might create confusion among the public. In 1946, however, physical medicine physicians chose the term 'physiatrist' for members of their medical specialty so the physiotherapists changed their organisation's name from the American Physiotherapy Association to the American Physical Therapy Association. See Murphy, *Healing the Generations.*
3. American Physical Therapy Association, "Direct Access to Physical Therapist."
4. Wrynn, "Under the Showers"; "'Re-constructing' Physical Education"; and "Whatever Happened to Corrective Gymnastics?"
5. Stanfield and Hui, *Introduction to the Health.*
6. Kahn. "Foreword."

7. Granger, "The Development of Physiotherapy"; Clein, "The Early Historical Roots."
8. Moyer, Rounds and Hannum, "A Meta-Analysis."
9. Amy Morris Homans to R. Tait McKenzie, personal correspondence October 31, 1908, UPT 50, McK 37, Box 1, FF 21, University of Pennsylvania Archives.
10. Nissen, *Practical Massage*.
11. Ibid.
12. Ibid.
13. Goldstein, *The Health Movement*.
14. Whorton, *Crusaders for Fitness*.
15. Park, "The Second 100 Years."
16. Wrynn, "The Contributions of Women."
17. Rathbone, *Corrective Physical Education*.
18. Hazenhyer, "Physical Therapy."
19. Epstein, *Woman's Place*.
20. Ibid., 7.
21. *Today's Physical Therapist*.
22. Murphy, *Healing the Generations*.
23. *Today's Physical Therapist*.
24. Murphy, *Healing the Generations*.
25. Rossiter, *Women Scientists in America*.
26. Hudak et al., "Dr. Frances A. Hellebrandt."
27. McCurdy, "Physical Training."
28. Lynn, "Marjorie Bouve," 88.
29. Rachel Keegan, "Collection Overview: Boston-Bouve College Records, 1892–2000," Archives and Special Collections Department Boston-Bouve College, Northeastern University, Boston, MA. http://www.lib.neu.edu/archives/collect/findaids/m41find.htm (accessed June 23, 2003).
30. Sweeney, "Reconstruction Work," 533.
31. Ibid.
32. For more on the involvement of the US government and the US military in the medical treatment of servicemen and women, see Department of Veterans Affairs, "VA History in Brief," Office of Public Affairs, Washington, DC. http://www.va.gov/opa/publications/archives/docs/history_in_brief.pdf (accessed July 17, 2013).
33. Ibid.
34. Sanderson, "Woman's Part," 367.
35. "Rehabilitation Medicine at the University of Pennsylvania, 1914–1918," *The History of Rehabilitation Medicine at UPHS*, Chapter 2. http://www.pennmedicine.org/physical-medicine-rehabilitation/about-us/history.html, 4, (accessed October 24, 2002).
36. Ibid., 3.
37. Rathbone, "The American Physiotherapy Association."
38. McKenzie, "The Functional Reeducation."
39. Mennell, "Massage in the After Treatment."
40. "U.S. Leads in Work for Disabled Men," *New York Times*, March 23, 1919, Part II, 2.
41. Palmer, "Remedial Reeducation."
42. Granger, "The Development of Physiotherapy," 16.
43. Gritzer and Arluke, *The Making of Rehabilitation*.
44. Beck, "Presidential Address."
45. "American Women's Physical," 3.
46. Nelson, "History of the Archives," 373.
47. Hazenhyer, "Physical Therapy."
48. Rathbone, "The American Physiotherapy Association," 9.
49. Gritzer and Arluke, *The Making of Rehabilitation*, 71.
50. Krusen, "Historical Development," 1.
51. Additon, "Work among Delinquent Women."
52. Foster, *The Social Emergency*.
53. Jennifer Ingham, Sally Brunette and Lauren Lassleben, "Timeline of Reed College Events to 1959." http://web.reed.edu/alumni/oral_hist_timeline.html (accessed July 16, 2013).
54. Kelly Her, "Massage Goes Mainstream," *Taiwan Review*. http://taiwanreview.nat.gov.tw/ct. asp?xItem=25052&CtNode = 1337&mp = (accessed July 17, 2013).

55. Nicholls and Holmes, "Discipline, Desire and Transgression."
56. Nicholls and Cheek, "Physiotherapy and the Shadow."
57. Ibid., 2343.
58. Murphy, *Healing the Generations.*
59. "The Massage Parlors," *Los Angeles Times*, May 26, 1917, II4.
60. "Lady Rubbers to the Front," *Los Angeles Times*, March 15, 1919, II3.
61. "Purity Raid Tip Starts Evacuation," *Los Angeles Times*, February 27, 1923, 12.
62. "Permit Sale Plot Charged," *Los Angeles Times*, March 11, 1925, A1.
63. "Editorial," 2.
64. Tuggle, "What Is a Physiotherapist?" 116.
65. "Editorials," 27.
66. Tuggle, "What Is a Physiotherapist?" 115.
67. "Enactment of Masseur Code Requested," *Los Angeles Times*, April 11, 1932, A14.
68. Police Battle Want Ad Vice," *Los Angeles Times*, February 14, 1932, A2.
69. Ruffin, "A History of Massage."
70. "Massage School Regulations Sought," *Los Angeles Times*, March 27, 1939, 10; "Police Board Asks Ruling on Power over Masseuses," *Los Angeles Times*, February 6, 1939, 9; "Curb Voted on Massagers," *Los Angeles Times*, August 16, 1940, 13.
71. Knopf, "Blinded Soldiers," 114.
72. Goldstone, "Massage," 171–2.
73. Ibid., 173.
74. Stevenson, "IV. The American Physiotherapy," 254.
75. Kelly Her, "Massage Goes Mainstream," *Taiwan Review*, http://taiwanreview.nat.gov.tw/ct. asp?xItem=25052&CtNode = 1337&mp = (accessed July 17, 2013); "China Asks If 'Happy Ending' Massage Services Are Illegal," *FoxNews.com*, http://www.foxnews.com/world/2013/06/28/china-asks-if-happy-ending-massage-services-are-illegal/ (accessed on July 17, 2013); Sally Schilling, "Millbrae Updating Massage Ordinance: City to Require One State Certificate, Not Two," *The Daily Journal*, http://www.smdailyjournal.com/articles/lnews/2013-07-11/millbrae-updating-massage-ordinance-city-to-require-one-state-license-not-two/1771569.html (accessed July 17, 2013).
76. Kahn, "Foreword."
77. "Editorials: What Is Happening," 523.

References

Additon, Henrietta S. "Work among Delinquent Women and Girls." *The Annals of the American Academy of Political and Social Science* 80 (1918): 152–160.
American Physical Therapy Association. "Direct Access to Physical Therapist Services." www.apta.org.
American Physical Therapy Association. *Today's Physical Therapist: A Comprehensive Review of a 21st Century Health Care Profession.* Alexandria, VA: American Physical Therapy Association, 2011.
"American Women's Physical Therapeutic Association." *The PT Review* 1 (1920): 3.
Beck, Dorothea M. "Presidential Address." *The PT Review* 4 (1924): 9–10.
Clein, Marvin I. "The Early Historical Roots of Therapeutic Exercise." *Journal of Health, Physical Education and Recreation* 41 (April 1970): 89–91.
"Editorial." *The PT Review* 5 (1925): 2.
"Editorial: What Is Happening to Massage?" *Archives of Physical Medicine* (1952): 31, 523.
"Editorials." *The PT Review* 8 (1928): 26–27.
Epstein, Cynthia Fuchs. *Woman's Place: Options and Limits in Professional Careers.* Berkeley: University of California Press, 1970.
Foster, William Trufant, ed. *The Social Emergency: Studies in Sex Hygiene and Morals.* Cambridge, MA: The Riverside Press, 1913.
Goldstein, Michael S. *The Health Movement: Promoting Fitness in America.* New York: G.K. Hall (MacMillan), 1991.
Goldstone, Leonard A. "Massage as an Orthodox Medical Treatment Past and Future." *Complementary Therapies in Nursing and Midwifery* 6 (2000): 169–175.
Granger, F. B. "The Development of Physiotherapy." *The PT Review* 3 (1923): 14–19.

Gritzer, Glenn, and Arnold Arluke. *The Making of Rehabilitation: A Political Economy of Medical Specialization, 1890–1980*. Berkeley: University of California Press, 1985.

Hazenhyer, Ida May. "Physical Therapy as a Career." *Bios* 17 (1946): 191–197.

Hudak, Anne M., M. Elizabeth Sandel, Gary Goldberg, and Alison M. Wrynn. "Dr. Frances A. Hellebrandt: Pioneering Physiologist, Physiatrist, and PM&R Program Visionary." *PM&R: The Journal of Injury, Function and Rehabilitation* 5 (August 2013): 639–646.

Kahn, Janet R. "Foreword." In *Massage Therapy: The Evidence for Practice*, edited by Grant Jewell Rich, xv–xviii. New York: Mosby, 2002.

Knopf, S. Adolphus. "Blinded Soldiers as Masseurs in Hospitals and Sanatoria for Reconstruction and Rehabilitation of Disabled Soldiers." *The Annals of the American Academy of Political and Social Science* 80 (1918): 111–116.

Krusen, Frank H. "Historical Development in Physical Medicine and Rehabilitation during the Last Forty Years." *Archives of Physical Medicine and Rehabilitation* 50 (July 1969): 1–5.

Lynn, Minnie L. "Marjorie Bouve." *Journal of Health, Physical Education and Recreation* 41 (1970): 88.

McCurdy, James H. "Physical Training as a Therapeutic Agent." *American Physical Education Review* 12 (1907): 205–222.

McKenzie, R. Tait. "The Functional Reeducation of the Wounded." *New York Medical Journal* 108 (1918): 1–16.

Mennell, James B. "Massage in the After Treatment of the Wounded." *Scientific American Supplement* 80 (December 1915): 358.

Moyer, Christopher A., James Rounds, and James W. Hannum. "A Meta-Analysis of Massage Therapy Research." *Psychological Bulletin* 130 (2004): 3–18.

Murphy, Wendy. *Healing the Generations: A History of Physical Therapy and the American Physical Therapy Association*. Alexandria, VA: American Physical Therapy Association, 1995.

Nelson, Paul A. "History of the Archives – A Journal of Ideas and Ideals." *Archives of Physical Medicine and Rehabilitation* 50 (July 1969): 367–405, 414.

Nicholls, David A., and J. Cheek. "Physiotherapy and the Shadow of Prostitution: The Society of Trained Masseuses and the Massage Scandals of 1894." *Social Science & Medicine* 62 (2006): 2336–2348.

Nicholls, David A., and Dave Holmes. "Discipline, Desire and Transgression in Physiotherapy Practice." *Physiotherapy Theory and Practice* 28 (2012): 454–465.

Nissen, Hartvig. *Practical Massage and Corrective Exercises.*, 5th ed. Philadelphia, PA: F.A. Davis, 1929.

Palmer, Charles A. "Remedial Reeducation – 'Overseas'." *American Physical Education Review* 23 (1918): 371–382.

Park, Roberta J. "The Second 100 Years: Or, Can Physical Education Become the Renaissance Field of the 21st Century?" *Quest* 41 (1989): 1–27.

Rathbone, Josephine L. "The American Physiotherapy Association." *The Journal of Health and Physical Education* 4 (September 1934): 7–8.

Rathbone, Josephine L. *Corrective Physical Education*. Philadelphia, PA: W.B. Saunders, 1934.

Rossiter, Margaret. *Women Scientists in America: Before Affirmative Action, 1940-1972*. Baltimore, MD: Johns Hopkins University Press, 1995.

Ruffin, Paula T. "A History of Massage in Nurse Training School Curricula (1860-1945)." *Journal of Holistic Nursing* 29 (2011): 61–67.

Sanderson, Marguerite. "Woman's Part in the Work of Reconstruction." *American Physical Education Review* 23 (1918): 367–370.

Stanfield, Peggy S., and Y. H. Hui. *Introduction to the Health Professions*. Sudbury, MA: Jones & Bartlett, 2002.

Stevenson, Jessie L. IV. "The American Physiotherapy Association." *Journal of Health and Physical Education* 17 (1946): 212–213, 256.

Sweeney, Miriam. "Reconstruction Work on Returned Soldiers." *American Physical Education Review* 23 (1918): 533–537.

Tuggle, Julia. "What Is a Physiotherapist?" *The PT Review* 15 (1935): 12–15.

Whorton, James. *Crusaders for Fitness: The History of American Health Reformers*. Princeton, NJ: Princeton University Press, 1982.

Wrynn, Alison M. "The Contributions of Women Researchers to the Development of a Science of Physical Education in the United States." PhD diss., University of California, Berkeley 1996.

Wrynn, Alison M. "'Re-constructing' Physical Education: The Education of Rehabilitation/ Reconstruction Aides in the United States during the First World War." In *Proceedings of the VIIIth ISHPES Congress*, edited by Gigliola Gori, Thierry Terret, and Sankt Augustin, 202–206. Germany: Akademia Verlag, 2005.

Wrynn, Alison M. "'Under the Showers': An Analysis of the Historical Connections between American Athletic Training and Physical Education." *Journal of Sport History* 34 (2007): 401–415.

Wrynn, Alison M. "Whatever Happened to Corrective Gymnastics? An Historical Analysis of Kinesiotherapy and Allied Fields." *Proceedings of the North American Society for Sport History* (2003): 21–22.

Discourses on the Production of the Athletic Lean Body in Central Europe around 1900

Rudolf Müllner

Centre for Sport Science, Sport and Culture, Vienna, Austria

The ideals of the athletic lean body are predominant in the public discourses and images of the present. They have an enormous normative power. There is a market of different techniques to enhance the body. Many people regard their own bodies as insufficient. This study interprets physicalness and its meanings as products of sociocultural discourses. These meanings therefore change over history. From the Renaissance to the middle of the nineteenth century, for instance, the ideal images of the body were predominantly corpulent. With the rise of the bourgeoisie around 1900, the lean body became desirable. During the same period, the idea came up that modern subjects are primarily self-responsible for fabricating their own lean and healthy body. The study will focus on the sociocultural contexts which led to the establishment of modern body discourses and shows how those are connected to sports.

Introduction

The methods used to maintain or to achieve a lean body have reached considerable dimensions in modern society. They have become a functional sector of substantial economic interest and are prominent in popular as well as scientific public discourses. On the one hand, the discourses emphasise the individual; on the other hand, possible interventions on the national or transnational level are contemplated.[1] The focus lies on the individual body, which can hardly comply with the normative standard set by society. Nevertheless, this discrepancy between the real and the ideal body should, as far as possible, be minimised by individual effort.[2] Meanwhile on the national level, extensive media efforts are made to permanently confront the public with unending advice on nutrition, exercise and weight loss, given by experts from different fields.[3]

On the European level, an emphasis is put on tackling childhood obesity. With European children becoming increasingly heavier and physically inactive, EU governments have declared childhood obesity to be 'one of Europe's most pressing public health challenges'. The figures presented by the European Commission document dramatic developments.

> Some 22 million children in the EU are considered overweight or obese, with the numbers growing by 400,000 per year. A report by the Organisation for Economic Cooperation and Development (OECD) showed that 13.3% of EU children aged 11–15 are overweight or obese.[4]

At the same time, the post-modern market of self – as well as externally applied techniques – features a wide range of 'attractions'. Aesthetic surgery, stomach stapling operations, liposuction, body shaping, doping, genetic manipulation of healthy bodies, anti-ageing products, Viagra, fat burning, anti-obesity programmes and many more serve the apparently omnipresent imperative of enhancement – and not just of the body. An essential part in the quest for physical optimisation lies in achieving a lean, sporting, preferably fat-free body. Body fat is perceived as a threat and in order to fight it, innumerable exercise methods, often supplemented by dietary concepts, are applied.[5]

However, the new culture of leanness also faces criticism. Some characterise it as 'anorectic, normative' and stigmatising of corpulent and fat people. It is an immensely complex, multi-layered topic which cannot be addressed with monocausal explanations. There are no clear patterns following the principle of 'one cause, one effect'. Karl-Heinz Bette,[6] for instance, refers to the fact that we are witnessing a valorisation of and at the same time an estrangement from the body. The historical origins of many of the facets described above, according to the hypothesis outlined in the following section, lie in the transition between pre-modern and modern times in the second part of the nineteenth century.

Research Questions

The historical perspective supplies three main questions which I will aim to answer in the following section. (1) When did modern discourses on lean body shapes first arise and when did the lean body become established as ideal? (2) What is characteristic of these discourses? Which meanings were attached to them? I then will focus on the question how individuals use self-applied technologies to implement inherent orders, values and norms of society in their own bodies. The analytical term 'self-applied technologies', coined by Michel Foucault, is used in this context to examine how a person conducts 'operations on their own body, soul, way of thinking and behaviour' in order to reach 'a certain state of satisfaction, purity, wisdom, wholeness or immortality'.[7] (3) What is the role of training techniques of self-optimisation in this context?

Approaches focusing on the social, cultural and historic aspects view the body, including its patterns of motion and action, as a cultural matter. The physique of and discourses on the body are considered to be the product as well as the producer of society.[8] As such, they always have a historical dimension. The body and its importance, the meanings attributed to it and finally the way it appears in discourses, change over the centuries. In short, the body has a history that cannot be interpreted independently of the specific ways power is allotted within society.

On the Constitution of Modern Body Subjects around 1900

When were modern discourses on leanness established? Relevant historic studies investigating the topic agree that change began around 1900. It was a consistent change, if not socially homogenous, pointing in the direction of increasing leanness and affecting the bodies of men and women alike.[9] The paradigm of having to battle body fat and obesity can be traced back to the eighteenth century. Previously, obesity and other problems related to body fat were issues concerning the upper class only. Since then, however, excessive overeating and gluttony were no longer regarded merely as individual misbehaviour. Instead, obesity began to be viewed as potentially harmful for the community and the nation as a whole and should therefore be curtailed.[10]

During the first half of the nineteenth century, body fat rarely had a negative connotation. Corpulent people were still regarded as healthy and agile, fat had not yet been equated with the lethargic, lazy and weak. However, from the second half of the nineteenth century onwards, radical changes to the ideal body images took place. These mainly concerned the bourgeoisie and the nobility and had strong gender-specific connotations. Finally, around 1900, 'the image of a lean figure and sportive maleness' became increasingly dominant.[11]

Female Bodies – Male Bodies

Images of the ideal female body are, in this process, inseparably connected with the social role of women. Throughout the whole nineteenth century the economic dependence of women on men was still very pronounced. Female bodies consequently were subjected to hegemonic male views and interests. This means that emphasising the female secondary sexual traits, for example broad hips, narrow waist and big breasts, was of particular importance for women wanting to be attractive to men. This 'Venus shape' had long been the ideal for female bodies, and eventually, in the nineteenth century, mechanical devices were used to make hips and breasts more prominent. The corset and the bustle proved especially efficient in achieving this. The corset acted as a 'super-optimal dummy'[12] in emphasising the most attractive female body parts.

Starting in 1880, a real paradigm change occurred. The public portrayal of women, for example in advertisements, changed from purely static, that is sitting, standing, posing or at best doing housework, to a more dynamic one. From 1890, women were occasionally portrayed engaged in physical exercise, as in advertisements for bicycles. At this time, the modern lifestyle of middle-class women already included rudiments of sport. Female body ideals became leaner and more flexible; producing a lean body became a new duty for the modern woman. The issue of fighting body fat was also broached explicitly: The magazine *Die Hausfrau* (The Housewife) recommended physical exercise such as juggling balls because 'an increased mental use of nutrients' would be the consequence, leading to a 'noticeable decrease of fat in the lower body'.[13]

In Wilhelminian times,[14] successful women began to emphasise their thin figures also in the non-training context. A lean, upright, proud figure was the ideal of Wilhelminian times, not only for women. Children and men, too, should stick out their chests and suck in their stomachs.[15]

Publicly presented leanness and uprightness were the embodied semantic expression of the political middle-class's increasing establishment. 'The rising middle-class utilised the symbolic value of uprightness representing authority. Walking proudly, upright and with their heads held high, their gaze wandering, they implemented their emancipation.'[16] By displaying the upright posture they were able to achieve by their own strength, members of the middle class sought to distinguish themselves from the nobility, and also from the workers and peasants, whose backs were bent from heavy labour. In regard to the female body, though, this was only the beginning of a further, radical slimming down. The emancipation movement, profound changes in the role of women as industrialisation continued rapidly and the taking over of male domains by women during World War I led to a convergence of male and female body images. This development reached its preliminary climax with the Garconne-type in the 1920s. The Garconne's body, slim and androgynous, hardly possessed any female traits at all. She wore trousers and a short haircut, was sporty and signalled independence to an extent which was hitherto unknown and without historic precedent.[17]

Compared to female bodies in the first half of the nineteenth century, male bodies were far less regulated by the need to appear attractive. There is no evidence supporting the existence of a consistent male body ideal during this period. On the contrary, male images and roles in society diverged across social classes. There was the wealthy, corpulent bourgeois man, existing in caricature-like sub-categories, such as the rich banker and the industrialist. The man with the bulging stomach basically had no negative connotation yet. The stomach of a portly man represented his 'wealth of body', an indicator of his actual wealth, influence and economic influence.[18] Variants of this type were the stout, cigar-smoking governor and the fat capitalist, the enemy of the starved, gaunt proletariat. The stereotype of a proletarian's body was wasted and thin, or alternatively depicted as a muscular fighter for solidarity in the class struggle.[19] Due to intense physical strain and, in part, acute malnutrition, body fat was not an issue for the working class.[20] Meanwhile, men of the lower middle class could strive for the ideal soldier's body propagated by German Gymnastics.

A special member of the middle class was the modern employee. Since the 1840s he could be encountered in the public, typically clothed in the uniform suit. The suit distinguished the employee from the nobleman, symbolising simplicity, plainness, rationality and efficiency.[21] Analysing the material of historic adverts for beauty products, it is apparent that around 1900, men were gradually included in the target group. Hair tinting lotions and corsets for restricting male bodies coming apart at the seams were advertised.[22] Moreover, from now on the bourgeois man was supposed to work on himself and exercise his body. For this purpose, advertisements around 1900 already offered men a choice of various equipment, such as 'Dr. Phelans-Exerciser' and rowing machines.[23]

Another sub-variant of the male body type could be found in acrobats and strength athletes. The most famous among them was undoubtedly Eugen Sandow (1867–1925), one of the earliest proponents of modern bodybuilding.[24] He developed his own strength training concept.[25] Sandow himself embodied the ideal image of the strong, muscular, yet lean man. A specific trait of Sandow's strength training programme seems analogous to the concept of Taylorism used in industrial manufacturing processes. It divided the body into different muscle groups, which were exercised sequentially and separately.[26] Modern strength training in its various forms became a useful tool for

> creating beautiful male bodies and to persist in the battle against body fat. A man must be athletic, lean and strong at the same time. The bodybuilding schools which had developed until then, with or without special equipment, suited the task of creating ideal 'male beauty' excellently and thus became more refined.[27]

The increasing popularity of bodybuilding during this period was no coincidence because it fitted perfectly with the new ethics of achievement predominant in the rising bourgeoisie of 1900. For Germany, between 50 and 100 bodybuilding studios existed between 1890 and 1910, each with several hundred members. These mainly belonged to the middle class.[28]

Exhibiting a fat body became increasingly problematic for men. The new man of the ambitious bourgeoisie should have a lean, flexible, powerful body.[29] For that reason, it became increasingly important around 1900 to improve one's body. The new physical activity of training for sport seemed one effective way in achieving improvement. The social figure of the sportsman (and in a very limited way the sportswoman) began to take form.

The Paradigm of Enhancement and Self-responsibility

All these developments took place in the context of a dynamic, highly complex transformative process impacting the whole of society to such an extent that no individual could physically avoid it. A few keywords may be applied for a cursory description of this process: Forced industrialisation,[30] Taylorism in the manufacturing chain, rationalisation and acceleration in virtually all areas of life, the bourgeoisie with all its specific values and views establishing itself as the new hegemonic class, radical changes in the views on matrimony and sexuality, beginning erosion of traditional gender roles, modification of public spaces, for example through a growing number of (body) pictures provided by photography and film technologies, the emerging sports movement and advances in egalitarianism and democratisation processes mark this period.[31] In regard to the physical ideal, a profound change took place. The formerly established ideal of the corpulent body was supplanted by the lean, dynamic body, which could be achieved through self-control and with diets, frequent weighing, sports and training.

Two basic patterns arose from the challenge of accomplishing a modern body. One was the whole spectrum of life reformatory schools of thought, propagating expression dance, light, air and nudism movements, gymnastics for natural healing, birds of passage, the youth and play movement, etc., combined with philosophical constructs and often accompanied by matching dietary concepts.

> The life-reformatory concept of problematic body fat was a historical prerequisite preparing the ground for the modern lean body cult. Fat bodies were made out to be 'against nature'. Natural healers ... opposed the modern industrial society with mineral water cures and biological anti-fat diets, combined with massages, gymnastic, dance, and sport exercises.[32]

Underlying all these approaches is, simply put, the assumption that industrialisation 'robbed' the human body of its 'natural' behaviour, which must actively be restored to its previous 'natural' state, however that is defined. From this perspective, the 'natural' body was a naturally slim body. If this shape was lost, it must be restored by natural methods. The standard recipe used for intervention was – overlapping with the social field of modern sports – a combination of dieting and exercise.

The second pattern of physical optimisation assumed that only those capable of keeping their body in shape through athletic training were able to cope with the pressure of performance on the modern middle class. Both approaches, in part, complement and overlap with each other, but they differ considerably in the argumentation and methods they use.[33]

Before taking any steps to improve one's body, it was necessary first to evaluate the current situation. Methods of modern science, documentation, measurement, quantification and comparison, were applied for this purpose.[34] As instrument efficiently supporting self-control and allowing self-assessment, the mirror entered the private area.[35] Over centuries, the mirror had been a symbol either of court privilege or of the brothel. Now it advanced into the intimate area of the bathroom. Mirrors, on the wall, integrated in cupboards or free-standing, became a frame for the naked body, an opportunity to view and control one's shape. The most powerful control force was thereby no longer provided by others, or by society in general, but by the subject's intimate review of the mirror image. The mirror's advance into private areas led to a 'democratisation of self-reflection' and facilitated increased self-control.[36]

Since the turn of the century other instruments serving the same purpose were scales which were placed either in private bathrooms or in public areas. Among the urban bourgeoisie of the late nineteenth century, the daily measuring of body weight gained in popularity.[37] This trend expressed an increasing nutritional consciousness. The scales were, along with modern eating regimens which already relied on nutrition tables, an important instrument of self-control, intended to support self-discipline and establish normal body weight. Which bodyweight should be considered normal was and still is a much-debated topic full of controversy which dates back to the second half of the nineteenth century. In 1868, the French physician and anthropologist Paul Broca invented the so-called 'Broca formula', the first reference point for calculating the normal human body weight. Broca calculated the normal bodyweight in kilograms by subtracting the value 100 from the body height in centimetres. Since this calculation yielded only rough results and was too inaccurate in regard to individual variation, numerous other formulae were soon invented to calculate normal or ideal bodyweight for men and women. Also dating back to the 1860s, William Banting and John Hutchinson calculated what they perceived as healthy bodyweights for an insurance company. The goal was to minimise risk and to provide optimal calculations of insurance fees. Measurement and quantification were also central tools of control in the strength athlete Sandow's training concept. In Sandow's popular guidebook, *Strength and How to Achieve It* (1897), he advises his readers to draw charts and to map the muscle development from month to month. Self-regulation and progression in performance had now become the subject's own responsibility.[38]

From the current point of view it is astonishing how well-defined the ideas of the malleability and amendability of the human body already were at the beginning of the twentieth century. Relevant information about plastic surgery for instance already appeared in a Berlin newspaper of 1907.[39]

In parallel to life-reforming practices, a new rational sporting paradigm coming from England appeared at the end of the nineteenth century. In it, specific knowledge about the formability and optimisation of the human body were realised. Producing a slim body was not necessarily the primary objective, the fat-free body, however, was always intended[40] and training was the central element. At the end of the nineteenth century there already existed specific knowledge about the plasticity of the muscle structure and how it changes under pressure – elicited by the carrying of heavy weights or by continuous strain. It was known that muscles could change, be strengthened and made more resilient and that external stimuli could change the muscle tone and increase muscle circumference. This, however, does not mean that systematic training regimens had been invented and were applied. Instead, the opposite was the case. Fatigue, according to common belief, was a sign that maximal capacity had been reached. To continue exercising at this point would endanger one's health. On the whole, though, in an age of expanding imperialism and increasing industrial productivity, the mechanisms of progress prevailed. Masculinity and especially the male body was subjected to the productive logic of a machine. This mechanical concept changed over time. In the second half of the nineteenth century, the image of the steam engine was the predominant one. Around 1900 it was replaced by the concept of the body as an electric motor.[41] Like the machine, the body was deployed to realise the belief in advancement, serving the purpose of increased industrial productivity. Controlled by volition, it may not tire anymore. One of the key issues of the ending nineteenth century utopia was accordingly the detachment of boundless power my man.[42] The bodily equivalent was to postpone the border of physical exhaustion. The goal was to strengthen the body through permanent systematical training, to raise the engine efficiency of the human body. The strengthened and exercised body became an integral part of 'the bourgeois effort to shape and exploit the world through rational and effective labour'.[43]

In the period around 1900 modern sports, labour medicine and sports physiology developed.[44] So-called ergometry soon became the centrepiece of clinical diagnostic research. Physiologists were not interested in boosting sporting performance at first, but in measuring and improving work performance. The Greek word 'ergon' translates as work and 'metron' as measure, or scale. For the first experiments measuring the cardiovascular system in 1883, the crank handle ergometer was invented. In 1889 the treadmill followed and finally in 1896 the cycling ergometer appeared.[45]

How inseparably modern sporting exercise and workout were linked to the development of the industrial society is demonstrated by a short example describing the origin of modern sports in England in the middle of the nineteenth century. Eisenberg[46] remarks on the surprising historical fact that until 1850 the British gentleman-sportsman did not engage in systematic training, but instead adamantly refused it. Why did they refuse to exercise? To British nobility and members of the gentry ambitions of athletic performance seemed not to befit their rank. Demonstrating disinterestedness and belittling defeats in sportive competitions – and also the use of amateur regulations – were efficient instruments of social distinction. 'Even in the new disciplines of track and field, swimming and rowing, targeted training for these sports was at first unusual.'[47]

Sport Training as a Technique for Self-optimisation in the Second Half of the Nineteenth Century

In the context of British sports, the contents and target groups of training for different sports were first described in the continental literature on hygiene in the second half of the nineteenth century. It contained detailed information about a strictly regulated training regimen combined with a meat diet. The goal of this innovation called 'entraînement' was, according to hygiene professional Michel Lévy, 1857, to 'reduce bodyweight and increase respiratory capacity. [. . .] Additionally, one should relieve the body of superfluous fat and liquid with the help of purges, diets and sweating induced by morning runs on a sober stomach followed by tea drinking.'[48] After this first intervention and purification, body and muscles should have been strengthened by further exhausting exercise.

Besides physical exercise, specific diets, for example of hard bread or meat and even emetics and purgatives, were recommended. Athletes' bodies and the means producing them became a role model for the general public. In magazines, the cycling world champion O. Duncan was cited to 'prevent fattening with purges and hot baths before training'.[49] The Austrian sports pioneer and influential publicist Victor Silberer used similar arguments in his 1883 *Handbook of Cycling*. The main concern of training should be 'to eliminate superfluous body fat; there are two ways to achieve this, either by sweating it out or by working it off'.[50]

A concept common to both modern training and diet programs was the rational submission to time regimes and previously defined goals. Observation, documentation and recording of each intervention, planning and its outcomes were essential.

> The individual training schedule is, like the diet plan, a central element of long-term, systematic bodystyling, which necessities detailed observation of the body and all its changes. These need to be registered in every detail and the training adapted accordingly. Muscle increase and body fat reduction are measured and noted down and sometimes commented upon in training diaries. Making one's self the subject of such a chronicle, as if writing of an autobiography of the body, was already a widespread practice in 1900.[51]

Able-bodied athletes represented the ideal of capability. Their workout plans, however, could rarely apply to citizens and workers, who had to deal with an exhausting daily working life. In addition, there still remained a lot of doubt about the pros and cons of physical exercise regarding health. The new body type of the athlete had entered the world and it was inconceivable that it might disappear again.[52]

The ways of disciplining the body described above had a hegemonic male connotation. Rigid self-control, strength, competition and stamina were male stereotypes. Men should steel their bodies, women should restrict themselves to playful and rhythmic exercises. Some kinds of gymnastics were mainly designated for women, to compensate their inactive lifestyle. Round dance, stretching, and also cycling, rowing, walking or tennis were recommended for women. The hygiene classic and bestseller by Anna Fischer-Dückelmanns *The Woman as a General Practitioner* published in 1901 even recommends dumb-bell training for older women. The aim clearly is to battle body fat:

> Men in their fifties practicing gymnastics – that is quite common, but women! What impertinence to ask a fifty-year-old German woman with her heavy, clumsy body, her stiff, fat extremities and her inevitable girth to exhaust herself with 25-pound lumps of iron! Beyond comprehension, what is demanded nowadays. ... *The Woman as a General Practitioner* aims to evoke the belief in today's women that they are not 'old' at 50, but should be physically and mentally fit. [...][53]

We should keep in mind that women were much more exposed to the imperative of leanness establishing itself around 1900 than were men. At the same time women's participation in modern sports was very restricted. Despite some improvements like the institutionalisation of tennis lessons for girls around 1880 and some female pioneers of the British sports movement acquiring expertise in a few sports, active women in general were still the exception.[54]

The most prominent model of an athletic woman at the turn of the century was the Austrian Empress Elisabeth Amalie Eugenie (1837–1898). When she started cycling – well after her 60th birthday – her main motive presumably was fat reduction. In a letter to her husband, Emperor Franz Josef, she wrote, 'do not forget to inform me if cycling really reduces fat'.[55]

Following Deak,[56] who detected three periods[57] of 'slimming down' in society over the twentieth century, we will finally review further developments from the mid–1920s to the beginning of National Socialism. Deak remarks on the emergence of an ideal body type tending towards the androgyne. Round, 'female' forms belonged to the past.[58] In this period, publications on diets, hunger cures, gymnastics for weight decrease, etc. flooded the market. Also, the first medical diagnosis of bulimia classifying it as an eating disorder was made in 1932.[59] Merta[60] confirmed this finding and additionally documented an abundance of guidebooks on life reform and topics relating to gymnastics. In the 1920s, leanness became a value in its own right. This cultural phenomenon became apparent in the cinema, in beauty contests and in the fashion and cosmetics industries. Ullstein first published the *Paper for the Housewife*, a precursor of the contemporary magazine *Brigitte*. In it, the predominant female ideal was that of the androgynous actress. Recipients of the magazine mainly belonged to the middle class. With the rise of National Socialism, this female body image was completely overturned. The ideal was radically changed and the androgynous type made out as an enemy. The National Socialist concept of the female body focused on efficient childbearing and motherhood, while the male body was required to adhere to the soldierly athletic demands of war.[61] In the post-war years just after 1945, which were marked by severe food shortage, plump body ideals re-emerged for a short time. Starting in the 1960s though, radical slimming down can again be noticed.[62]

Summary – Results

The lean body ideal developed in the context of cultural and social changes in the wake of industrialisation and modernisation starting in the second half of the nineteenth century. Its emergence is linked to trends like rationalisation, acceleration, flexibility, Taylorisation and optimisation, affecting all areas of life. Central to the logic of all these transformative processes is the subjection of modern bodies to the imperative of permanent self-optimisation. One efficient technique to achieve optimisation, to increase efficiency, to improve one's body is rational training for sport. Since the beginning of modernisation it was used as a means for obtaining a lean body. Discourses on body optimisation and leanness at the beginning of industrial modern times differentiate along gender and social classes. Future research should aim for a detailed analysis of these changes, supplemented by consolidated empirical data. Further focus should lie on the 'sport-for-all' – and the fitness movements that emerged in the 1970s.[63]

Notes

1. Günter, "Fitness als Inklusionsprämisse," 2.
2. Möhring, "Bodystyling," 73; Spiekermann, "Übergewicht und Körperdeutungen," 47.
3. http://bewusstgesund.orf.at/oe_speckt_ab/, accessed May 5, 2012. As a reference for Germany, see the study initiated by Künast in 2004 with the programmatic title 'Fattening foods: Why the Germans become fatter and fatter and what we have to do against it' (Künast, *Die Dickmacher*). For many further campaigns and studies in Germany see Günter, "Fitness als Inklusionsprämisse."
4. Program of the Congress 'Tackling Childhood Obesity in Europe: Comparative Perspectives on Prevention and Policy Implementation', Brussels, April 3, 2012, available at http://www.pu blicpolicyexchange.co.uk/events/CD03-PPE2.php, accessed December 22, 2013.
5. Ach and Pollmann, *No Body Is Perfect*, 9–13.
6. Bette, *Körperspuren*.
7. Foucault, "Die politische Technologie," "Technologien des Selbst," 26; Günter, "Fitness als Inklusionsprämisse," 3.
8. Gugtzer, *Body Turn*, 14–20.
9. Grauer and Schlottke, *Muß der Speck weg*; Thoms, "Dünn und dick," "Körperstereotype"; Deak, "Schöner Hungern," 210; Spiekermann, "Übergewicht und Körperdeutungen," 48–50.
10. Thoms, "Körperstereotype," 296.
11. Penz, *Metamorphosen der Schönheit*, 19, 55.
12. Thoms, "Dünn und dick," 245.
13. Quoted in Ibid., 251.
14. Approximately from 1880 to 1914.
15. Thoms, "Dünn und dick," 253–4.
16. Alkemeyer, "Aufrecht und biegsam," 49.
17. Dorer and Marschik, "Sportlerinnen in Österreichs"; Grauer and Schlottke, *Muß der Speck weg*, 121–4.
18. Grauer and Schlottke, *Muß der Speck weg*, 151.
19. Thoms, "Körperstereotype," 285.
20. Deak, "Schöner Hungern," 211.
21. Penz, *Metamorphosen der Schönheit*, 32.
22. Thoms, "Dünn und dick," 254.
23. Ibid., 255.
24. Wedemeyer, *Starke Männer, starke Frauen*, 94–106; Sicks, "Muskelmänner."
25. Between 1895 and 1910 a whole new genre of strength sports literature was created. Apart from Sandow, Sicks ("Muskelmänner," 174f) names 10 further corresponding German monographs.
26. Möhring, "Bodystyling," 73.
27. Merta, *Schlank! Ein Körperkult*, 340.

28. See note 26.
29. Penz, *Metamorphosen der Schönheit*, 55f.
30. The complex term industrialisation initially described the transformation of a society dominated by agriculture into a society depending primarily on industrial production. This process began to spread from Great Britain in the eighteenth century and reached its climax on the continent at the end of the nineteenth century. The radical changes to production processes and the technical innovations had far reaching social consequences, leading to changes like the rise of the bourgeoisie, the appearance of the working class, rationalisation of daily life, specialisation and the capitalist ethics of performance.
31. Terms like machine age, industrial system, age of technology or factory system all indicate a dynamic development affecting all areas of peoples' lives. A multitude of innovations, technological and otherwise, like the telephone, the typewriter, the cinema, massively accelerating motorisation, the spreading railway net, the beginnings of air travel and tourism, urbanisation and household technologies, higher social mobility, higher standards of hygiene and electricity, further characterise this era. Eigner and Helige, *Österreichische Wirtschafts*, 55–124.
32. Merta, *Schlank! Ein Körperkult*, 363.
33. Sicks, "Muskelmänner," 180; Marschik, "Transformationen der Bewegungskultur"; Müllner, "Moderne und Sport"; Shorter, "Sport, Körper und Körperimage."
34. Windgätter, "KraftRäume," 109; Spiekermann, "Übergewicht und Körperdeutungen," 43–5, 47.
35. See note 26.
36. Penz, *Metamorphosen der Schönheit*, 34; Wagner, *Blicke auf den dicken Körper*, 68–70; Günter, "Fitness als Inklusionsprämisse." Remarkable in this context is the dominance of reflecting surfaces in modern fitness and dance studios. Compare the recent discussion concerning the so-called 'quantified self-movement', in which individuals use modern digital information measuring instruments (e.g. Apple 'I-watch') to permanently generate data on their somatic status. This allows them to modify their situational activities (for top athletes their training) accordingly.
37. See note 20.
38. Sicks, "Muskelmänner," 180.
39. Thoms, "Dünn und dick," 279. Appropriate surgical techniques for the removal of fatty tissue were published in 1911 in the *Journal for Diets and Physical Therapy*.
40. Evidently modern sport diversified immensely during its development from the nineteenth to the twenty-first century. We cannot consider all the details here, but would instead like to suggest an analysis of the genesis of modern health-, recreational- and fitness sports with its specific sub-categories such as 'fatburning' and 'bodystyling'. Focus should first and foremost be put on the discovery of physiological fat burning by medicine and scientific training concepts and their utilisation by the fitness industry. An early book on 'training sciences' by Johann Christoph Friedrich GutsMuths (1759–1839) called "Gymnastics for the Youth" *Gymnastik für die Jugend* (1793) in which he elaborates on the 'sweating out of useless flesh' as a means of optimising training processes.
41. Möhring, "Bodystyling," 75; Windgätter, "Euphorie und Erschöpfung," 17–9.
42. Windgätter, "KraftRäume," 108; Gödde, "Der Kraftbegriff bei Freud," 228–32.
43. Sarasin, *Reizbare Maschinen*, 315; Sicks, "Muskelmänner," 171f.
44. Sicks, "Muskelmänner," 171f. Starting around 1880, numerous works focus on the efficient use of energy by athletes. Studies on endurance in race cyclists appear in France, Germany and Austria. Eisenberg ("Der Sportler," 97f) observe that many natural scientists in Germany were also active sportsmen and often made their sport the subject of scientific enquiries. Physicians, chemists and physiologists frequently underwent self-experimentation for their studies of anthropometry, electrocardiography, respiration and x-ray technology. From this early starting point of scientific research there developed in Germany even before World War I a new field in natural science – sports science. See Court, "Deutsche Sportwissenschaft," 36–149. A central role in this context is taken by modern muscle dynamography which emerged around this time. Studying the limits of human performance had become the main objective of research shortly before 1900. See Windgätter, "KraftRäume."
45. A basic and still heavily contested paradigm of modern physiological research on athletic performance is, for almost a century now, the 'sports heart'. In 1899, the Finnish physician

Henschen already described systematically occurring enlargements of the heart. Through clinical observations of endurance sportsmen he reached the conclusion that 'this heart, which is enlarged through sports, achieves greater performance than a normal one and consequently there exists a physiological enlargement of the heart through sports …' (Hollmann, "Herz und Sportmedizin," 501.) Despite this opinion, almost all hygiene experts until the end of the nineteenth century consider exhaustion of muscles exceeding the pain threshold and increased respiration and heart frequency to have adverse health effects.

46. Eisenberg, "Der Sportler," 91, 96.
47. Ibid.
48. Levy quoted in Sarasin, *Reizbare Maschinen*, 332.
49. Ibid., 334.
50. Silberer and Ernst, *Handbuch des Bicycle-Sport*, 279f.
51. Möhring, "Bodystyling," 75.
52. Eisenberg, "Der Sportler." This coincides with the establishment of gymnastics classes in schools in the 1860s and initiates the popularisation of sports, which becomes a mass phenomenon after World War I.
53. 'Die Frau als Hausärztin', quoted in Sarasin, *Reizbare Maschinen*, 341.
54. Pfister, "Die Anfänge des Frauenturnens," "Körper, Sport."
55. Quoted in Praschl-Pichler, *Kaiserin Elisabeths Fitneß*, 140; Müllner "Sportivität einer Kaiserin." An almost identical picture is drawn by Pfister ("Sir Galahad, Skiing," 621–2) of the exercise practices of the well-known writer Bertha Eckstein-Diener (1874–1948), who belonged to the Viennese bourgeoisie. She was an enthusiastic sportswoman and for her, too, the production and maintenance of a lean, fat-free body were lifelong motives guiding her actions.
56. Deak, "Schöner Hungern," 210.
57. According to Deak, Phase 1 begins around 1900, Phase 2 circa in 1925 and Phase 3 lasts from 1960 until today.
58. Grauer and Schlottke, *Muß der Speck weg*, 121–4.
59. Deak, "Schöner Hungern," 213.
60. Merta, *Schlank! Ein Körperkult*, 340–58.
61. Penz, *Metamorphosen der Schönheit*, 92.
62. Grauer and Schlottke, *Muß der Speck weg*, 157–60; Spiekermann, "Übergewicht und Körperdeutungen," 50–1.
63. Dilger, *Die Fitnessbewegung*.

References

Ach, Johann Stefan, and Arnd Pollmann, eds. *No Body Is Perfect: Baumaßnahmen am menschlichen Körper – Bioethische und ästhetische Aufrisse*. Bielefeld: transcript, 2006.
Alkemeyer, Thomas. "Aufrecht und biegsam: Eine politische Geschichte des Körperkults." In *Sport Studies: Eine sozial- und kulturwissenschaftliche Einführung*, edited by Matthias Marschik, Rudolf Müllner, Otto Penz, and Georg Spitaler, 47–59. Wien: Facultas utb, 2009.
Bette, Karl-Heinrich. *Körperspuren: Zur Semantik und Paradoxie moderner Körperlichkeit*. Bielefeld: transcript, 2005.
Court, Jürgen. *Deutsche Sportwissenschaft in der Weimarer Republik und im Nationalsozialismus*. Vol. 1 of *Die Vorgeschichte 1900–1918*. Münster: Lit Verlag, 2008.
Deak, Alexandra. "Schöner Hungern: Über den Zusammenhang von Diät und Wahn." In *No Body Is Perfect: Baumaßnahmen am menschlichen Körper–Bioethische und ästhetische Aufrisse*, edited by Johann Stefan Ach, and Arnd Pollmann, 207–224. Bielefeld: transcript, 2006.
Dilger, Erika. *Die Fitnessbewegung in Deutschland: Wurzeln, Einflüsse und Entwicklungen*. Schorndorf: Hofmann, 2008.
Dorer, Johanna, and Matthias Marschik. "Sportlerinnen in Österreichs Medien 1900-1950: Das 'Sportgirl' als Symbol für die moderne Frau." In *Sind's froh, dass Sie zu Hause geblieben sind*, edited by Matthias Marschik, and Rudolf Müllner, 238–247. Göttingen: Verlag die Werkstatt, 2010.
Eigner, Peter, and Andrea Helige, eds. *Österreichische Wirtschafts- und Sozialgeschichte im 19. und 20. Jahrhundert*. Wien: Verlag Christian Brandstätter, 1999.

Eisenberg, Christiane. "Der Sportler." In *Der Mensch des 20. Jahrhunderts*, edited by Ute Frevert, and Heinz-Gerhard Haupt, 87–112. Frankfurt: Campus Verlag, 1999.

Foucault, Michel. "Die politische Technologie der Individuen." In *Technologien des Selbst*, edited by Luter H. Martin, Huck Guttman, and Patrick H. Hutton, 168–186. Frankfurt: S. Fischer, 1993.

Foucault, Michel. "Technologien des Selbst." In *Technologien des Selbst*, edited by Luter H. Martin, Huck Guttman, and Patrick H. Hutton, 24–62. Frankfurt: S. Fischer, 1993.

Gödde, Günter. "Kraftbegriff bei Freud: Physiologische und psychologische Verwendungen." In *Zeichen der Kraft: Wissensformationen 1800–1900*, edited by Christof H. Windgätter, 228–246. Berlin: Kulturverlag Kadmos, 2008.

Grauer, Angelika, and Peter F. Schlottke. *Muß der Speck weg? Der Kampf ums Idealgewicht im Wandel der Schönheitsideale*. München: dtv, 1987.

Gugutzer, Robert, ed. *Body Turn: Perspektiven der Soziologie des Körpers und des Sport*. Bielefeld: transcript, 2006.

Günter, Sandra. "Fitness als Inklusionsprämisse? Eine Diskursanalyse zur Problematisierung adipöser Kinder- und Jugendkörper in sportwissenschaftlichen Gesundheitsdiskursen." *Forum Qualitative Sozialforschung/Forum: Qualitative Social Research* 14, no. 1 (2013). http://www.qualitative-research.net/index.php/fqs/article/view/1800/3465/

Hollmann, Wildor. "Herz und Sportmedizin – historische Entwicklungen und Perspektiven." *Herz* 31, no. 6 (2006): 500–506.

Johann Christoph Friedrich GutsMuths. *Gymnastik für die Jugend* [Gymnastics for the Youth]. Schnepfenthal: Verlag der Buchhandlung der Erziehungsanstalt, 1793.

Künast, Renate. *Die Dickmacher: Warum die Deutschen immer fetter werden und was wir dagegen tun müssen*. München: Riemann, 2004.

Marschik, Matthias. "Transformationen der Bewegungskultur." In *Sport Studies: Eine sozial- und kulturwissenschaftliche Einführung*, edited by Matthias Marschik, Rudolf Müllner, Otto Penz, and Georg Spitaler, 23–34. Wien: Facultas utb, 2009.

Merta, Sabine. *Schlank! Ein Körperkult der Moderne*. Stuttgart: Franz Steiner Verlag, 2008.

Möhrig, Maren. "Bodystyling. Körperkonzepte und Körperpraktiken der Fitnessbewegung." In *Auf die Plätze: Sport und Gesellschaft*, edited by Susanne Wernsing, Katarina Matiasek, and Klaus Vogel, 73–77. Dresden: Wallstein Verlag, 2011.

Müllner, Rudolf. "Moderne und Sport: Historische Zugänge zur Formierung des sportlichen Feldes." In *Sport Studies*, edited by Matthias Marschik, Rudolf Müllner, Otto Penz, and Georg Spitaler, 35–46. Wien: Facultas.wuv, 2009.

Müllner, Rudolf. "Sportivität einer Kaiserin: Elisabeth fährt Rad." In *Motor bin ich selbst: 200 Jahre Radfahren in Wien*, edited by Bernd Hachleitner, Matthias Marschik, Rudolf Müllner, and Michael Zappe, 32–33. Wien: Metro Verlag, 2013.

Penz, Otto. *Metamorphosen der Schönheit: Eine Kulturgeschichte moderner Körperlichkeit*. Wien: Turia+Kant, 2001.

Pfister, Gertrud. "Die Anfänge des Frauenturnens und Frauensports in Österreich." In *Turnen und Sport in der Geschichte Österreichs*, edited by Ernst Bruckmüller, and Hannes Strohmeyer, 86–104. Wien: ÖBV, 1998.

Pfister, Gertrud. "Körper, Sport und Geschlecht aus historischer Sicht." In *Handbuch Sportgeschichte*, edited by Michael Krüger, and Hans Langenfeld, 337–344. Schorndorf: Hofmann Verlag, 2010.

Pfister, Gertrud. "Sir Galahad, Skiing and a Woman's Quest for Freedom." *The International Journal of the History of Sport* 30, no. 6 (2013): 617–633.

Praschl-Bichler, Gabriele. *Kaiserin Elisabeths Fitneß- und Diätprogramm*. Wien: Amalthea, 2002.

Sarasin, Philipp. *Reizbare Maschinen: Eine Geschichte des Körpers 1765–1914*. Frankfurt am Main: Suhrkamp Verlag, 2001.

Shorter, Edward. "Sport, Körper und Körperimage um die Jahrhundertwende." In *Sport zwischen Disziplinierung und neuen sozialen Bewegungen*, edited by Hubert C. Ehalt, and Otmar Weiß, 15–29. Wien: Böhlau, 1993.

Sicks, Kai Marcel. "Muskelmänner: Kraftsport und Sportmedizin um 1900." In *Zeichen der Kraft: Wissensformationen 1800-1900*, edited by Christof H. Windgätter, 170–184. Berlin: Kulturverlag Kadmos, 2008.

Silberer, Victor, and George Ernst. *Handbuch des Bicycle-Sport*. Wien: Verlag der "Allgemeinen Sport-Zeitung", 1883.

Spiekermann, Uwe. "Übergewicht und Körperdeutungen im 20. Jahrhundert – Eine geschichts-wissenschaftliche Rückfrage." In *Kreuzzug gegen Fette: Sozialwissenschaftliche Aspekte des gesellschaftlichen Umgangs mit Übergewicht und Adipositas*, edited by Henning Schmidt-Semisch, and Friedrich Schorb, 35–55. Wiesbaden: VS Verlag für Sozialwissenschaften, 2008.

Thoms, Ulrike. "Dünn und dick, schön und häßlich: Schönheitsideale und Körpersilhouette in der Werbung 1850-1950." In *Bilderwelt des Alltags: Werbung in der Konsumgesellschaft des 19. und 20. Jahrhunderts*, edited by Peter Borscheid, and Clemens Wischermann, 242–281. Stuttgart: Franz Steiner Verlag, 1995.

Thoms, Ulrike. "Körperstereotype: Veränderungen in der Bewertung von Schlankheit und Fettleibigkeit in den letzten 200 Jahren." In *Körper mit Geschichte. Der menschliche Körper als Ort der Selbst- und Weltdeutung*, edited by Clemens Wischermann, and Stefan Haas, 281–307. Stuttgart: Franz Steiner Verlag, 2000.

Wagner, Ursula. *Blicke auf den dicken Körper: Gegen die Unterwerfung unter die Schönheitsnorm.* Frankfurt am Main: Brandes & Apsel Verlag GmbH, 1989.

Wedemeyer, Bernd. *Starke Männer, starke Frauen: Eine Kulturgeschichte des Bodybuildings.* München: C.H. Beck, 1996.

Windgätter, Christof, ed. "Euphorie und Erschöpfung: Das Paradigma der Kraft im 19. Jahrhundert." *Zeichen der Kraft: Wissensformationen 1800-1900*, 7–23. Berlin: Kulturverlag Kadmos, 2008.

Windgätter, Christof, ed. "KraftRäume: Aufstieg und Fall der Dynamometrie." *Zeichen der Kraft: Wissensformationen 1800-1900*, 108–137. Berlin: Kulturverlag Kadmos, 2008.

Women Boxers: Actresses to Athletes – The Role of Vaudeville in Early Women's Boxing in the USA

Gerald Gems[a] and Gertrud Pfister[b]

[a]HPE, North Central College, Naperville, USA; [b]Department of Sport and Exercise Sciences, University of Copenhagen, Copenhagen, Denmark

This article fills a gap in the very limited literature on women's boxing by examining the gendered space in which women engaged in the sport as participants in saloons, vaudeville theatres and the prize ring. In doing so, they challenged the contemporary gender order and disputed the notion of women as the weak sex. Vaudeville provided women with an opportunity to present physical performances that surpassed the restrictions placed on women within the mainstream middle-class society. This article includes biographical sketches of some of the outstanding female boxers of the era by drawing upon new primary sources and embedding the findings within various gender theories.

Introduction

In recent decades, women's boxing has become increasingly popular as a fitness exercise or as a competition. Boxing had previously been presumed to be a masculine activity; but women's boxing has a long history. This examination intends to ascertain the early development of women's boxing and its affinity with vaudeville, and identify some of the participants and analyse their motivations.

Boxing bouts between women occurred regularly in early eighteenth century England.[1] Some female boxers became well known. Elizabeth Wilkinson married James Stokes, a pugilist, fencer, promoter and owner of a boxing venue.[2] She published challenges in newspapers, and can be considered an entrepreneur who advertised her fights and earned not only a measure of fame but also a considerable amount of money. Other female participants in fist fights seem to have been extremely poor and willing to provide a cruel spectacle for a sensation-seeking audience. William Hickey, an observer at such a bout, reported that he observed two women 'engaged in a scratching and boxing match, their faces entirely covered in blood, bosoms bare, and the clothes nearly torn from their bodies. For several minutes not a creature interfered with them … and the contest went on with unabated fury'.[3] Such battles continued among working class women over the course of the nineteenth century, and appeared in the USA by the 1860s.

Historians, however, have focused almost entirely on the male boxers and the role of this sport as a marker of masculinity and its social Darwinian symbolism.

Very little is known about the female pugilists who challenged gender boundaries and the assumption of women as the 'weaker sex'. Only after its formal acceptance as a competitive sport at the turn of the twenty-first century did women's boxing become a focus of scientific debates and a topic of publications attracting attention, not the least because boxing still seems to be incompatible with femininity.[4]

In this essay, we focus on women's boxing in the USA at the end of the nineteenth century and provide new insights into the backgrounds and biographies of female boxers. Opportunities and challenges of women are always dependent on the social and material conditions, the norms and rules of the society and, in particular, the gender order. Therefore, women's boxing has to be interpreted against the background of the American society and in the context of the existing gender arrangements.

Theoretical Framework

Societies are organised via norms and rules, structures and institutions which define the spaces of and relations between individuals and groups.[5] Besides age, gender is a universal concept, which is embedded in the social order legitimating the distribution of work and power. Although gender arrangements vary across historical periods and societies, the notion of women as caregivers and the image of men as warriors were and are a common feature.

Boxing, which requires physical strength and aggressiveness, seemed to be characteristics which were claimed by men and traditionally denied to the 'weak' sex. However, in many cultures and societies, there were women with various motives and backgrounds who disregarded gender norms and participated not only in non-competitive sparring but also in fights for fame and money.

Similar to the male prizefighters of the era, the female boxers expressed and valued their physicality. Pierre Bourdieu, the French sociologist, developed the concepts of habitus and taste and the respective amount and forms of capital (economic, social and cultural). Habitus and taste are dispositions which refer to one's lifestyle and values, and provide a perspective in which to see the world as well as to act and to react in a given situation and environment.[6]

According to this perspective, individuals who were born and grew up in a working-class environment have embodied specific values and lifestyles, among them a respect for physicality and an identity which rests upon physical prowess, whereas an upper-class person's social and cultural capital is dependent upon wealth and/or educational attainment. Gender is a fundamental dimension of the habitus which is socially constructed, embodied and 'gendered', and experiences are adopted and lived, evaluated and perceived differently depending not only on social class, but also on gender.[7] By 'doing gender', individuals re-create the gender order, i.e. the norms, ideals and roles allotted to men and women, which are embedded in culture and society. In Western countries, similar gender hierarchies and similar notions of femininity and masculinity prevailed in the period under research; these notions decisively influenced not only women's access to men's activity such as boxing, but also the messages and meanings which women displayed and conveyed in specific cultural spaces, e.g. in the boxing ring [8]

Women's Roles in the Nineteenth-Century USA

The Gender Order in the American Society

In the nineteenth century, Western societies were structured via strict class and gender hierarchies. Women had no political rights and few options beyond marriage; they were subordinated to their husband as head of the family. Throughout the nineteenth century, women were denied suffrage and property rights in most states of the USA. In the unlikely event of a divorce, the husband was entitled to the children. An early feminist movement emerged in a women's convention in 1848 and aimed to formally object to the deplorable conditions of the 'other sex'; however, the women's initiatives had little success. The gender arrangements closely connected with rules of propriety and decency and restricted women's aspirations. The tasks as middle-class women were to be wives and mothers and their domestic duties dominated their everyday lives. Their home was (or should be) their world and women's appearances in the public were guided by rules of decency and propriety. Only the daughters of upper-class families had access to higher education and by 1870 only 1% of college-age Americans attended the universities and four of every five students were men. Few of the educated women were admitted to professions; their career choices were limited to that of teachers, nurses and social workers. Women from lower classes had to earn money to make ends meet, and they often worked in dingy factories for long hours with minimal pay, or in service occupations such as laundresses and domestic helpers in the homes of the wealthy. Working-class families often had many children, who were a financial burden when young, but later worked to help support their families.[9]

Despite numerous variations, at the end of the nineteenth century, the gender order in the USA emphasised gender duality and gender differences. Women, at least members of the middle classes, were considered the weak sex, which had to be protected and therefore excluded from strenuous and potentially dangerous activities such as sport in general and boxing in particular. Theirs was a world of gentility and refinement. Not only in the ballrooms, but also on the sporting grounds they had to 'do gender', i.e. display femininity in addition to a middle-class taste which was mirrored in the choice of pastimes. Acceptable activities such as cycling, croquet, tennis and golf were not too strenuous and did not allow body contact.[10] In contrast, boxing was vigorous and exhausting and considered as taboo for women because it displayed unfeminine qualities such as strength, power and aggressiveness. In addition, skimpy attire, ripped clothes, battered bodies and sometimes even the bare breasts of the female boxers aroused the sexual fantasies and appealed to the voyeurism of the male audiences. Respectable women were not expected to participate or even attend prizefights.

In contrast, working-class women, employed in factories, living on farms, frontier women or women working in the entertainment business could not and did not have to comply with middle-class standards of femininity. Their lives encompassed physicality with little economic and social capital to be gained.

This is particularly true for the female boxers, who were in this period of time entertainers, attractions in saloons and stars in vaudeville shows throughout the USA.

Women in the World of Vaudeville Theatres, Circuses and Fairgrounds

People working in the entertainment business, e.g. in a circus or in a vaudeville show, live in a world which does not function according to the rules of the mainstream society. It is a world of illusions, of glitter and glamour, but also a world where the artists present unbelievable performances – with regard to strength, skills and risk taking. Within such an environment, girls and women are not considered as the 'weak sex' which has to be protected; on the contrary, women have to assume their share of work and have to develop specific skills such as equestrianism, balancing on a rope and weight lifting. They work in all fields and on all levels of a circus, as strongwomen, lion tamers or even as circus directors. Children of circus artists grow into the professions of their families and learn from a young age to ride or work on a trapeze, lift weights, perform club-swinging routines or to box. Thus, it is not surprising that many female boxers learned their skills from family members and performed together with their relatives on the vaudeville circuit.[11].

Vaudeville emerged in North America in the mid-nineteenth century. The shows included a large variety of 'attractions ranging from concerts, to freak shows and to athletic displays such as wrestling, boxing or club swinging'. At a time without radio, movies and television, circus and vaudeville shows soon became formidable businesses; they provided work for thousands of artists and entertainment for the masses. In contrast to the bachelor subculture of the saloons, vaudeville theatres, halls or tents attracted families of the middle classes to the readily available shows. The popular programmes as well as the low entrance fees contributed to the huge success of this form of entertainment.[12]

A few thousand women worked in this business, adopting various roles from managers to singers, but largely by displaying physical prowess. Depending on their genre, top performers could have a high social status. In Europe, this was particularly true for the circus equestriennes, who were accepted even in aristocratic circles. In the USA, female rodeo riders or sharpshooters exhibited their physical skills as popular participants of Wild West shows; but vaudeville only began to merge high and low culture in the early twenty-first century with the introduction of celebrated actresses who agreed to perform on the vaudeville stage in exchange for exorbitant fees. With the rise of movie theatres in the 1920s, live entertainment at variety theatres lost its appeal and during the 1930s vaudeville was replaced by the cinema.[13]

Circuses, fairgrounds and vaudeville theatres were places where the extraordinary was the rule and where performances were expected which seemed to be impossible in real life. Thus, also the gender roles became more fluid and women could and did perform in ways which were unacceptable in the 'real' world. On the vaudeville circuit, female performers were admired for deeds which exceeded men's strength and skills. Here, they could not only make a living, but also even gain recognition and a measure of fame.[14]

In the second half of the nineteenth century, numerous extraordinary women began earning fame and money through sporting endeavours; pedestrians, long-distance cyclists and strong women made a considerable income by performances which seemingly transcended the possibilities of most men. Among the strongest women of the era was Katharina Brumbach who named herself Sandwina after she had defeated the famous strongman, Eugen Sandow, in weightlifting. Working with the Barnum & Bailey Circus, she offered money to any man in the audience who could defeat her in wrestling. Nobody ever won the prize.[15]

Long-distance walking and running provided another opportunity for women to distinguish themselves in the second half of the century. By the 1870s, a number of female pedestrians won acclaim and a measure of celebrity by defeating men in endurance walking contests. Ada Anderson travelled from England to the USA to display her abilities and walked 675 miles (about 1085 kilometres) over the course of a month. By the end of the decade, more than 100 female pedestrians appeared in professional races.[16] At the same time, the bicycle gained popularity. Louise Armaindo became acclaimed as the champion female bicycle rider of the world, as she set endurance records and defeated male competitors in the 1880s. Armaindo challenged 'any lady in America, or will take five miles start in a fifty mile race from any man'.[17] Annie Sylvester, too, was a successful bicycle racer and, in addition, a famous 'trick and fancy rider who even mastered the unicycle', a feat beyond the capacities of the vast majority of men.[18] Such public displays of women's capacities clearly refuted the myths of the 'weak sex'; but because the strong women, the female bicycle racers and endurance runners were professional performers, they were accepted and considered as extraordinary and their achievements had little impact on the gender stereotypes and the gender order in the society as a whole. Whereas women exhibiting extraordinary skills may have been – although sometimes reluctantly – tolerated, females engaging in combat still faced a strong, often even an insurmountable resistance. Much more than endurance athletes, female boxers confronted traditional notions of femininity, broke the rules of Victorian propriety, but carved out a space for themselves within a presumably male domain.[19] Women in the boxing ring counteracted the contemporary gender order and dispelled the myth of women as the weaker sex.

Women's Boxing in the USA

The Beginnings

In the second half of the nineteenth century, boxing was extremely popular in the USA, with numerous fights in saloons, arenas and theatres all over the country. Reports about boxers and bouts filled the newspapers.[20] Whereas the male boxers were heroes, women who participated in the sport offended Victorian norms of the middle and upper classes. However, since the 1860s working-class women have engaged in fights for money which emulated the brutality and ferocity of male bruisers, and journalists indulged in descriptions of 'disfigured faces and battered bodies'.[21]

By 1869, the lawmakers in Chicago considered it necessary to ban all boxing contests, adopting the arguments of journalists:

> Prize fights between men are beastly exhibitions, but there is an unutterable loathsomeness in the worse brutality of abandoned, wretched women beating each other almost to nudity, for the amusement of a group of blackguards, even lower in the scale of humanity than the women themselves.[22]

Despite the opposition to women's boxing in many American cities, female boxers found an enthusiastic audience in athletic clubs or saloons such as at Harry Hill's Exchange in New York, an establishment favoured by the members of the bachelor subculture between 1854 and 1886. Harry Hill featured a variety of attractions for his clientele, which included a stable of female as well as male prizefighters. The women could earn 15 to 25 dollars a week which was a sizeable income for that era and better than other options such as manual labour and prostitution. Therefore, Hill had no problems recruiting female pugilists.[23]

The first women's boxing contest at Hill's Theater took place between two of the dancers in 1876. Nell Saunders, tutored by her husband, a boxer, beat Rose Harland in a narrow decision after three rounds. Saunders won a $200 prize and a silver butter dish, almost a year's wages for a male worker. The exuberant male spectators granted Harland $10 for her efforts.[24] An illustration shows Hill's female boxers in 1879 wearing blouses and knickers, but a report about a fight between a Ms Burke and a Ms Wells emphasised that they were 'attired in unmentionables made of silk'.[25] Their fight ended in a draw after six rounds, but the boxing seemed to have been secondary to the titillation provided to the male spectators by the appearance and the clothing, or lack thereof, of the combatants.

Such reports were regularly published by the *National Police Gazette*, an American weekly 'covering crime, sports, celebrities, and all things sensational since 1845'. It claimed to be 'The Leading Illustrated Sporting Journal in America'. [26] The editor and proprietor, Richard K. Fox, was a formidable promoter of boxing and he fuelled men's and women's matches by offering cash prizes and championship belts as trophies. Women engaged in men's sports such as boxing, wrestling and weightlifting were a popular topic of the Gazette; they were displayed in various sorts of combative postures and accepted as professional entertainers. Alice Jennings, Daisy Daly, Anna Lewis, Ada Sandry, the Gordon sisters, Hattie Stewart, Hattie Leslie and many other more or less well-known female boxers were covered, often with illustrations, in the Gazette.[27] The lurid presentations of these and other women and the focus on sex and crime drew a multitude of largely working-class readers to this salacious newspaper.

Harry Hill's saloon as well as the *Police Gazette* and its owner played a crucial role in the development of women's boxing. Hill's cast of female fighters included Libbie Ross and Libby Kelly. Libbie Ross still boxed in 1891, in the Leadville Theater, where her 'show was very popular'.[28] Libby Kelly, praised because of her 'prowess with the boxing gloves', appeared in Harry Hill's Exchange in 1878 and made a name for herself as a proficient pugilist 'by the science she displayed ... she always proved victorious. She was tall and athletic, possessed a long reach, understood how to hit, stop and counter'.[29] Allegedly, her fame and glory caused numerous other females to follow in her footsteps. Among her successors were Nettie Burke, Jennie Meade and Hattie Edwards as well as 'Mlle. D'Omer who came to this country under the management of Harry Webb and appeared with varied success at the numerous theatres'.[30]

By the end of the 1870s, the opportunities for female boxers increased, as a growing number of saloons, theatres and public halls all over the country hosted women's boxing contests. The San Francisco Chronicle of January 26, 1879, announced, for example, a fight between two novices for a prize of $250. Jessie Lewis from England and Mollie Berdan from California were 'yet untrained in the fistic warfare, but will be given the requisite discipline by competent trainers'. Both women were described as feminine and pretty; unfortunately, we are not informed about the outcome of the bout.[31]

Prizefights and Championships

Although prizefights were outlawed in most parts of the USA, numerous boxing matches took place, often in clandestine places and sometimes disrupted by the police. Prizefighting between men was considered a crime, but bouts between women were condemned as especially disgusting and brutal in the extreme. In spite of the law, many women announced challenges for prize money. One of them was Alice Jennings, 'a powerful amazon with a great left hook, who issued a challenge to any woman in America in 1883'.[32] Daisy Daly, allegedly the women's champion of California, fought Jennings under the Queensberry rules at Hill's establishment that year. The bout resulted in a victory for Daly, who was well known in the theatrical profession as a singer.[33] At Hill's she engaged in boxing matches with male and female boxers and at 'a lively afternoon during a vigorous sparring she was knocked down twice by one of the male boxers'.[34] Her picture was published in the *National Police Gazette* and the sketches of other famous female boxers of the time reveal that they wore a one piece tight fitting short dress, which violated the clothing norms of polite society.[35] According to the *Police Gazette*, Nellie (sic, likely Hattie) Stewart of Norfolk, Virginia, became the first female boxing champion of the world in 1884 although many women, including Hattie Leslie, claimed such distinction as a marketing device.[36]

In 1888, a prizefight between women ended in a court case and caused quite a stir in the American press. Hattie Leslie and Alice Leary, both vaudeville performers, appeared in their tights for a bout on an island in the Niagara River. Fifty male 'sports' from Buffalo came with a boat to enjoy this sensational spectacle which had to be conducted at a clandestine place due to the laws banning prizefights.[37] Both boxers claimed extensive experience in the ring, with Leslie boasting a record of 34-0 with 29 knockouts and Leary asserting that she had 52 wins, with no losses and 47 knockouts. It proved to be a brutal affair despite the use of gloves. According to the press, Leslie suffered two knock-downs and had her nose broken, while Leary also dropped to the canvas on two occasions. When Leary tried to give up, the spectators demanded a final knockout. Despite her injury, Leslie rebounded to win by a knockout in the seventh round.[38]

At least one reporter found reward in the beauty of the two competitors if not their pugilistic skills. They were

> better looking than half the damsels one meets on the street, peeled off good clothes and fought seven rounds with kid gloves in the presence of fifty as tough, bad men as Divine Providence ever allowed to congregate on a Sabbath morning.[39]

At the conclusion of the bout, both the boxers and their male attendants were arrested. In the interrogation, Leslie revealed that Alice Leary (her real name was Barbara Dillon) had dropped out and that Rosetta Biebler, a Dutch girl, who never had sparred in her life, had taken her place. However, this is unlikely given her performance in the fight. Leslie also insisted that there was no prize money and that she participated in the fight because she wanted the newspaper notoriety.[40]

The district attorney did not buy the story of a fake fight, but he did not want to

> blame the women so much, though they are indicted. It is these men, these creatures who are at fault. It is a disgrace ... to think that men are so brutal, so lost to every instinct of manhood should engage in such an enterprise .... Prize-fights between men have perhaps been tolerated, but prize-fights between women never.[41]

The fight had been organised by John G. Floss, an official of the Buffalo Athletic Club, and John Spahn (alias John Leslie), the husband and manager of Hattie.[42] The district attorney's arguments mirror the middle-class ideals of femininity and standards of propriety. Such verdicts also reinforced the dominant belief that women could be manipulated by malevolent men. The judge sentenced the men to several months in prison. The attorney's judgment of the female boxers mirrors widespread opinions and prejudices. According to a journalist of a sexist tirade against female pugilists (who should rather work as washers or scrubbers), boxing is a 'degradation of women' and women who box are 'unsexed creatures' supported by men who have a personal or pecuniary interest in the women champions they manage.[43]

The 'World Champions' and Other Female Boxing Pioneers

The strong women of vaudeville and female boxers did not fit the gender norms and ideals of the time. They were proclaimed as a giantess or amazons and seemed to meet the stereotypes about female boxers as unfeminine hulks. At the same time, it was often emphasised that they were good looking and attractive. With few exceptions, press reports of women's bouts refer to the appearance of the boxers and many seem to meet the standards of feminine attractiveness (at least before the fights). Hattie Leslie, for example, was described as 'the famous Amazon and a tall, powerful specimen of humanity'.[44] Later reports describe her as 'trimmed and neat, with distinct and refined features, bright eyes and well-rounded arms'.[45]

An examination of Leslie's life reveals the circumstances and motivations of such working-class boxers. Hattie was illiterate, which indicates her underclass social background.[46] She had been in athletic training since she was a child and she did a club swinging act in a theatre which kept her in good physical condition.[47] After her victory over Leary (or whoever her opponent was), Hattie Leslie, 'champion female pugilist of the world',[48] made a living from sparring exhibitions and competitions on the vaudeville circuit, as well as from boxing and wrestling matches. She was one of the 'attractions of the Irwin Brothers vaudeville company', and staged a show with her 'American lady athletes, ten in number'.[49] In 1891, she sent out a challenge to wrestle any woman for $100. Alice Williams, a star wrestler, accepted, but the match ended in a draw. In1892, they wrestled again, this time for the alleged world championship, and Leslie lost.[50] Hattie Leslie died later that year from 'typhoid fever' in a hotel in Milwaukee.[51]

Hattie Stewart had a similarly powerful physique as her rival. She was born in Philadelphia and, according to her narrative in an interview, 'was always fighting with boys …'.[52] Stewart also developed her boxing skills by sparring with her partner, Dick Stewart, and female opponents in boxing clubs and variety theatres. Both Stewarts lived for a time in Norfolk where they worked at a gymnasium. After Stewart distinguished herself in an 1884 bout with Anna Lewis, the *Gazette* claimed 'This package of muscular dynamic was the first woman to become World Female Boxing Champion'.[53] According to the *Police Gazette*, 'she appeared at all the variety and music halls throughout North America, and not only did the young giantess knock out female rivals, but held her own with professional male boxers'.[54] Stewart was one of the women acclaimed as the 'female John L. Sullivan': the other one was Hattie Leslie. In 1890, Stewart issued a challenge to Hattie Leslie to fight for the female championship of the world and a sizeable side bet of $500. Leslie answered and accepted the challenge.[55] However, it seems that this fight did not take place.

Boxing for both males and females at the time was a haphazard business due to widespread prohibitions and police interference, not unlike working-class life in general, as evidenced by the career of Gussie Freeman. Gussie Freeman (alias Gus Lony, Lonely or Loony) fought against Leslie several times. In 1891, Leslie, the 'Champion Female Boxer', found 'a Fierce Brooklyn Opponent in the Pride of the Waterbury Ropewalks'. In an 'Unprecedented Spectacle at a Theatre' watched by 2000 spectators, she won the fight.[56] According to another report, a police officer stopped the fight in the third round and it was declared a draw. Gussie defeated Hattie Leslie three nights later. She knocked her out which reveals her abilities as a boxer.[57] She seems to be one of the few top female boxers who did not have a background in the world of show business, but started work as a rope maker when she was only 12 years of age. In an interview she revealed that she did not like women's work and that she was skilled in sports such as ball games, running and swimming. She was proud that she prevailed over men in gambling, drinking and fighting, a clear indication of her working-class habitus. Gussie was a 'born fighter and the strongest and most masculine woman in the city, if not in the world … who has completely stepped into man's place'.[58] Drawing on constructivist gender theories and Judith Butler's notion of 'gender trouble makers', Freeman's appearance and behaviour can be interpreted as a disruption of the binary oppositions of masculinity and femininity, and its heterosexual connotations.[59] She was a 'gender trouble maker' who found niches, i.e. boxing, where she could act out her inclinations and aspirations.

The match between Gussie and Leslie attracted a large audience, among them many men, who were eager to watch this 'scrap' between women 'bruising each other …. They had a four-rounder at a theater on Grand Avenue in Williamsburg, Brooklyn, that was talked about for decades'. Gussie won the bout and was invited by John Leslie, Hattie's husband and the manager of the dramatic combination, to travel with them. After having been cheated out of her salary, she joined another group. Although she drew crowded houses and defeated 12 men in two weeks, among them some allegedly famous pugilists, she still had problems to get her pay. This was the end of her boxing career; she went back to Brooklyn, opened a saloon and later returned to her work at the rope factory.[60]

At least one of the prominent female boxers of the era deviated from the working-class norm and complied – at least to a certain degree – with the gender ideals of the time. Chicagoan Cecil Richards was one of the four serious claimants of the world championship in women's boxing in the late nineteenth century. However, the lack of a governing body derogated the value of such titles. She was an exceptional boxer, not only because of her performances, but also because of her middle-class background. Allegedly, her father was a dry goods merchant. According to a newspaper biography, Richards was born into an athletic family; the men had been fighters, athletes and gymnasts, the women had dabbled with dumbbells and were fond of fencing. Two of her brothers have been 'particularly prominent with the gloves'. She seemed to have 'inherited the biceps' and began her pugilistic career at the age of 14.[61]

According to the newspaper reports, Cecil Richards was a pretty and 'feminine' woman, a 'devout Christian' and at the same time an accomplished boxer.[62] She seems to have never been knocked out, but sent numerous opponents to the ground, among them Hattie Moore, the female champion of Australia, which allowed her to claim to be the world champion.[63] Tired of fighting with women, Richards sparred with men.[64] She had a 'personal trainer', a featherweight boxer, with whom she performed in public exhibitions.[65]

Hattie Stewart lost her claim to the championship to Richards in 1887. The new champion allegedly defended her title 87 times until she lost a bout with Hattie Leslie on September 6, 1890, in Detroit.[66] However, those accounts have to be considered carefully as there are numerous discrepancies in newspaper reports and claims by both male and female boxers. For example, Richards claimed a knockout of Lansing Rowan; but Rowan asserted that they had never met each other.[67]

Challenging Male Boxers – Challenging Feminine Propriety

In the attempt to gain attention by rebelling against of the norms and rules of propriety and femininity, several female pugilists challenged men – at least to sparring bouts. Lansing Rowan, allegedly an opponent of Cecil Richards, was the daughter of a banker and an actress in a travelling theatre company. Rowan gained fame as the 'woman who challenges Corbett'. In an interview, she stated that she wanted to compete for points with the famous boxer, who had dethroned John L. Sullivan to become the heavyweight champion in 1892.[68] At the same time, the interview showed that Rowan had little or no boxing experience and that her challenge was a marketing ploy. Corbett did not react to this challenge. The next headlines were produced by the suicide of her father and the press brought forward the assumption that he killed himself grieving over a daughter who publicly transgressed the gender norms and the etiquette of her social class.[69] Although she claimed that her father was sick and had financial problems,[70] the story of the deviant behaviour of a young lady and its impact on her family was more attractive than the truth. Women's boxing was considered such a scandal that it may even have caused the suicide of a father.

Cecil Richards seems to have been more serious in her challenge to male boxers. In an article entitled 'She wants to box men', Richards is portrayed as the 'newest of all new women' and as 'an expert in the art which has heretofore been known as merely manly'. She is 'wonderfully well muscled', 'her cheeks are rosy', 'her lips are red, her eyes are soft, but her arms are hard' and she is an 'embodiment of health and strength'.[71] As stated above, Richards participated in exhibition rounds with men. However, in two articles issued in 1897, she challenged 'all the light weight boxers in the world, in particular Jack

McAuliffe', the undefeated lightweight champion from 1886 to 1893, to a six round contest. In addition, she bet $1000 that she would be 'on her feet at the end of the sixth round with any lightweight pugilist'.[72] Although these top professional male boxers refused to answer such proposals, their publication represented a symbolic challenge to the dominant gender order whereby the 'feminine' image of Richards contrasted with the blatant violation of the gender arrangement in the mainstream society. This contrast added to a morbid fascination of beautiful female risk takers in vaudeville.

Boxing – Fitness and Self-defence

New challenges to the gender order emerged when young, middle-class women invaded the male domain of sport in greater numbers in the 1890s. Known as 'Gibson Girls' due to the artist Charles Dana Gibson's popular illustrations of independent, vivacious, active women who departed from the sedate, domestic, Victorian gender norms of the past, some of these 'new women' expressed their physicality by taking boxing lessons. According to the *New York Times*, society girls, tired of golf, basketball and tennis, detected their interest in boxing. 'The boxing girl is to have her day'. The long article details the aims, opportunities and limitations of women's boxing, the 'very best exercise in the world'. However, the article ends with a warning: 'not that the boxing girls are to invade the ringside. Heaven forbid!'[73]

Women engaged in boxing for various reasons. Some tried to achieve a sense of self-empowerment and some hoped to use boxing as a means of self-defence. At a time when women were considered weak and in need of a male protector, a female student of the art of boxing declared 'If you are insulted in the street, knock your insultor down'.[74] Such conviction to be able to defend oneself contributed to a new sense of female empowerment. As early as 1895, newspapers encouraged women to spar to improve their health.[75] Fitness and slimness, 'to knock off pounds that are not needed', was an important incentive to engage in the new fad of boxing.[76] This provided second-class male boxers and female boxers such as Hattie Stewart with an income as instructors. In 1913, the *Atlanta Constitution* reported: 'Boxing is the latest fad among St. Louis society women … Bob Douglas, ex-prizefighter, gives them private lessons … his fair pupils … are mostly suffragettes'.[77] However, many of the male boxing teachers devalued the skills and the intentions of their students. As one of the instructors complained, women lacked men's aggressiveness and did not hit hard enough; but they were more graceful in the ring. Another boxing teacher had similar impressions about female's lack of mental and physical tenacity.

> They go at boxing like a boy who tries to swim dog fashion. To box well one must think and keep cool, and that is something women have to learn …. Then, too, they are timid. They are afraid of black eyes, and stiff jaws, and bruised bodies.[78]

It is an open question, if these female dilettantes threatened the gender dichotomy or surpassed the gender divide by engaging in a men's sport.

Boxing on the Vaudeville Circuit

Performances of strength and other physical skills have been central features of vaudeville shows. Besides club swinging and wrestling, boxing as an exhibition, a burlesque or sparring for points were among the popular entertainment acts. Many famous male pugilists from John L. Sullivan to Jack Johnson performed on the vaudeville circuit with boxing acts, but also with other performances, and there they gained additional fame and money. Vaudeville boxing had a specific appeal for female audiences because women were not admitted to 'real' boxing contests.[79] Boxing had to be de-brutalised in order to be an appropriate spectacle for the 'weak sex', but in particular the women seem to have been excited by the bodily encounters of strong and well-built men. Even middle-class women attended boxing films in great numbers at afternoon matinees in Chicago, Dallas, San Francisco and Boston to see Gentleman Jim Corbett.[80]

In variety theatres, female boxers, too, were welcomed as performers, appreciated and rewarded for their physical abilities. They adhered in particular to scientific boxing where their skills and techniques, similar to the male boxers, were displayed. Besides boxing exhibitions, they took part in sparring competitions, also referred to as sparring for points, and competed against both women and men. In the programme announcements, champion female sparrers are often highlighted, such as Alice Jennings, 'the champion female sparrer of the world who won the grand female tournament …' at Clark's Olympic Club in 1883.[81] In November of 1882, she competed with Carrie Edwards in a gloved contest in the same club. She also performed there with her partner, Eddie O'Brien, who claimed to be the champion featherweight of America. They started a tour at Nashman's Vaudeville Theater in Baltimore and were scheduled to appear throughout the South. However, as other announcements of this and other theatres show, there were numerous fighters who marketed themselves as world champions on the vaudeville circuit. In March 1884, Alice Jennings and O'Brien appeared in what was termed an instructive glove contest, but in April of the same year their show was billed as an 'assault at arms' at the Vine Street Opera House in Cincinnati.[82] Ten years later, the *Cincinnati Enquirer* praised the 'emerald trio', O'Brien, Jennings and O'Brien, as one of the best: 'The boxing between Alice Jennings and Edward O'Brien would be a credit to a more pretentious pugilist. Miss Jennings is an accomplished and scientific pugilist'.[83]

Some establishments focused on sport performances, as at Clark's Club Theatre in Philadelphia where on December 6, 1884, 'the final contest in Clark's successful boxing tournament took place. Besides Fritz Gonawein and Professor Schmidt, Miss Hattie Stewart, female champion boxer and a select company of 40 new specialty artists and boxers were among the attractions'.[84]

Several female boxers and their partners even had their own shows, e.g. Dick and Hattie Stewart who performed in many American cities. The *Parsons (Kansas) Daily Sun* published, for example, an announcement of a show where 'Hattie Stewart, the female Sullivan and champion female athlete of America and Prof. Dick Stewart, champion lightweight athlete of East (sic) Virginia were named as highlights'.[85] In 1886, the Richard and Hattie Stewart All Star Specialty Company performed in St. Paul.[86] In the same year, a soft gloves contest with Annie Lewis, a competition for points, was announced in the *Galveston Daily News* with a purse of $300. Boys had no access to this event which seemed to violate middle-class rules of propriety.[87]

At the end of the nineteenth century, female boxers were attractions in the boxing ring, but even more on the stages of the vaudeville circuit. Here a large and mixed audience could admire their skills and they could earn salaries well beyond those of most women, gaining a measure of economic and social capital although they disrupted the gender order, but this was expected in the world of show business.

Backgrounds and Motives

Since the 1870s, more or less serious combats among thespians, bargirls and more dedicated pugilists in the saloons provided a lascivious form of entertainment for male patrons and reports of such matches often derided the participants as bawdy women, unworthy of polite society. However, as the reports in the *Police Gazette* show, women's boxing became an encounter of skilled athletes and as such a sporting performance.

Female boxers used pseudonyms and only in exceptional cases their real names were revealed, e.g. in the reports about the court case following the Buffalo fight. In an article about Cecil Richards, it is stated: 'Of course Richards is not her really, truly name, she has adopted this name because she did not want to bring her "well-to-do" family in disrepute'.[88] The short glimpses of the boxers' lives revealed that most had a working-class background and that many had relatives, i.e. parents or siblings, who worked in the vaudeville circus. A large percentage had husbands who were their partners in boxing exhibitions, their trainers and their managers. Many female pugilists performed in a circus or a vaudeville theatre not only in boxing, but also in other artistic acts, e.g. dumbbell or Indian club exercises or wrestling. Their abilities and skills as young adults indicate that they started physical training in childhood, most likely in a vaudeville environment. Some of them, e.g. Cecil Richard or Gussie Freeman, refer to their upbringing as athletes. Gussie Freeman was one of the few outsiders drawn to boxing because her preference for and skills in men's sports. However, despite her abilities and her success as a boxer, her background as a rope maker and the lack of insight as to the rules of show business made it impossible to survive in the vaudeville world.

What were the motivations of Stewart, Leslie and other female boxers to engage in such an unfeminine endeavour? Earning a living via sport, in particular via boxing, was not a common practice among women in this period of time. However, performing in vaudeville may have been the profession which they had learned from childhood. Using their skills for encounters in boxing meant also earning considerable sums of money which greatly exceeded the annual wages for working-class women of the era.[89] Boxing also allowed these women greater independence and promised even a measure of fame unattainable by the vast majority of females, including those of the upper class who were dependent upon the wealth and social prestige of their husbands.[90]

The working-class origin of female boxers and their involvement with vaudeville influenced their career paths and allowed them to defy middle-class gender norms and ideals. As professional athletes, they complied with the expectations of the world of vaudeville with its own rules, although this meant to be 'gender trouble makers'.

Conclusion

Women's boxing emerged in a specific time period during the latter decades of the nineteenth century in the USA. During this era, it gained a measure of acceptance, at least among working-class men and the 'sports' of the better sort. Nearly all of the early female boxers in the USA had a background in show business, i.e. they had performed athletic feats in saloons, in vaudeville theatres or circuses.

Gender arrangements as well as women's opportunities and constraints in the show business world were different from the gender relations and situations of middle-class women. Like their male counterparts, the women who chose to box did so for monetary remuneration and local celebrity. If girls and women had skills which helped to support the income of the family or to increase the profit of the managers or entertainment enterprises, they were appreciated and supported, thus gaining a measure of social and economic capital within the confined community in which they lived.

Drawing on Pierre Bourdieu's concept of habitus and capital as well as the notion of gender as a social construction, the behaviour of the female boxers was not discordant with the values and tastes as well the physicality of show business and working-class life despite the different demands and settings. For both women in vaudeville and the working class, the dominant gender order did not apply. For vaudeville women displaying their half-naked bodies, working in environments dominated by men or engaging in a masculine sport such as boxing clearly violated rules and norms of middle-class femininity, but at the same time their strength, endurance and skills were valued among their peers and their audiences. In that sense, it was possible for female boxers to gain a measure of respect within their closed society and thus contribute to incremental gender changes in the mainstream culture as well.

Notes

1. For example, Thrasher, "Disappearance"; there are several good web pages on the topic, e.g. http://www.cyberboxingzone.com/blog/?p=7612.
2. See in particular Thrasher, "Disappearance," and the excellent article of Christopher James Shelton who emphasised the skills of Wilkinson-Stokes in mixed martial arts, http://www.cyberboxingzone.com/blog/?p=7612; see also https://www.facebook.com/Boxologyhistory/posts/408836575913191?stream_ref = 10.
3. There is much information about women involved in boxing and other forms of fighting in the eighteenth century.
4. See Heiskanen, *The Urban Geography*. Exceptions to the negligence are Guttmann, *Women's Sports*, and Park, "Contesting the Norm."
5. Lorber, *Paradoxes of Gender*; Connell, *Gender*.
6. Bourdieu, *Distinction*.
7. Krais, "Gender and Symbolic Violence"; Jenkins, *Pierre Bourdieu*; and Thorpe, "Bourdieu."
8. Heiskanen, *The Urban Geography*.
9. Garraty, *The American Nation*, 281–4; McMillen, *Seneca Falls*; Blum et al., *The National Experience*, 259–61, 483–4; Woloch, "Women's Education"; Brownlee and Brownlee, *Women in the American Economy*; Mintz and Kellogg, *Domestic Revolutions*; and Jones, *Daily Life*.
10. Guttmann, *Women's Sports*.
11. Adams and Keene, *Women of the American Circus*; Hedenborg and Pfister, "Écuyères and 'Doing Gender'."
12. Lewis, *From Traveling Show*.
13. Hedenborg and Pfister, "Écuyères and 'Doing Gender'."; Kibler, *Rank Ladies*.
14. Hedenborg and Pfister, "Écuyères and "Doing Gender'."
15. Park, "Contesting the Norm"; Todd, "Center Ring."
16. Shaulis, "Women of Endurance"; Park, "Contesting the Norm."
17. Reel, *The National Police Gazette*, July 29, 1882, 12; http://www.thelizlibrary.org/undelete/woa-spotlight/02-pedestriennes.html-10.
18. *Sporting and Theatrical Journal*, August 16, 1884, 1, 219.
19. Toulmin, *A Fair Fight*; Kim, "Fighting Men"; Park, "Contesting the Norm"; and Connell, *Gender*.
20. Gems, *Boxing*, 214–21.
21. *Chicago Tribune*, March 13, 1869, quoted in Gems, *Windy City Wars*, 15; Kim, "Fighting Men."
22. Gems, *Windy City Wars*, 14–5.
23. Chudacoff, *The Age of the Bachelor*; see the numerous articles in Reel, *The National Police Gazette*.
24. *New York Times*, March 17, 1876, 8.

25. Reel, *The National Police Gazette*, November 22, 187. A Miss Burke is also mentioned as one of the early female boxers in *Logansport Pharos-Tribune*, September 24, 1892, 7.
26. http://www.policegazette.us.
27. Park, "Contesting the Norm."
28. Scanlon, *A History of Leadville*, 114.
29. Reel, *The National Police Gazette*, September 24, 1892, 11; see also http://www.fscclub.com/history/fame-championess-e.shtml (accessed June 5, 2014).
30. *Hamilton Journal News*, September 24, 1892, 7.
31. Quoted in *New York Herald*, February 4, 1879, 5.
32. *Mason City Globe Gazette*, December 30, 1955, 14.
33. Park, "Contesting the Norm."
34. *Cincinnati Enquirer*, March 30, 1883, 2.
35. Reel, *The National Police Gazette*, February 1883, 12; *Logansport Pharos-Tribune*, August 12, 1893, 15.
36. *The Times*, Philadelphia, December 6, 1884, 5. As the notice in the *Police Gazette* is the only one about a boxer named Nellie Stewart, it can be assumed that the *Gazette* mixed the names and that Hattie Stewart who lived and worked for a time in Norfolk was the champion. See Hargreaves, "Women's Boxing."
37. For an extensive report, see also e.g. Warren, "An Outlaw Practice" and the information in the *New York State Reporter*, New York (State), Courts, Willard Smith Gibbons, Rowland M. Stover. W.C. Little & Company, 1890, 225.
38. For the fight, see the *Buffalo Courier*, September 17, 1888, 6; and other papers, e.g. the *San Francisco Chronicle*, September 25, 1888, 1.
39. *Buffalo Courier*, September 17, 1888, 6.
40. Ibid., October 4, 1888, 5.
41. Ibid.
42. John G. Floss was the owner of bowling alleys and an official of various sport organisations; see e.g. a report about a bowling congress, the *Brooklyn Daily Eagle*, January 14, 1896, 1. The two corner men were well-known pugilists, George La Blanche and William Baker.
43. *Logansport Pharos-Tribune*, August 12, 1893, 15.
44. *Buffalo Courier*, October 4, 1888, 5; see also http://onmilwaukee.com/sports/articles/hattieleslie.html?24620.
45. *Brooklyn Daily Eagle*, November 21, 1891, 1.
46. *Buffalo Courier*, October 4, 1888, 5.
47. *Cincinnati Enquirer*, July 22, 1888, 16.
48. *Winnipeg Free Press*, September 25, 1890, quoted in http://www.womenboxing.com/NEWS2009/news050509firstchallenge.htm; *New York Dramatic Mirror*, November 18, 1891, 8.
49. *New York Clipper*, June 11, 1892, 6.
50. Beekman, *Ringside*, 6.
51. Her death was announced in many newspapers, e.g. *Logansport Pharos-Tribune* (Indiana), October 15, 1892, 15.
52. *Omaha Daily Bee*, December 28, 1887, 2.
53. Quoted in http://www.zoominfo.com/p/Hattie-Stewart/10920177.
54. Reel, *The National Police Gazette*, September 24, 1892.
55. Kim, "Fighting Men," 120; see *Winnipeg Free Press*, September 25, 1890.
56. The *Brooklyn Daily Eagle*, November 21, 1891, 1.
57. *Daily Argus News*, June 11, 1895, no page.
58. Ibid.; see her biography, http://www.newyorkshitty.com/tag/gussie-freeman (accessed June 4, 2014).
59. Butler, *Gender Trouble*.
60. http://www.newyorkshitty.com/tag/gussie-freeman (accessed June 4, 2014).
61. *The Ledge,* July 1, 1897, 6.
62. Ibid.
63. *Galveston Daily News*, Sunday, May 30, 1897, 20; *San Francisco Chronicle*, January 30, 1897, 9; *The Ledge*, July 1, 1897, 6.
64. See the information at http://www.fscclub.com/history/zhened-old2-e.shtml (accessed June 4, 2014).

65. *Galveston Daily News*, May 30, 1897, 20; *San Francisco Chronicle*, January 30, 1897, 9; *The Ledge*, July 1, 1897, 6.
66. http://www.fscclub.com/history/fame-championess-e.shtml (accessed June 4, 2014).
67. *San Francisco Chronicle*, January 30, 1897, 9; February 10, 1897, 8.
68. *Kansas City Daily Gazette*, June 29, 1896, 1.
69. Ibid.
70. *North Adams Transcript*, June 29, 1896, 1.
71. *Logansport Pharos-Tribune*, February 22, 1897, 6; *San Francisco Chronicle*, January 30, 1897, 9.
72. *San Francisco Chronicle*, June 30, 1897, 9; *Logansport Pharos-Tribune*, February 22, 1897, 6.
73. *Topeka Daily Capital*, October 2, 1904, 13..
74. *Washington Post*, August 31, 1890, cited in Kim, "Fighting Men," 117.
75. *Atlanta Constitution*, February 10, 1895, 6.
76. *New York Times*, September 25, 1904, 42.
77. Kim, "Fighting Men," 119–20; *The Washington Post*, March 19, 1913, 7.
78. *New York Times*, September 25, 1904, cited in Kim, "Fighting Men," 117.
79. Isenberg, *John L. Sullivan*; see e.g. *Daily Capital Journal*, February 5, 1916, 9, about "special arrangements" for female spectators.
80. Kibler, *Rank Ladies*, 51; Streible, *Fight Pictures*, 81–90.
81. *The Times*, Reading, March 9, 1883, 4; see also the *Louisville Courier-Journal*, August 19, 1883, 3. The paper presents Jennings as star of the Whalen's Buckingham Theater with Eddie O'Brien.
82. *Daily Commonwealth*, December 11, 1883, 2; *Cincinnati Enquirer*, March 30, 1884, April 1, 1884, 11.
83. *Cincinnati Enquirer*, February 12, 1894, 7.
84. *Philadelphia Times*, December 6, 1894, 5.
85. *Parsons Daily Sun*, June 26, 1885, 4.
86. *St. Paul Daily Globe*, October 10, 1886, 3.
87. *Parsons Daily Sun*, June 26, 1885, 4.
88. *Logansport Pharos-Tribune*, February 22, 1897, 6; *The Ledge*, July 1, 1897, 6.
89. The $250 in the San Francisco fight between Mollie Berdan and Jessie Lewis was nearly a year's salary for men; see Park, "Contesting the Norm," 740.
90. See e.g. the reports about Hattie Stewart or Hattie Leslie. Both had managers/partners and travelled extensively; they had to deal with the press and they seemed to have been accepted as attractive women.

References

Adams, K. H., and M. L. Keene. *Women of the American Circus, 1880–1940*. Jefferson, NC: McFarland, 2012.

Beekman, S. *Ringside: A History of Professional Wrestling in America*. Westport, CT: Praeger, 2006.

Blum, J. M., E. S. Morgan, W. L. Rose, A. M. Schlesinger, Jr, K. M. Stampp, and C. V. Woodward. *The National Experience: A History of the United States*. New York: Harcourt Brace Jovanovich, 1981.

Bourdieu, P. *Distinction: A Social Critique of the Judgment of Taste*. Cambridge, MA: Harvard University, 1984.

Brownlee, W. E., and M. M. Brownlee. *Women in the American Economy: A Documentary History, 1675 to 1929*. New Haven, CT: Yale University Press, 1976.

Butler, J. *Gender Trouble: Feminism and the Subversion of Identity*. New York: Routledge, 1990.

Chudacoff, H. P. *The Age of the Bachelor: Creating an American Subculture*. Princeton, NJ: Princeton University Press, 1999.

Connell, R. W. *Gender*. Cambridge: Polity, 2002.

Garraty, J. A. *The American Nation: A History of the United States*. New York: Harper & Row, 1983.

Gems, G. R. *Boxing: A Concise History of the Sweet Science*. Lanham, MD: Scarecrow Press, 2014.

Gems, G. R. *Windy City Wars: Labor, Leisure, and Sport in the Making of Chicago*. Metuchen, NJ: Scarecrow Press, 1997.

Guttmann, A. *Women's Sports: A History*. New York: Columbia University Press, 1991.

Hargreaves, J. "Women's Boxing and Related Activities: Introducing Images and Meanings." *Body and Society* 3, no. 4 (1997): 33–50.

Hedenborg, S., and G. Pfister. "Écuyères and 'Doing Gender': Presenting Femininity in a Male Domain – Female Circus Riders 1800–1920." *Scandinavian Sport Studies*, no. 3 (2012): 25–47.

Heiskanen, B. *The Urban Geography of Boxing: Race, Class, and Gender in the Ring.* New York: Routledge, 2012.

Isenberg, M. T. *John L. Sullivan and His America.* Urbana: University of Illinois Press, 1988.

Jenkins, R. *Pierre Bourdieu.*, Revised edition London: Routledge, 2002.

Jones, M. E. *Daily Life on the Nineteenth Century American Frontier.* Westport, CT: Greenwood Press, 1998.

Kibler, M. A. *Rank Ladies: Gender and Cultural Hierarchy in American Vaudeville.* Chapel Hill: University of North Carolina Press, 1999.

Kim, Y. "Fighting Men and Fighting Women: American Prizefighting and the Contested Gender Order in the Late Nineteenth and Early Twentieth Centuries." *Sport History Review*, no. 43 (2012): 103–127.

Krais, B. "Gender and Symbolic Violence: Female Oppression in the Light of Pierre Bourdieu's Theory of Social Practice." In *Bourdieu: Critical Perspectives*, edited by Craig Calhoun, Edward LiPuma, and Moishe Postone, 156–177. Chicago, IL: University of Chicago Press, 1993.

Lewis, R. M. *From Traveling Show to Vaudeville: Theatrical Spectacle in America, 1830–1910.* Baltimore, MD: Johns Hopkins University Press, 2003.

Lorber, J. *Paradoxes of Gender.* New Haven, CT: Yale University Press, 1994.

McMillen, S. G. *Seneca Falls and the Origins of the Women's Rights Movement.* New York: Oxford University Press, 2008.

Mintz, S., and S. Kellogg. *Domestic Revolutions: A Social History of American Family Life.* New York: Free Press, 1988.

Park, R. J. "Contesting the Norm: Women and Professional Sports in Late Nineteenth-Century America." *The International Journal of the History of Sport* 29, no. 5 (2012): 730–749.

Reel, G. *The National Police Gazette and the Making of the Modern American Man, 1879–1906.* New York: Palgrave Macmillan, 2006. http://site.ebrary.com/id/10155131

Scanlon, G. *A History of Leadville Theatre: Opera Houses, Variety Acts and Burlesque Shows.* Charleston, SC: The History Press, 2012.

Shaulis, D. "Women of Endurance: Pedestriennes, Marathoners, Ultra-marathoners, and Others: Two Centuries of Women's Endurance (1816-1996)." *Women in Sport & Physical Activity Journal* 5, no. 2 (1996): 1–29.

Streible, D. *Fight Picture: A History of Boxing and Early Cinema.* Berkeley, CA: University of California Press, 2008. http://public.eblib.com/EBLPublic/PublicView.do?ptiID=837235

Thorpe, H. "Bourdieu, Feminism and Female Physical Culture: Gender Reflexivity and the Habitus-Field Complex." *Sociology of Sport Journal* 26, no. 4 (2009): 491–516.

Thrasher, C. "Disappearance: How Shifting Gendered Boundaries Motivated the Removal of Eighteenth Century Boxing Champion Elizabeth Wilkinson from Historical Memory." 2012. http://ejournals.library.ualberta.ca/index.php/pi/article/view/19438

Todd, I. "Center Ring: Katie Sandwina and the Construction of Celebrity." *Iron Game History* 10, no. 1 (2007): 4–13.

Toulmin, V. *A Fair Fight: An Illustrated Review of Boxing on British Fairgrounds.* Oldham: World's Fair, 1999.

Warren, I. J. M. "An Outlaw Practice: Boxing, Governance and Western Law." PhD diss., Victoria University of Technology 2005.

Woloch, N. "Women's Education." In *The Reader's Companion to American History*, edited by E. Foner, and J. Garraty, 324–327. Boston, MA: Houghton Mifflin, 1991.

British Cultural Influence and Japan: Elizabeth Phillips Hughes's Visit for Educational Research in 1901–1902

Keiko Ikeda

Faculty of Education, Yamaguchi University, Yamaguchi-city, Japan

The ideal of Japanese womanhood was created according to an educational ideology suited to a modern nation state. One regularly used concept was 'ryōsaikenbo', a mixed ideology, drawing together idealised images of the British lady and traditional Japanese women. Another imitated concept was Japanese athleticism called new *Bushidō* influenced by British boys' public school morality during the era of the Anglo-Japanese Alliance. However, there was a strong sense of Japanese cultural nationalism that grew in reaction to the threat of foreign enemies and the hardship of two wars, the Sino-Japanese War, 1894–1895, and the Russo-Japanese War, 1904–1905. This created a potential problem. Despite an occidental veneer, those new values were combined with traditional Japanese religion. Elizabeth Phillips Hughes' articles published in Japan during 1901 and 1902 reflect this process of inventing a tradition of both Japanese women's and men's ideal that was originally influenced by the values of the British middle class and the fact that early feminism was trapped within imperialistic ideology. Eventually, girls' physical exercises were recommended as long as they did not damage femininity. Less feminine sports took popular underground paths. Girls' physical exercises flourished after the First World War in Britain and the Second World War in Japan.

Introduction: Invented Tradition of Japanese Women's Athleticism

A new form of idealised Japanese women was created as part of the emerging educational ideology required to build a modern Japanese nation state during the late nineteenth and early twentieth centuries. British cultural forms were involved in this process. One regularly used concept was 'ryōsaikenbo', a mixed ideology, drawing together idealised images of the 'British Lady' and 'traditional' Japanese women. This term literally meant 'a good wife and wise mother', a great administrator at home, and was initially formed for educational purposes within girls' secondary education including girls' physical education. Despite an occidental veneer, the new values were combined with traditional Japanese religion.[1] This process was in parallel with the creation of the image of the ideal boy. The Japanese *bushi*-spirit, which was thought to be the long traditional chivalry of a Japanese ruling class (popularly the so-called samurai-spirit) in the feudal era, was reinterpreted and integrated into an indigenous Japanese 'athleticism' – this word was literally translated from 'the spirit of athletic world' expressed in a Japanese sporting journal with the English title *The Athletic World*. This phrase was thought to be a translation of 'athleticism' as it had the explanation that the spirit was originated from the characters of the people at British school. As it is well known, athleticism was strongly influenced by British public school morality closely associated with the games field.[2] Along with this nature, Japanese 'Undō no Seisin' (the spirit of the athletic world) meant 'athleticism' in the journal entitled *The Athletic World* as explained below:

Athleticism:

What made his character? At first, it is 'manliness' ... the second is 'pluck', invincible spirit, ... the third is 'fair play' ... the fourth is 'magnanimity', in other words, 'generosity' ... the fifth is 'order'.[3]

This article was based on the speech made by the President of Tokyo Imperial University, Dr Dairoku Kikuchi. Later, Kikuchi combined this character with the concept of the traditional Japanese moral code *Bushidō*. He described *Bushidō* as fair play, 'What is called fair play, means playing fair by a person with character in all competitions, which should be sought more widely in Japan. In other words, *Bushidō*, what I desire, signifies this'. He also used phrases such as 'British peoples' *Bushi*-like competition', 'Competition without cowardice', 'British *Bushi*-spirit appeared in Competition'.[4]

At this time imperialistic politics demanded that women's roles should fit the ideological needs of building the modern nation state. The emperor-centred Japanese Constitutional Monarchy and Parliamentary Democracy were attempting to adopt a more British model. But while British-veneered institutional frameworks were referred to in Japanese politics, this was accompanied by a strong sense of cultural nationalism which had been aroused in reaction to the threat of foreign enemies and the hardships of two wars, the Sino-Japanese War (1894–1895) and the Russo-Japanese War (1904–1905) at the turn of the century.[5] This created a potential problem. Therefore, British influence was concealed by the Japanese elite to make their people believe it was a traditional Japanese creation. Yet, in this period, Japanese political and ideological values shaped the philosophy of many educational institutions, which actively introduced British moral values, ethical standards and social beliefs. However, imported British moral codes were reinterpreted in order to allow the Japanese people to adjust to a mixture of British and traditional Japanese values during the period of the Anglo-Japanese Alliance (1902–1922). This was an 'invented tradition' as described and illustrated by the British historians, Eric Hobsbawm and Terence Ranger.[6]

Elizabeth Phillips Hughes' articles published in Japan during 1901 and 1902 reflect this process of an invented tradition of both Japanese women's and men's ideal originally influenced by the values of British middle class and the fact that early feminism was trapped into imperialistic strategy.

Elizabeth Phillips Hughes, 1851–1925

Elizabeth Phillips Hughes, 1851–1925, was born in the South Wales as a daughter of the Methodist family. Her brother was the President of the Methodist Conference in 1894 and her father was a doctor in Carmarthen, the son of a Methodist preacher. She broke away from the family tradition of Methodism, became a member of the Church of England and developed radical views and came to the notice of Miss Beale, principal of the Cheltenham Ladies' College. Her active public service later brought her 'The degree of LL.D'. (*honoris causa*) conferred on her by the University of Wales in 1920.[7]

Hughes visited Japan during 1901 and 1902 after retiring as the principal of the Cambridge Training College (CTC) for Women (later Hughes Hall). She gave lectures, taught English in various colleges and helped to promote teacher training during her stay in Japan for about 15 months from 1901 to 1902.[8] Although contemporary Japanese newspapers explain that she was trusted to investigate Japanese education by the British government for a year, her visit appears to have been motivated partly by a meeting with Tetsuko Yasui, a professor at Tokyo Women's Higher Normal School, who had studied at the CTC prior to her visit to Japan and partly by the research demands of educationalists linked to the British government.[9]

Hughes, a graduate of Newnham College at Cambridge, had been appointed principal of the newly created CTC for Women in 1885. She had earlier spent four years on the staff of Cheltenham Ladies' College, under Miss Dorothea Beale, headmistress of the College from 1858. The CTC was established as a Secondary Training College especially suited for the needs of university women who planned to teach in girls' secondary schools.[10] Although Hughes was not a specialist in the idea of physical exercises, her lectures on women's exercise appear to have reflected the ideals of influential pioneers during her early teaching in the Cheltenham Ladies' College in London. Miss Beale, headmistress of the college, had been an early pioneer of female education who influenced the general pattern of physical education in other schools. Miss Beale continued to encourage the callisthenic exercises included in the school's first prospectus and improved facilities, providing a large room for calisthenics in 1876, and abolished croquet, believing that it led girls to physical deformity and idleness. She also believed that competitive games were incompatible with girls' activities as they damaged essential feminine characters and enhanced masculinity.[11] However, in 1898, in the book entitled *Work and Play in Girls School*, co-authored by Beale and Jane Frances Dove, Headmistress of Wycombe Abbey School, a girls' boarding public school, she accepted Dove's idea that 'I think I do not speak too strongly when I say that games, i.e., active games in the open air, are essential to a healthy existence', and ' I have said that games are essential to a healthy existence; of course I mean that they are so under the circumstance of school life'.[12] Hughes was also influenced by another pioneer, Miss Frances Mary Buss, headmistress of the North London Collegiate School from 1850. Miss Buss encouraged the musical gymnastics of the American Diocletian Lewis (1823–1886) and equipped a gymnasium with a range of apparatus including a giant stride, parallel bars and a wall-mounted ladder. These pioneers' sensitivity to health helped to alleviate anxiety about the female constitution. It was Miss Buss's belief that 'the health of the pupils is the first consideration of this school'.[13]

The physical exercises of girls and women in Britain by the end of the 1890s varied with social class, education and early work experiences. These varied activities may be gathered into five principal types.

- Games played in the gardens of middle-class homes included tennis, ninepins, badminton, fives, battledore and shuttlecock. Working-class games were often played on the streets.
- Organised games played in the middle-class schools at game clubs and lunchtime might include hockey, netball and tennis, alongside other outdoor activities such as swimming, boating and climbing.[14]
- Games played by young adults at working-class factory clubs such as football followed an underground popular path, although more evidence for the prevalence of this game was after the First World War when munitions-factory clubs for women increased.[15]
- Gender-biased exclusive sports such as women's cricket had been first witnessed in the eighteenth century but declined in the nineteenth century except at elite schools such as girls' public boarding schools where the curriculum was almost identical to

boys' public schools. Some of the games pursued by girls at school were still inaccessible to most girls in the 1990s.[16]

- Physical education at schools in which callisthenics, Swedish exercises and musical gymnastics were taught with regular physical examinations by a qualified doctor who prescribed treatment by exercise to cure postural defects.[17] 'What is the right exercise for girls?' Physiology and psychology were used in answering that fundamental question.

Therefore, what Hughes introduced to Japan during her stay in Japan were those physical activities identical to the second and the last categories, which were encouraged in some British schools on the occasion of PE class, games clubs and other outdoor activities on Sports Day. Hughes regularly recommended them through her lectures given at Japanese educational institutes located both in urban and rural towns. Although her ideas were based on English educational objectives from the view of her position as an educationalist, it is worth considering the process of introducing them to Japanese society as both their transmission and reception were sensitive to the prevalent ideologies in Britain and Japan in the period between the Sino-Japanese War and the Russo-Japanese War.

The history of *Hugh's Hall 1885–1985* (1985) at Cambridge has material on Hughes but fails to acknowledge the importance of Hughes' connections with this process of creating this significant 'invented tradition'[18] in Japan. It states only that Hughes resigned from her post in the spring of 1899 on grounds of ill health, although she was still relatively young, at 47. She required rest on account of intensive works until then and 'it was in Japan that Miss Hughes was met with a warm welcome after she left Cambridge. She spent several months in Japan in 1901 and 1902, giving lectures, teaching English in various colleges and helping to promote teacher-training'.[19]

The Places and Influences Brought by Hughes

During 1901–1902 she visited more than 20 towns all across Japan including Kyūshū, Honshū and Hokkaidō islands as well as universities and educational societies in Tokyo. This provided her with an extremely wide influence throughout all Japan.[20]

For example, in the case of one local town, Yamaguchi, located in the far west of the main island, her lecture was presided over by the Educational Society of Yamaguchi on October 26, 1902 and the local ladies' society invited her to return the next day. At Yamaguchi School (now Yamaguchi University), according to a newspaper, about 500 primary school teachers and invited local notables assembled to listen to her lecture. She explained to the audience that, 'before the conclusion of the Anglo-Japanese Alliance, British people had been interested in Japan's educational system and I was trusted to investigate it by the government' ... 'Japan is now politically equal to Britain, therefore Japanese higher education for women should be firmly established', 'To equalize Japanese home education to the West, girls' education is necessary'. She criticised the old approaches to Japanese education which had been exclusively inclined to intellectual infusion and pointed out the need for active commitment to the practical field in terms of appropriate educational methodology. She also pointed out the issue of the deficiency of women's social activities and the need for scientific education at both school and home because an uneducated mother damaged the need for scientific school education. She discussed possible ways of adopting the newly introduced methods and put an emphasis upon the importance of the fusion of already-established useful ways and newly available concepts.[21]

Hughes's Lectures and Inspecting Activities in Tokyo

What was her main commitment to Japanese educational system during her stay? Hughes taught at Japan Women's University and advised the university founder, Jinzo Naruse. Naruse had studied abroad at Andover Theological Seminary and Clark University in Worcester, Massachusetts, and became a pioneer in the field of higher education for women in Japan. Japan Women's University was established in 1901. It was the same year when Hughes first came to the university on September 28, 1901, and was designated as professor at the university next year to teach 'English Life and Poems' for three months from April to July, 1902.[22]

According to *The Report of the Japanese Imperial Society of Education* issued on November 15, 1901, Hughes made a speech at the meeting of the *Japanese Imperial Society of Education* on October 12, 1901. *The Report* indicates the names of the invited notables to the meeting. They included the educationalists of the era, Chief of the Council of Higher Education, politicians of the House of Peers, professors of the university, the director of the Central Gymnastic Institute, Jigorō Kano, a founder of Kodōkan Judo, Tetsuko Yasui who had studied at the CTC, a professor of Tokyo Women's Higher Normal School and Umeko Tsuda who studied in the USA, a founder of Tsuda College in 61900. Hughes later gave a lecture at Tsuda College on November 30, 1901.[23] In particular, Kano, who was then President of Tokyo Higher Normal School, wrote a preface to a book entitled *Miss Hughes' Lectures on Her Teaching Methods* published on August 15, 1902. The content of the book was based on note-taking by the audience of her lectures that were given more than 10 times at Tokyo Higher Normal School, for about two hours a day, twice a week during February and March,1902.[24] These facts show that Hughes was accompanied by politically, educationally and culturally influential people and Japanese educationalists attempted to diffuse her idea into the general public in terms of translating it into Japanese as a printed matter. In practice, the contents of her articles published in Japan provide more details of her ideas and the intention of Japanese translators in which a required value of the era in both countries was reflected.

The Emerging Japanese Discourse of Women's Physicality and Tradition

Even though English and Japanese secondary sources minimise her contribution, close study of Japanese primary sources offers the possibility of a much more revisionist interpretation. Good sources were readily available. Many of her lectures given at Japanese educational institutions and societies were published in ladies' and educational journals immediately. For example, her 'Physical Exercise of Women I & II' and 'Modern British Ladies I & II' were published as articles of the journal entitled 'Women'.[25] Her lecture on 'The Methods of Gymnastics' organised by the Society for Japanese Physical Education (*Nihon Taiiku-kai*) on May 24, 1902 in Tokyo was published as an article of the journal *Physical Education*.[26] 'The Ethical Ideal of the English Public School Boy' was published as an article of the journal *Kokushi*, which meant *Japanese people who dedicated themselves to the Nation*.[27]

'Physical Exercise of Women I & II' (1901)

In 'Physical Exercise of Women I & II', Hughes insisted that physical education improved the physical component of motherhood as a national force and domestic administrator, coupling the modern value of sound recreations and outdoor activities with scientific knowledge based on physiology, psychology and ethical practices. She explained that politicians and social improvers were highly concerned about the importance of physical exercises. As shown previously with the five principal types of the physical exercises of girls and women in Britain by the end of the 1890s and what was introduced to Japan was included in the second and last categories. She classified gymnastics as the most important and, second, organised games and outdoor games such as boating and climbing as essential. She recommended the exercises as useful in developing physical harmony, fitness and agility as well as in fostering self-control, which brings a pleasant feeling in terms of pursuing recreations. In addition, she asserted that it brought psychological gains, improvement of accuracy, agility, imagination and attention in daily life. Therefore, 'active physical exercises for girls should not be restrained for the reason of their clothes … it is the matter that civilisation requires'. 'Physical exercises should be adopted at school with the scientific basis well-organized'. She made a particular point of recommending Swedish exercises from the view of physiology and psychology. She thought of them as the most proper exercises for physical education at school and distinguished them from other organised games such as women's basketball, hockey, cricket, tennis and outdoor activities such as rowing, riding horse and walking. She valued those games and outdoor activities because they reflected how much the daily exercises fostered ability, arguing that

> basketball fosters courage, cooperation and self-control, cricket has highly-educational purposes although high technique is required. Tennis requires it as well, although it brings less cooperation; rowing and riding-horse are recommendable, unless over-doing; walking is more appropriate if it were coupled with geology, botany or historical heritage-visits.

Cycling and mountaineering were also encouraged as a complete physical training for long distances.[28] In practice, Hughes herself exemplified the usefulness of mountaineering through climbing Mt Fuji and Mt Asama in Japan together with Tetsuko Yasui, a professor at Tokyo Women's Higher Normal School, who had studied at the CTC before Hughes came to Japan and gave her accommodations for her stay in Japan.[29] Before climbing Mt Fuji, Hughes and Yasui had climbed the Alps together during Yasui's time studying at the CTC from March 1897 to April 1900.[30]

'Modern British Ladies I & II' (1902)

Hughes's 'Modern British Ladies I & II' further supplements her idea of physical education, in this case from the view of the women's ideal. The article explains the tendency of increasing British women's responsibility, duty and rights during the previous 50 years as well as people's inclination both in Britain and Japan to preserve old customs and traditions. Considering these aspects, she advised Japanese people to maintain the merit of old customs and recommended ways of mixing old and new aspects effectively into Japanese characteristics. She also introduced her Japanese audiences and readers to an understanding of the important role of politically and educationally influential middle-class women in Britain. In particular, the significant purpose of physical exercise for women was emphasised again, mentioning tennis and cycling as activities which bought bravery, skill, cooperative mind, self-control and cultivated essential character as a woman fit for the required role of a 'queen-like' administrator at home. It was not surprising that Hughes's idea of the women's ideal and Japanese educational ideology of *ryōsaikenbo* were based on very similar ideas with respect to a concept of 'wise mother' who was to be a strong administrator and rational director at home. Therefore, it would be rather natural to consider it as an introduction from the same source. In practice, the mixed concept of *ryōsaikenbo* was firmly established during and after this period. This process also required scientific education at the nursery level. The difference pointed out by Hughes was the deficiency of social activities for Japanese women. Her way of suggesting the improvement was gentle as she appears to have been clever enough to understand her position as a diplomat as well as an investigator on the customs of Japanese society. She recommended a slow progress and moderate improvement. They were all appropriate to the Japanese approach to innovation.[31]

Whether her influence was effective or not, the fusion of new and old ideas, the mixture of western and eastern values, was seen conspicuously in and after this period in Japanese society. However, to make people believe in its Japanese origin was the most important political and educational task during the time when strong cultural nationalism arose under the Anglo-Japanese Alliance following the hardship of the two wars, the Sino-Japanese War and the Russo-Japanese War.

'On the Methods of Gymnastics (Taisōhō-ni-tsuite)' (1902)

Hughes's lecture on 'the Methods of Gymnastics' was organised by the Society for Japanese Physical Education (*Nihon Taiiku-kai*) on May 24, 1902 in Tokyo. It was published one month after the lecture as an article of the journal, *Physical Education*.[32] It was Hughes who first introduced the importance of Swedish exercises and encouraged the improvement of the clothes worn for girls' exercises.[33] According to the journal, she appears to have studied gymnastics, psychology, medicine, physiology and pedagogy in Germany, the USA and Sweden. She believed that Swedish exercises initiated by Pehr Henrik Ling (1776–1839) were 'the best gymnastics for all people of civilised countries in the twentieth century', and that it is 'proper for people of all ages and all ranks in both sexes ... teaching the right way of walking and sitting' and 'the order of the exercises are reasonable in view of physiology, stimulate their attentions and contribute to the education of our mind'.[34] Hughes added that 'German gymnastics are fit for the muscle training of soldiers but they lack elegance'.[35] In addition, she encouraged the improvement of clothing worn by girls to make exercise more easily accessible. After a few years, this was implemented. A leading educationalist, Miss Akuri (Aguri) Inokuchi (1870–1931) who was studying in New York in 1902, returned to Japan in 1903, later becoming a professor at Tokyo Women's Higher Normal School and introduced the bloomer style and Swedish exercises through her *Theory and Practice of Physical Education* published by the Japanese Investigation Committee for Gymnastics and Games in 1905.[36] Both were based on the same idea.

'The Ethical Ideal of the English Public School Boy' (1902)

'The Ethical Ideal of the English Public School Boy' was written by Hughes and published as an article of the journal, *Kokushi: Japanese people who dedicated themselves to the Nation* (No. 41 and 42, 1902) in the same year. This article indicates that her lectures were not only restricted to the topics of women's education, but also introduced a wider knowledge of the purposes of British middle class including boys' ideal that was suitable for the Japanese elites. This fact is more important in understanding 'what was introduced by Hughes' and 'what was accepted as women's education' in the era of the imperialistic political alliances of the two countries. This article suggests that, although Japanese girls' education was influenced by the ideal of the British Lady, it should be comprehended as a part of a pair of concepts significantly constructed as values of the British middle class. Her lecture explained that British middle-class ideology was composed of both the ideal types of men and women which were linked with each other through imperialism. What was essential education for boys who were to become future administrators of the Great British Empire? As was well known, men's character was imbued by simple manliness influenced by athleticism associated with the game field, while women's ideal was based on the concept of 'a queen at home'. Together these ideals provided the basis for building a strong modern nation state and imperialistic strategy. This structure was to become more intelligible when Japanese society attempted to imitate the British educational moral code, so as to copy the strong British Empire and try to exceed all foreign countries by establishing political educational institutions in order to create a much stronger Japanese Empire.

Hughes's lecture on 'the English Public School Boys' is worth considering from this point of view. In practice, Hughes referred to boys' education required for the British Empire and said that boys 'grown up into the manhood in the atmosphere of public school' to become the statesmen 'who have governed India and the British colonies ... the literary men who have made her literature, and her greatest military commanders'. She was a leading educationalist who contributed her life to establishing higher female education. On the other hand, she could not escape from the ideology of imperialism, the dominant idea of the era. The extent to which Hughes had internalised the ideology of British imperialism is made explicit in much of her writing as, for example, in the passage below:

> This class of school has for centuries educated a very large proportion of them who have made English history. The statesmen who have governed India and the British colonies, the politicians who have made the laws of England, and the judges who have administered them, the literary men who have made her literature, and her greatest military commanders, have as a rule grown up into manhood in the atmosphere of her big Public Schools.[37]

In addition, Hughes mentioned ethical criteria for boys' education. She said, 'Character', 'the strongest esprit de corps', 'a passionate and permanent devotion for their old school' and 'sacrifice' with 'no pride in his worldly prosperity' were so fundamental that the English school boy became a man who pursued things according to his ethical creed:

> Character is valued by the English school boy as far beyond knowledge or even learning. This can be clearly illustrated. The strongest esprit de corps exists and the pupils feel a passionate and permanent devotion for their old school, while the old school feels the great interest and pride in the prosperity and success of its old pupils. But if fame be won by a sacrifice of principle, by dishonour and corruption, then the old school will feel the shame of the ignoble character of its former pupil, and have no pride in his worldly prosperity.[38]

She also stressed three dominant virtues: 'truth' as the sign of a gentleman; 'a proper regard for the weak and helpless' as the feeling of responsibility, the great moral safeguard of England; the third was 'physical endurance and courage' which were contrary to being 'a coward' or 'a sneak'.[39] Thus, she explained the ethical ideal of English gentlemen. These were the personal characteristics so often repeated by later historians in explaining the role of the British moral code which functioned to aid the integration of a ruling class.[40]

British Men's Athleticism Linked to Japanese *Bushidō*

Early feminism was unconsciously trapped into probable imperialistic strategy as long as what Hughes' articles provided was relevant as well. In particular, her 'Ethical Ideal of the English Public School Boy' (1902) provides the boys' ideal as a pair ideology of the ideal womanhood along with her other articles such as 'Physical Exercise of Women I & II' (1901) and 'Modern British Ladies I & II' (1902). As it is well known, the concept of 'muscular Christianity' has propelled a social hierarchy as an imperialistic strategy of a ruling class in terms of the elite schools' educational concept and the influence of health education. It embraced the reason why the middle class must have sought it, linked with an idea of emerging social Darwinism.[41] This has not been fully considered as the former studies were inclined to focus on innovative aspects rather than the conventional feminine type and illustrate the difference from men's character. However, Hughes articles clearly reflect commonalities in both British and Japanese imperialism which influenced educational principle in both sexes during the era when the Anglo-Japanese Alliance concluded in 1902. Moreover, the following was the most important part of her assertion which made a link to the similarities to the Japanese traditional ideal: she continued that 'Mr. Nitobe, in his book on *Bushidō*, mentions correctly that there is very much in common between the "honour" of the Samurai, and the "honour" of the English Public School boy' and the Japanese traditional ideal. The year 1902 was the period just after Inazō Nitobe's influential book, *Bushidō: The Soul of Japan*, was published in English (Philadelphia in 1900), which later impressed President Theodore Roosevelt into 'distributing several dozens of copies among his friends'.[42] Nitobe had studied at Johns Hopkins University in Baltimore, Maryland. While in Baltimore, he became a member of the Religious Society of Friends (Quakers) and married an American woman, Mary Patterson Elkinton.[43] In addition, his *Bushidō* was not a recovery of *Bushidō* as a Japanese long tradition, but rather a modern version of principles of Japanese men's ideal invented by Nitobe who was more familiar with western religion and sciences. However, his idea became increasingly influential among the Japanese elite. For example, in 1908, six years after Hughes's visit to Japan, Dr Tairoku Kikuchi, President of the University of Tokyo, wrote an article with headings of '*Bushidō* in Competitions', 'British peoples' *Bushi*-like competition', 'Competition without cowardice', 'British *Bushi*-spirit appeared in Competition', 'British Students' Manly Spirit', 'Brilliant *Bushidō* was accomplished through competitions', with an advertisement for Nitobe's preface for Kohō Yamagata's *New Bushidō* (Tokyo: Jitsu-gyo-no-Nihonsha,1908) at the corner of his column, when Nitobe's *Bushidō* was also translated into Japanese in the same year 1908.[44] The similarity is never a casual coincidence as, in practice, a feminist of the era, Hughes herself diffused the idea: 'There are of course important virtues ignored in this school boy's ideal, but his simple creed is sound as far as it goes and his three virtues are necessary elements in any really civilized society'. [45] This was obviously the elements of the values diffused through and beyond the British Empire and imitated in early Japanese elite schools such as former bodies of The University of Tokyo.[46] Therefore, it was the era the new *Bushidō* started to become an invented tradition of men's education and women's ideal, '*ryōsaikenbo*, a good wife and wise mother', influenced by ideals of the British ladies and gentlemen. This shows that a modern nation state was attempting to prepare itself in terms of education, drawing on idealised concepts of boys and girls which were needed for imperial Japanese politics relating to the middle-class ethos in England. In other words, both the masculinity for boys and physical exercises encouraged for girls were associated with an imperialistic ideology understood as an educational principle which produced the future administrators to drive the intentional expansion of the British and the Japanese empires.

'*The Russo-Japanese War and Development of Japanese People' (1905)*

What happened soon after her return to Britain? Hughes contributed an article entitled 'The Russo-Japanese War and Development of Japanese People' to a Japanese weekly home journal, *Katei Shūhō*, issued by the alumni association of Nihon Women's University in 1905.[47] This article reflected the results of her investigation during her stay in Japan, her idea of the respectable characteristics of Japanese women and her suggestions to shape their prosperous future, associated with the increasing occupational participation of British women in manufacturing factory labour in the early twentieth century:

> In the situation of exhausted national resources brought by the war, all Japanese people need to engage in producing national wealth. Women and even children will not be able to escape from participating in the required manufacturing labour work force, in particular, for silk and silk fabrics. In this climate, this industry will be increasingly developed as the wage paid for workers in lower living standards is not high. Not to mention, the manufacturing industry will be further progressed.

> … Homes would become in essence factories, and as a home produces more products, factory-made products are finally able to be exported overseas. When society encourages more manufacturing labour at home and this way of procuring finances is more exploited, it contributes to advancing interests brought by the war. Although women have not been directly engaged in the force of arms during the war, why don't they contribute themselves to industrious battles with foreign countries? I believe that Japan will conquer many civilized countries in the battles of producing the industrial arts as well.

> … In conclusion, ladies should foster various faculties in terms of learning, interest in all disciplines to be wise and agile enough to enjoy every aspect of society. I wish my dearest Japanese ladies' success as they prepare to endeavour for this great important purpose and be sure to succeed at it in practice in the future.[48]

As well known, it was the year 1905 when western people were astonished by Japan's unexpected victory against Russia – this marked the first time in the modern era that an eastern power defeated the west militarily – after the recently agreed-upon Anglo-Japanese Alliance. Hughes appraised the development of Japanese women's industrial commitments and encouraged their further contributions to compensate for the national resources exhausted after the war. However, the promotion of women's vocational participation and encouragement of physical exercises for women had limitations. It was not a perfect emancipation from the subordination of men's dominance. Women's sound body was recommended towards the power of the empire as a healthy mother for a warrior and a clever wife administrating the home would benefit the empire and national wealth. Her idea was venerably adopted in the context of a receptive country of the allied Japanese empire. After the war, gender issues looked as if they were changing from early feminism, *ryōsaikenbo* to a next stage as long as women were involved with factory labour. However, their occupational participation had the destiny to lose the meaning of women's independence and implicate with the principles of the forthcoming fascism which encouraged the mobilisation of labour and proliferation for the national strengths. Eventually, it was conservatively replaced by maternal feminism.[49]

Concluding Remarks

Overall, Hughes' articles concerning Japanese society show the need of an integrated history in order to make world history more intelligible. Hughes's visit to Japan was a part of British history at the turn of the century and the influential part of the conflicting era of Japanese history during the political alliance between Britain and Japan. However, analysing the structure of cultural fusion created by the impact of her lectures has been difficult. Previously it has been interpreted one-sidedly in the context of Japanese educational history. For example, in the ways that Japanese notables and educationalists were involved with the construction of Japanese higher education. In practice, former studies on Hughes were mostly attempted by Japanese educational histories. They have lacked the wider international cultural context to comprehend the coincidences with more global commonalities beyond the framework of their country's history, not mere comparative studies between the UK and Japan, but to illustrate agents of change, an understanding of a history at the turn of the century and a history of the 1900s. Combining British history with Japanese contexts through Hughes's visit to Japan, it becomes much clear that her visit provided not just a case study of gender history between Britain and Japan, but an important part of the way a modern nation state was attempting to prepare itself in terms of education, drawing on idealised concepts of boys and girls which were needed for imperial Japanese politics relating to the middle-class ethos in England. In other words, it shows that the British political culture in a wide sense was not only adopted in integrating the British nation, but was diffused, adopted and adapted well beyond the British colonies. In addition, the structure of fusion was completely different from the other areas of the British colonies in Asia. In the case of Japan, more intelligently, the evidence of such an imperialistic intervention was soon obscured by Japanese cultural nationalism during the process of importing western values. The concept of women's ideal, Japanese 'rōsaikenbo' borrowed from the ideal of a 'British lady' and integrated into Confucianism, and 'simple manliness' influenced by British athleticism in the game field and reinterpreted as Japanese spirit of a new *Bushido* reinforced the structure of the fusion of western and Japanese values. As with other intellectuals of her period, Hughes referred to Mr Nitobe's *bushidō* and accentuated its commonalities of men's and women's ideal types both in Britain and Japan. Thus, Japanese people accomplished the mixture of western culture without losing their pride as a nation, and culturally mixed sense of modernisation contributed to fasten the establishment of a modern nation state and further secured their realm of the Japanese Empire.

In gender studies, notions of masculine and feminine types are inclined to focus on the difference between them. However, this study shows that both were affected by imperialistic ideology. Early feminism which made it possible to establish secondary education for girls should be carefully discerned. In particular, gymnastics in PE classes and games at school were recommended as long as they did not damage the femininity of girls who were encouraged to be healthy middle-class women to be mothers to foster future elite administrators for the British Empire and the Japanese Empire. Another discovery was the complicate construct of the cultural fusion in which cultural nationalism was linked to and eventually obscured the western origin. There were women who wanted less feminine sports and pursued these sports through a popular underground path. They flourished after the First World War in Britain, and the Second World War in Japan, which will be another important story to be continued and explored by more studies.

Notes

1. Ikeda, "'*Ryōsai-kembo*'," 539–40.
2. The concept of 'athleticism' is well known among sport historians all over the world in terms of the following influential studies. Mangan, *Athleticism*; Mangan, *The Games Ethic*; and Mangan, "Social Darwinism." In addition, Allen Guttmann and Lee Thompson pointed out the diffusion of British 'athleticism' into the Japanese society. Guttmann and Thompson, *Japanese Sports*, 81.

3. *The Athletic World 3*, no. 2, February 1899, np. The article of 'Undō no Seisin' (Athleticism) was introduced as a speech of Dairoku Kikuchi. Kikuchi, "Undō no Seisin' (Athleticism)."
4. Kikuchi, "Kyōsō-jō-niokeru-Bushidō."
5. Fukaya, *Ryōsai-kembo-shugi-no-kyō-iku*, 11.
6. The term 'invented tradition' is based on the explanation by Eric Hobsbawm. Hobsbawm, "Introduction: Inventing Traditions," 1–14.
7. Bottrall, *Hugh's Hall 1885–1985*, 29–30.
8. Ibid., 33–4; and Ōno, "E. P. Hughes in Japan (1901–1902)," *passim*, in particular, 340.
9. *Bo-cho-shinbun* (local newspaper), Yamaguchi, on October 28, 1902; Aoyama, *Collected Issue*, 53; and Ōno, "E. P. Hughes in Japan (1901–1902)," 323.
10. Bottrall, *Hugh's Hall 1885–1985*, 4, 30.
11. Hargreaves, *Sporting Females*, 63.
12. Dove, "Section III. Cultivation of the Body," 398.
13. Hargreaves, *Sporting Females*, 64.
14. Ibid.
15. Williams, *A Game for Rough Girls?*, 4.
16. As Jennifer Hargreaves remarks, 'middle-class girls were now able to participate in forms of exercise which would have been unimaginable for them only a few decades before, and which were still inaccessible to most girls in British society'. Hargreaves, *Sporting Females*, 64.
17. Ibid., 64–5.
18. Hobsbawm, "Introduction: Inventing Traditions," 1–14.
19. Bottrall, *Hugh's Hall 1885–1985*, 28, 33–4.
20. She visited Japanese towns such as Nagoya, Kanazawa, Kyoto, Kobe, Tottori, Chiba, Fukushima, Sendai, Hokkaido, Matsumoto, Wakayama, Himeji, Okayama, Hiroshima, Yamaguchi, Fukuoka, Kumamoto, Kagoshima, Nagasaki, Saga and Kokura. Ōno, "E. P. Hughes in Japan (1901–1902)."
21. Bo-cho-shinbun, October 28, 1902.
22. Ōno, "E. P. Hughes in Japan (1901–1902)," 327, 335.
23. Ibid., 329.
24. Kimura, "Misu-Hūsu-niyoru-Suwedenn-shiki-Taiso-no-Susume," 4.
25. Hughes, "Physical Exercise of Women I"; "Physical Exercise of Women II"; and Hughes, "Modern British Ladies I"; "Modern British Ladies II."
26. Hughes, "A Translation of Her Lecture, 'Taisōhō-ni-tsuite'."
27. Hughes, "The Ethical Ideal," 6–9; and Hughes, "A Japanese Translation of 'The Ethical Ideal'," 4–7.
28. Hughes, "Physical Exercise of Women I."; and Hughes, "Physical Exercise of Women II."
29. Yasui, "Natsukashii-Jū-nenn-maeno-Natsu,"; Aoyama, *Collected Issue*, 45–6; Ōno, "E. P. Hughes in Japan (1901–1902)," 329, 337–9; and Shibanuma, *Jurisconsultus*, issued by The Institute of Law at Kanto Gakuin University, no.21, (2012), 135–7, 140.
30. Yasui, "Arupusu-tozann-no Tsuikai,"; and Shibanuma, *Jurisconsultus*.
31. Hughes, "Modern British Ladies I."; and Hughes, "Modern British Ladies II."
32. Hughes, "A Translation of Her Lecture, 'Taisōhō-ni-tsuite'."
33. Kimura, "Misu-Hūsu-niyoru-Suwedenn-shiki-Taiso-no-Susume,", *passim*.
34. Hughes, "Taisōhō-ni-tsuite."
35. Ibid., 2.
36. Inokuchi, *Taiiku-no-riron-oyobi-jissai*, 403–4; and Ikeda, "'Ryōsai-kembo'," 541.
37. Hughes, "The Ethical Ideal," 4. cf. Hughes, "A Japanese Translation of "The Ethical Ideal'," 6–7.
38. Hughes, "The Ethical Ideal," 4–5. cf. "A Japanese Translation of 'The Ethical Ideal'," 7.
39. Hughes, "The Ethical Ideal," 5–6; cf. "A Japanese Translation of "The Ethical Ideal'," 8–9.
40. Mangan, *Athleticism, passim*; Mangan, *The Games Ethic, passim*; Mangan, "Social Darwinism"; and Holt, *Sport and the British*, in particular, Chap. 2. "Amateurism and the Victorians" and Chap. 4 "Empire and Nation".
41. Abe, "Muscular Christianity,"132.
42. The first edition was published in Philadelphia in 1900. Nitobe wrote the preface in "Malvern, Pa., Twelfth Month, 1899" (Inazo Nitobé, *Bushido: The Soul of Japan*. "Author's preface to the tenth and revised edition" for 1905, in revised and enlarged 13th edition).

43. Ibid. (the preface for the first edition in 13th edition and "Author's preface to the tenth and revised edition" for 1905); Cf. Abstract in an Inventory of the Inazo Nitobe Papers.
44. Nitobé's *Bushidō* was translated into Japanese by Ōson Sakurai (Nitobé, *Bushidō*,). Nitobe wrote a preface for Yamagata's *New Bushidō*. Kikuchi, "Kyōsō-jō-niokeru-Bushidō."
45. Hughes, "The Ethical Ideal," 7; cf. "A Japanese Translation of 'The Ethical Ideal'," 9.
46. Abe and Mangan, "'Sportsmanship' – English Inspiration," 100–2; and Takahashi, *Rondon-kara-kita-Spōtsu-no-Dendōshi, passim.*
47. Hughes, "The Russo-Japanese War," 6.
48. Ibid.
49. Ikeda, "'*Ryōsai-kembo*'," 545–8.

References

Abe, Ikuo. "Muscular Christianity and Formation of the Concept of Modern Sportsmanship in the Case Study of Charles Kingsley." In *Taiiku-shi-no-Tankyū* [Exploring the study for the history of physical education], edited by The Editorial Board for the Commemoration of Retirement of Professor Yūzō Kishino, 117–140. Sakura-mura: Publishing Board of University of Tsukuba, 1982.

Abe, Ikuo, and J. A. Mangan. "'Sportsmanship' – English Inspiration and Japanese Response: F.W. Strange and Chiyosaburo Takeda." *The International Journal of the History of Sport* 19, nos 2–3 (2002): 99–128.

An Inventory of the Inazo Nitobe Papers, 1890–1991. Swarthmore, PA: Friends Historical Library of Swarthmore College. http://www.swarthmore.edu/library/friends/ead/5107nito.xml

Aoyama, Nao. *Collected Issue of Nao Aoyama's Works Volume 3: Yasui Tetsu-to-Tokyo-Joshi-Daigaku* [Tetsuko Yasui & Tokyo Women's University]. Tokyo: Keiō Tsūshin, 1982.

Bottrall, Margaret. *Hugh's Hall 1885–1985.* Cambridge: Rutherford, 1985.

Dove, Jane Frances, "Section III. Cultivation of the Body." In *Work and Play in Girls Schools*, edited by Dorothea Beale, Lucy H. M. Soulsby, and Jane Frances Dove. London, New York, and Bombay: Longmans, Green, and Co., 1898, in: edited and introduced by Kagawa, Setsuko, *Women's Body, Health and Physical Education in Nineteenth to Early Twentieth-Century Britain*, Vol. 4, 396–423. Kyoto: Eureka Press, 2011.

Fukaya, Masahi. *Ryōsai-kembo-shugi-no-kyō-iku* [Education based on the principle of Ryōsai-kembo]. Nagoya: Reimei Shobo, [1965] 1990.

Guttmann, Allen, and Lee Thompson. *Japanese Sports: A History.* Honolulu: University of Hawaii Press, 2001.

Hargreaves, Jennifer. *Sporting Females: Critical Issues in the History and Sociology of Women's Sports.* London: Routledge, 1994.

Hobsbawm, Eric. "Introduction: Inventing Traditions." In *The Invention of Tradition*, edited by Eric Hobsbawm and Terence Ranger, 1–14. Cambridge: Cambridge University Press, 1983.

Holt, Richard. *Sport and the British: A Modern History.* Oxford: Oxford University Press, 1989.

Hughes, E. P., "A Translation of Her Lecture, 'Taisōhō-ni-tsuite' (On the Methods of Gymnastics)." Presented at the meeting for Nihon Taiiku-kai (Society of Japanese Physical Education), May 24, 1902, Tokyo, Japan, *Taiiku* (*Physical Education*), no. 103, Dōbunkan, Tokyo, June 25, 1902, 1–10.

Hughes, E. P. "Modern British Ladies I." *Onna [Women]* 2, no. 2 (1902): 10–17.

Hughes, E. P. "Modern British Ladies II." *Onna [Women]* 2, no. 3 (1902): 24–29.

Hughes, E. P. "Physical Exercise of Women I." *Onna [Women]* 1, no. 10 (1901): 1–8.

Hughes, E. P. "Physical Exercise of Women II." *Onna [Women]* 1, no. 11 (1901): 1–6.

Hughes, E. P. "The Ethical Ideal of the English Public School Boy." *Kokushi [Japanese people who dedicated themselves to the Nation]* 5, no. 41 (1902): 4–7.

Hughes, E. P. "A Japanese Translation of 'The Ethical Ideal of the English Public School Boy'." *Kokushi [Japanese people who dedicated themselves to the nation]* 5, no. 42 (1902): 6–9.

Hughes, E. P. "The Russo-Japanese War and Development of Japanese People." *Katei Shūhō [Weekly Journal of Home]*, no. 23 (1905): 6.

Ikeda, Keiko. "'*Ryōsai-kembo*', 'Liberal Education' and Maternal Feminism under Fascism: Women and Sports in Modern Japan." *The International Journal of the History of Sport* 27, no. 3 (2010): 537–552.

Inokuchi, Akuiri. *Taiiku-no-riron-oyobi-jissai* [Theory and practice of physical education]. Tokyo: Kokkō, 1906.

Kikuchi, Dairoku. "Kyōsō-jō-niokeru-Bushidō [*Bushidō* in competitions]." *The Japanese Trade Journal [Jitsugyo-no-nihon]*, nos. 11–12 (June 15, 1908): 20–22.

Kikuchi, Dairoku. "'Undō no Seisin' [Athleticism]." introduced as a speech of Dairoku Kikuchi, *The Athletic World* 3, no. 2, Tokyo: Kōbundō, February (1899), 1–3.

Kimura, Kichiji. "Misu-Hūsu-niyoru-Suwedenn-shiki-Taiso-no-Susume [Swedish exercises recommended by E.P. Hughes]." *Chukyo Taiikugaku-ronsō [Research journal of physical education by Chukyo University]* 14 (1973): 1–19.

Mangan, J. A. *Athleticism in the Victorian and Edwardian Public School: The Emergence and Consolidation of an Educational Ideology.* Cambridge: Cambridge University Press, 1981.

Mangan, J. A. "Social Darwinism and Upper-Class Education in Late Victorian and Edwardian England." In *Manliness and Morality: Middle-Class Masculinity in Britain and America, 1800–1940*, edited by J. A. Mangan and James Walvin, 135–159. Manchester: Manchester University Press, 1987.

Mangan, J. A. *The Games Ethic and Imperialism: Aspects of the Diffusion of an Ideal.* Harmondsworth: Viking/Penguin Books, 1986.

Nitobé, Inazo. *Bushido: The Soul of Japan*, Revised and Enlarged 13th ed. Philadelphia, PA: The Leeds and Biddle, 1908.

Nitobé, Inazo. *Bushido* [Japanese Translation by Ōson Sakurai]. Tokyo: Tcibi, 1908.

Ōno, Nobutane. "E. P. Hughes in Japan (1901–1902)." *The Annual Collection of Essays and Studies, Faculty of Letters, Gakushuin University*, no. 36 (1989): 323–346.

Shibanuma, Akiko. *Jurisconsultus*, issued by The Institute of Law at Kanto Gakuin University, no. 21 (2012): 135–149.

Takahashi, Kozō. *Rondon-kara-kita-Spōtsu-no-Dendōshi [A great missionary of modern sports from London: F.W. Strange].* Tokyo: Shogakukan, 2012.

Williams, Jean. *A Game for Rough Girls? A History of Women's Football in England.* London: Routledge, 2003.

Yamagata, Kohō. *New Bushido.* Tokyo: Jitsugyo-no-Nihonsha, 1908.

Yasui, Tetsuko. "Arupusu-tozann-no Tsuikai [The memory of climbing the Alps]." *Shin-jo-kai [New women's world]* 1, no. 5 (August 1, 1909): 4–8.

Yasui, Tetsuko. "Natsukashii-Jū-nenn-maeno-Natsu [Old summer ten years ago]." *Shin-jo-kai [New women's world]* 3, no. 8 (August 1, 1911): 42–45.

Index

Abdurahman, Dr. Ishmael 38
Abrahams, Dan J. 43
Absentee Property Owners Law (1950) 12
Adhikari, Mohamed 38
aesthetic surgery and the self 65–6
Afrikaanse Nasionale Bond (Afrikaans
    National Organisation) 38
Alexander, Morris 39
Alexander Cup Sports Competition 39, 40
All Africa People's Conference, 1958 2
Allied Travel Commission of NATO 24
AMA (American Medical Association) 54, 56
American Physical Education Association, the
    54, 55
ANC, the 11
Anderson, Ada 81
Andrianov, Konstantin 27
Anentia, Arere 39
Anglo-Japanese Alliance (1902–1922) 95, 97,
    103
anti-apartheid boycott movement 1–2, 4–7, 11
anti-racism campaigns of UEFA 14
APA (American Physiotherapy Association),
    the 57, 58, 59, 60
apartheid definition 2, 12, 17
APO (African People's Organisation) 42
APTA (American Physical Therapy
    Association) 51–2, 54, 60n2
Archives of Physical Medicine (journal) 60
Armaindo, Louise 81
Asian Games, the 26
athletic lean body, the 65–6, 69–71, 72–3,
    75n55
Athletic World, The (journal) 94–5
Athlone School Sports Union 40
Atlantic Constitution (newspaper) 87

Bandung conference, the 26, 29
Banting, William 70
BDS (Campaign for Boycott, Divestment and
    Sanctions) 2, 11–18
Beale, Dorothea 95, 96
Beck, Dorothea 56
Berdan, Mollie 83

Bette, Karl-Heinz 66
Biebler, Rosetta 84
Bitong, Ernesto T. 30–1
body and meanings attached to it, the 66
bodybuilding 68
body discipline 72
body fat 66–7, 69, 72, 74n40
body weight ideals 70, 72
Boston Normal School of Gymnastics, the 53,
    55
Bourdieu, Pierre 79, 89
Bouve, Marjorie 55
Boycott Movement Committee 2
boycotts in sport 1–2, 4–5
Braun, Frank 4
Brazilian participation in GANEFO 31
Brigitte (magazine) 72
British idea of the respectable characteristics of
    Japanese women 103
British imperialism as ideology 101, 102, 104
British influence in Japanese institutional
    frameworks 95, 97–104
British physical sports introduced to Japan as
    an 'invented tradition' 96, 97–100
Broca, Paul 70
Brumbach, Katharina (Sandwina) 81
Brundage, Avery 24
Brutus, Dennis 39
BSPE (Boston School of Physical Education)
    55
bulimia 72
Bushido 95, 102, 104
Bushido: The Soul of Japan (book) 102
bushi-spirit of the Japanese feudal era 94–5
Buss, Frances Mary 96
Butler, Judith 85

Caldecott, A.F. 38–9
Cape Corps Gifts and Comforts Fund 40
Carlos, John 23
CDTU (Cape and District Tennis Union), the
    43–4
Chakrabarty, Dipesh 30
Cheltenham Ladies College 95, 96

Chen Yi 30
Chicago Daily World (newspaper) 25
childhood obesity 65
China Sport (magazine) 26
Chinese support for GANEFO 21–2, 23–7, 28–32
CIA, the 29
Cincinnati Enquirer (newspaper) 88
civil campaign groups against apartheid 6
Clark's Club Theatre, Philadelphia 88
Cold War anxieties and GANEFO 26–7, 30
collaborationsit politics by South African Whites 44
'colonization' charge against Israeli actions in Palestine 12
Coloured Primary School Union of the Transvaal 38
Commonwealth Games Association 8
communism and the non-aligned movement 27
Connolly, Chris 24
constructive engagement with South Africa by the UK, Australia and New Zealand 5–6
Corbett, Jim 86, 88
Corbusier, Harold 56
corset, the 67
crank handle ergometer, the 71
cricket as favoured sport at South African mission schools 39, 40
cricket tours to South Africa 4, 6, 9
CSRU (City and Suburban Rugby Union) 42
CSU (Central School Sports Union) 37–8, 40–1, 42–3, 44, 45
CTC (Cambridge Training College) 95, 96
cultural boycotts in sport 10–11
cultural nationalism in Japan 95, 104
Currie Cup, the 9

Daly, Daisy 83
Die Hausfrau (The Housewife, magazine) 67
Diener, Bertha Eckstein 75n55
diet and sport 71–2
D'Olivera, Basil 4
Doman, E.J. (Ned) 43–4
dominoes in South Africa 44
Douglas, Bob 87
Dove, Jane Frances 96
Dudley, Richard 39, 42
Dudley, Samuel 43
dumb-bell training for women 72
Duncan, O. 71
Dyreson, Mark 25–6

Eastern bloc and Third World influence in sporting bodies 4, 5, 7
Educational Society of Yamaguchi 97
Edwards, Carrie 88
EJ (Educational Journal) 39, 41, 46n43
embargoes 8, 10

English public school boy and Bushido 102
'entraînment' 71–2
Epstein, Cynthia Fuchs 54
ergometry and clinical diagnostic research 70–1, 74n44
Ethical Ideal of the English Public School Boy (article) 100–1
EU, the 65
Eugenie, Elizabeth Amalie 72
exercise as therapy for the injured 54
exhibition shows by female boxers 88–9

Fataar, Allie 43
February, Victor 42
female body idealizations 67, 72
female cycling 81
female pugilist challenges to men 86–7
FIFA 15
Fischer-Dückelmanns, Anna 72
Floss, John G. 84, 91n42
football as integrative enclave in Israel 17 *see also* Israel 2013 UEFA Under-21 championships boycott
Foster, William Trufant 57
Foucault, Michel 66
Fox, Richard K. 82
Freeman, Gussie 85, 89
Friendship Games, the 9

Galveston Daily News (newspaper) 88
GANEFO (Games of the New Emerging Forces) 8–9, 21, 22–5, 26–7, 30–2; implications of rift with IOC 25–6, 30; and Sino-Soviet tensions 27, 28–30, 31
Garconne-type female body, the 67
gender arrangements in nineteeth century US society 79–80, 89
gender segregation in science 54
gender studies and imperialism 104
geopolitical Second World role of China 22
German Gymnastics 68, 100
Gibson, Charles Dana 87
'Gibson Girls,' the 87
Gitersos, Terry 24
global sports system and South African sports boycott 6–7
Golding, George 43, 44, 48n107
Goldstein, Michael 53
Goldstone, Leonard 60
governing bodies in sport for each racial group 5
Green, Rev. Arthur 42
Group Areas Act (1950, South Africa) 3
GutsMuths, Johann Christoph Friedrich 74n40

Handbook of Cycling (book) 71
Harland, Rose 82
Harry Hill's Exchange 82, 83

HART: NZAAM 6
Henschen 74–5n45
Heywood, Rev. C.R. 41
Hickey, William 78
Hill, Harry 82
Hippocrates 52
Hobsbawm, Eric 95
Homans, Amy Morris 53
Howa, Hassan 4
Hughes, Elizabeth Phillips 95–6, 97–104
Hutchinson, John 70

IFA (Israeli Football Association), the 15, 16
IFs (international federations) 9, 24
illicit massage practices 57–9, 60
implications of an Olympic rift between the
    IOC and GANEFO 25–6, 30
Inazo Nitobe 102, 104
Indonesia and use of sport as a political tool 23,
    24, 25, 30, 31
Indonesian conference and the GANEFO
    project 22
industrialisation 68–9, 74n30
Ingram, Fred 39
Inokuchi Akuri 100
International Court of Justice, the 2
international sport as a monopoly 8, 9
Intifada, the 13
'invented tradition' of British sports as native
    Japanese origin 97, 100
IOC, the 4, 5, 9; and GANEFO 22, 24, 26, 28, 29
IRB (International Rugby Board) 6
Islamic football league in Israel 17
Israel 2013 UEFA Under-21 championships
    boycott 2, 11, 12, 13–16
Israeli actions in the Gaza Strip 11–12
Israeli Defence Force, the 13

Japanese Imperial Society of Education 98
Japanese veneer of its institutions 95
Japan Women's University 98
Jennings, Alice 83, 88
Jeux d'Afrique (1965) 24
Jones, Griffith 59
Josef, Franz, Emperor 72
Joyner, Safrona 58–9

Kano Jigoro 98
Kay, Johnnie 41
Keino, Kipchoge 39
Kelly, Libby 83
Khama, Seretse 39
Kies, Benjamin 43
Kikuchi Dr. Dairoku 95, 102
Kinesiology and Physical Therapy 51–2

Lambrechts, N.E. 42
Leary, Alice 83–4

lectures of Elizabeth Phillips Hughes in Japan
    98–101
legislative impacts on South African sport 3–4
Lenin Club, the 42
Leslie, Hattie 83–5
Leslie, John 85
Lewis, Annie 88
Lewis, Jessie 83
LGBT call to boycott the Sochi Olympics 16
Ling, Per Henrik 52, 100
Little, Gilbert Samuel 43
Liu Shaoqi 25
Los Angeles massage parlours 58–9
Los Angeles Times, The (newspaper) 58, 59
Lyman, David 59

male body idealizations 67–8, 70
malleability of muscle structure, the 70
Manuel, George (Uncle Jim) 41, 42
Massage and the Original Swedish Movements
    (book) 59
McAuliffe, Jack 86–7
MCC (English) cricket team tour of South
    Africa 4
McCurdy, James Huff 54
McKenzie, R. Tait 54, 56
media coverage of GANEFO 28–9, 30–1
medicine and physical education 53
middle-class standards of femininity 80, 90
mirror as instrument for self-assessment, the 69
Miss Hughes' Lectures on Her Teaching
    Methods (book) 98
mission schools 38, 39
Mitchell, Weir 52
Modern British Ladies I & II (article) 99–100,
    101
modern discourses on the leanness of the body
    66–7, 69–71
monopsony 9, 11; in the international sports
    market 14, 16
Montreal 1976 Olympics boycott 1, 4–5
Moore, Hattie 86
Moses, Ernest 40, 41, 42, 43
motivations of female boxers 89
Mphahlele, Ezekiel 39
Muir, Thomas 45
Muscular Christianity 41, 101–2

Natal Open golf championship (1963) 3–4
National Party (South Africa) 37
National Police Gazette (magazine) 82–3, 89,
    91n36
National Socialism and the female body 72
NATO 24
New Democratic Party of South Africa 3
New Era Fellowship, the 43
Nihon Women's University 102
Nissen, Hartvig 53, 54

INDEX

Northern California Association of Physiotherapists 59
Northern Schools Union 40
NZRFU (New Zealand Rugby Football Union) 6

O'Brien, Eddie 88
Olympic boycotts 1, 4–5, 10
On the Methods of Gymnastics (lecture) 100
OPT (Occupied Palestinian Territories) 13
Ostrum, Kurre 59

PA (Palestinian Authority), the 13
Palestinian admission to FIFA 15
Palmer, Capt. Charles 56
Park, Roberta 53
PFA (Palestine Football Association) 15, 16
PFA (Playing Fields Association) 41, 42
physical education, emergence of 53
physical education for British women 96–7, 99
Physical Exercise of Women I & II (article) 98–9, 101
physical therapy, emergence of 53–7, 59
Physical Therapy as a career 51
physiological fat burning 74n40
physiotherapists and massage 59
Pietersen, A.F. 43
Pinetown and Suburban Indian Schools' Sports Association, Natal 38
PLO (Palestine Liberation Organisation), the 13
political motives of Coloured People 42, 45
politics of international sport and Third World grievances 22–3, 29–30
politics of Israel and Palestine 12–13
popular political protest movements and sports boycotts 10
Population Registration Act (1950, South Africa) 3
Posse, Baron Nils 54
Practical Massage and Corrective Exercises (book) 53
Prashad, Vijay 22, 27, 29
prizefights between female boxers 83–4
product substitution in sports boycotts 8–9
proprioceptive neuromuscular facilitation 60
Prosser, Dr. Charles A. 56
PT Review (journal) 59

RA ('Reconstruction Aides') 52, 54, 55–6, 57, 58
racial presentation of APTA 54
racism in Israeli football 14
Ragland, Dr. D.C. 58–9
Ranger, Terence 95
'rebel' leagues across sport and monopsonistic cartels 9

'rebel' sports tours to South Africa 6, 7, 10
reconstructionism 38
Reed College 57
Report of the Japanese Imperial Society of Education, The 98
Richard and Hattie Stewart All Star Specialty Company, the 88
Richards, Cecil 86–7, 89
Roosevelt, Theodore, 102
Ross, Libbie 83
Rossiter, Margaret 54
Rowan, Lansing 86
rugby union in South Africa 5–6, 11
Rusk, Dean 26
Russo-Japanese War (1904–05), the 95, 97, 103
Russo-Japanese War and the Development of Japanese People, The (article) 102–3
ryosaikenbo (idealised image of the Japanese woman) 94, 99–100, 102, 103, 104

sanctions definition 7–8, 10
Sanderson, Marguerite 55
Sandow, Eugen 68, 70
SANOC (South African National Olympic Committee) 4
Saunders, Nell 82
Sayre, Lewis 52
School Board Act (1905, South Africa) 38, 44
scientific boxing 88
segregation 3
'self-applied' technologies 66
separate education systems in South Africa 38
Separation Wall in the OPT 2, 12
Sewgolum, Sewsunker 'Papwa' 3–4
Sihanouk, Prince 31
Silberer, Victor 71
Sino-Japanese War (1894–95) 95, 97
Sino-Soviet split, the 27, 28–30, 31
Smith, Eddie 44
Smith, Tommie 23
Smuts, Gen. Jan 3, 38
social class and body shape 67, 68, 71
social Darwinism in education 45, 102
Social Emergency: Studies in Sex Hygiene and Morals, The (book) 57
social responsibility in sport of mission schools 40, 41, 45
Society of Trained Masseuses 58
Sorek, Tamir 17
South African Council on Sport 5
South African Non-Racial Olympic Committee 5
South African Olympic and British Empire Games Association 39
South African rugby tour of New Zealand (1981) 6–7
South African Sports Association 5
South African sport under apartheid 3

112

Spahn, John 84
sport and interference with church and school growth 41
sport at mission schools in Cape Town, South Africa 37–43, 44–5
sporting paradigms for a slim, strong body 70–1
sports boycotts in the context of a wider set of cultural boycotts 7–10, 16, 17
Sports Illustrated (magazine) 25
sports physiology and body efficiency 70–1, 74n44
standards required to qualify as a Physical Therapist 52
Steenveld, Ernest 43
Stewart, Hattie (Nellie) 83, 85, 86, 87, 91n36
Stokes, James 78
Strength and How to Achieve It (book) 70
strength training 68
Sukarno, Achmed 23, 25, 26, 27, 29, 30, 31
Sullivan, John L. 86, 87
suspension of the Indonesian NOC 26
Swedish gymnastics 52–3, 99, 100
Swedish massage 58
Sweeney, Miriam 55
SWSSU (Somerset West School Sports Union) 42
Sylvester, Annie 81

Taylorism concept of the manufacturing process 68, 69, 73
tennis in South Africa 43–4
TEPA (Teachers' Educational Professional Association) 48n95
Theory and Practice of Physical Education (book) 100
therapeutic massage as a mode of treatment 52–3, 55–6, 57–8, 59–60
Third World grievances and the politics of international sport 22–3, 29–30
Tlatelolco massacre in Mexico 4
TLSA (Teachers' League of South Africa) 38, 39, 40, 43, 44–5, 48n95

Torres, Caesar 25
Trafalgar High School Bursary Fund 43
training regimen for sport 71–2, 73

UEFA 14–15, 16
Universals Domino Club, Cape Town 44
USA Olympic boycotts 10
US concern over GANEFO 26, 27, 28–9, 30
USSR and GANEFO, the 27–8
USSR Olympic boycotts 10

van der Ross, David 40
van der Ross, Richard 44
van Niekerk, D.B. 40, 43
van Schoor, Willem 43
vaudeville and early women's boxing 78–9, 80–1, 82–90

weighing scales as instrument of self-assessment 69–70
Wilkinson, Elizabeth 78
Williams, Alice 85
Woman as a General Practitioner, The (book) 72
women in the professions 54
women's boxing and vaudeville 78–9, 80–1, 82–90
women's roles in the modern Japanese state 95
Work and Play in Girls School (book) 96
Workers Party of South Africa 42
working-class origins of female boxers, the 82, 84, 85, 89–90
World War I and rehabilitation measures 55–6, 59
WPDA (Western Province Domino Association) 44

Yamaguchi School 97

Zhou, Taorno 25, 29
Zonnebloem College 41, 42, 47n45
Zonnebloem College Magazine 45